No Return
TICKET
Leg Two

No Return TICKET Leg Two

A TRUE STORY

Captain Skip Rowland

© 2017 by Skip Rowland

All rights reserved. No part of this book may be reproduced or transmitted in any form or by any means, electronic or mechanical, including photocopying, recording, or by any information storage and retrieval system, except in the case of brief quotations embodied in critical articles and reviews, without prior written permission of the publisher.

Although the author and publisher have made every effort to ensure the accuracy and completeness of information contained in this book, we assume no responsibility for errors, inaccuracies, omissions, or any inconsistency herein.

Printed in the United States of America

ISBN Paperback: 978-0-9991836-0-1
ISBN eBook: 978-0-9991836-1-8

Original photo of boat on cover: © William Murphy
Cover artwork: Bogdan Maksimovic
Cover and interior design: Ghislain Viau

This is for the restless ones, the gallant fools who follow the path of the sun across blue waters to distant shores.
—Don Blanding – 1928

CONTENTS

Prologue		xi
Chapter 1	Serious Blending	1
Chapter 2	Chicken! You're Getting Chicken, So Shut Up!	7
Chapter 3	Selecting Our Youth In Training	10
Chapter 4	Christmas In Sydney Town—Aussie Style	15
Chapter 5	Maintenance In The Pretzel Position	18
Chapter 6	The Dunalley Canal Bandit	21
Chapter 7	Hobart, Tasmania Pre-Race Day	25
Chapter 8	An Aging Vessel Coughs Up A Diamond	31
Chapter 9	The Gun Goes BOOM!	35
Chapter 10	What The Weather Guy Didn't Tell Us	46
Chapter 11	Mid Sea Apple Sauce Caper	55
Chapter 12	ABC Television—Chopper Bafoon	60
Chapter 13	Non Triumphant Finish	65
Chapter 14	Thank You Australia	70
Chapter 15	Life Beyond Sydney	76
Chapter 16	Gunkholing Northbound In "Fine" Weather	83

Chapter 17	The Amazing Pipe Cleaners Story	88
Chapter 18	Up A Not So Lazy River	93
Chapter 19	The Big Wet	97
Chapter 20	Surfers Paradise Was Special For Denise	105
Chapter 21	Sneaky Pub— Tell Em Tall Peter sent Ya!	111
Chapter 22	Mooloolaba	115
Chapter 23	Wanted For Murder	119
Chapter 24	A Deckies Life Aboard A Modern Prawn Trawler	124
Chapter 25	Surprises In The Coral Sea	130
Chapter 26	Whale Bones, Whales and Bombs	134
Chapter 27	Return Engagement in Mooloolaba	145
Chapter 28	Whitsunday's And the Great Barrier Reef	148
Chapter 29	Rainbow Bridge	151
Chapter 30	Joy Love and Prayers	160
Chapter 31	The Rich Lady At Hamilton Island Race Week	163
Chapter 32	Hook Island Overfalls	172
Chapter 33	Roo Returns	178
Chapter 34	An Inconvenient Theft	182
Chapter 35	Life Goes On—To Darwin	186
Chapter 36	Darwin to Ambon Yacht Race	189
Chapter 37	Heads on Sticks—I Want Heads On Sticks	193
Chapter 38	The Kid Who Will Someday Be King	201
Chapter 39	Komodo Dragons	203
Chapter 40	Lombok Island—Impressions	207
Chapter 41	The Bali Cock Broker	210

Chapter 42	'Buried' Above Ground	216
Chapter 43	Jakarta	222
Chapter 44	Mysterious Krakatoa—After a Bus Ride From Hell	229
Chapter 45	Friday the 13th—Equator Crossing	235
Chapter 46	Not So Secret Navy Base	243
Chapter 47	Singapore: City Of Contrasts	249
Chapter 48	Northbound In The Malacca Strait	261
Chapter 49	Pirates	266
Chapter 50	Had We Killed a Man?	278
Chapter 51	Reporting To Authorities	282
Chapter 52	Botulism—The Erie Aftermath	285
Chapter 53	Dealing With Submerged Debris	288
Chapter 54	A Cruising Friend Journeys to Heaven	292
Chapter 55	In the Andaman Sea	297
Chapter 56	Headed To Phuket	301
Chapter 57	Thailand—The Magic Kingdom	305
Chapter 58	An Awesome Sea Nomad	312
Chapter 59	Reaching Out With Love—14,000 Miles Out	316
Chapter 60	Flee If You're The Driver	320
Chapter 61	Kings Cup Regatta	323
Chapter 62	A Life So Precious	326
Epilogue	Where Are They Now?	333
Glossary		339

PROLOGUE

You are stepping aboard *Endymion* on our first morning in Australia following an eleven-month Pacific crossing from California. (*No Return Ticket, Leg One: Outward Bound California to Australia*). What a voyage! If trouble was to be found we managed to source it. From a close encounter with a rogue freighter, to sailing into a military uprising, encountering hellish storms and taking a mid-Pacific knock-down we figured sailing the Australian coastline would be a cake walk. Little did we know.

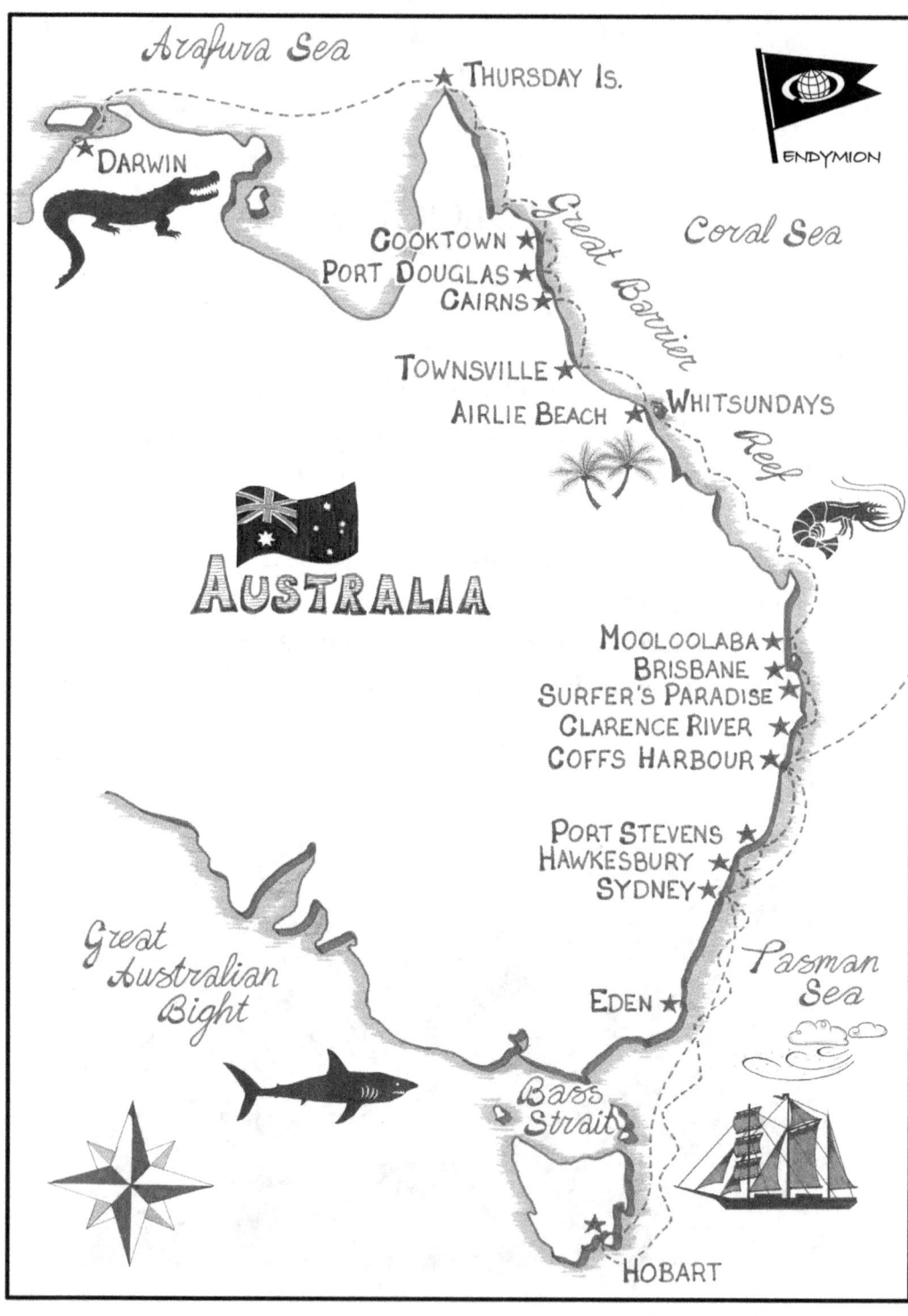

CHAPTER 1

SERIOUS BLENDING

As you delve into this book I have a question for you; Were you to arrive in a distant country who would you *least* expect to become your first group of friends? I'm guessing you didn't say Customs and Immigration officers.

Following our clearing officials went out of their way to make us welcome. However, I can't say it started well.

Our Q Flag (quarantine flag) hung in clear, windless air when Australia's Customs, Immigration and Agriculture inspectors came aboard at 0800. We had arrived at Coffs Harbor, New South Wales, Australia at 0500 that morning, long before the sun gave birth to morning traffic. In our homeland America, it was Thanksgiving Day 1987.

Mike was passed out in a forward V-berth, a victim of too much arrival celebration rum. Larry, Denise and I were still awake—barely. We expected this port clearing to be easy and informal. Somehow, we had missed advance warnings of the countries extremely strict regulations.

✻ Captain Skip Rowland ✻

My first shock was being ordered to surrender our canned goods, sixty-three of which were still sealed, containing everything from fine meats to refried beans. These were our staples, potential survival foods.

"I don't get it. Why surrender these? American canned goods are the safest in the world!" I was addressing a customs official.

"Sorry—it's policy."

"So you're telling me I just hand these over—let you cart them away. What happens to them next?"

"They're incinerated."

"You mean burned?"

"Yes, that is correct. We prefer incinerated."

"Jesus, that's a crappy answer. Why not say cremated."

"Calm, Skip, be calm." Denise spoke softly, nudging me.

The next line of our 'welcome to Australia' greeting was this crowd pleaser;

"Sorry, Captain. You'll have to either crack and cook, or crack and dispose of your remaining fresh eggs. Looks like three dozen."

"You gotta be ..."

"AND," his voice rose above mine, pointing to a pile of goods on the salon table, "make a choice, either pop or destroy the popcorn, all of it."

"Come on!" I was upset. Popcorn was our favorite treat.

"No exceptions. It's policy."

Close to a thousand dollars worth of restricted items were piled around the salon as we sat silently watching officials fill out forms. I thought to myself, *They'll probably take it home and split it. How could anyone justify destroying quality canned goods from America?* Tension loomed. No one was speaking. Denise was popping popcorn and frying eggs.

Mike, always a goofball, picked that moment in eternity to drag his weary body from the forward cabin. His bleary eyes slowly focused on the crisply dressed authorities. "Hey, you guys wouldn't have any spare bullets would ya?"

Bad quickly escalated to worse. Not smart, Mike. For the next hour we sat in frustration, watching *Endymion* being torn apart in a search for weapons or contraband. None was found. Gradually those who had made our entry to Australia so unpleasant began to ease up on we weary travelers.

The lead inspector sounded sincerely courteous; "Before you sign these documents Captain, is there anything else you wish to declare?"

Denise innocently blurted, "There may be a few more cans under the navigation station floorboards."

It was one place they hadn't looked and sure enough there were. I could have killed her. I felt violated and insulted. They departed with a boatload of our supplies, all quality goods, nothing suspicious.

"Hell of a way to welcome us down under," said Larry.

We agreed, but at least it was over. Our rum & Pepsi splurge had lost its luster. We all needed a day to sleep and re-energize. The seven days and nights passage from New Caledonia had been the stormiest since leaving Newport Beach, California, nearly a year ago. While others put their heads to pillows I made a slow inspection tour of *Endymion*. She had proved a strong, seaworthy, trusted and comfortable companion. I mentally noted to write Henri Wauquiez a letter of praise. His outfit builds one hell of fine yacht. Since leaving Newport Beach I had never found a manufacturer's problem to cause concern.

I sat alone in the cockpit in morning sunshine, looking at people looking at our huge American colors and me while they walked the path to the Coffs Harbor entrance. I thought about my granddad and his original 130-foot schooner *Endymion*. He'd made several Atlantic crossings between 1902 and her demise from electrolysis in 1910.

The original *Endymion* had been a grand old vessel, requiring many men of might to sail her. I wondered: *Had he experienced clearing difficulties? Were rules even in force? Had Grandpa felt the same kinship to his ship as I have with mine? There are times when I feel this boat is a part of me, or vice-versa—like we are two parts of one being, if you get my drift. It's a bond between man and fiberglass that to me at least, is love.*

I truly loved my yacht.

Slowly I drifted off without sugarplums but recognizing it was the Aussie inspectors who, in the end flew better colors. It had been wrong to believe what wasn't true, that we were above their rules and mistaken again for refusing to believe what was true, that we were the same as anyone else.

The same three officers returned the next day to invite us to a weekend BBQ at one of their homes. The blending had begun. Our ships stores, not on the menu had been properly disposed of, whatever that means—I hoped it wasn't wasted. Over the next few weeks we joined the inspectors, their wives and children for dinners and beach volleyball, even a trip to an historical cemetery to examine bits and pieces of Australian history. I appreciated the epitaph on one exceptional marker. It read: "On June 22, 1867 Jonathon Fiddle went out of tune.

While docked at Coffs Harbor we reunited with a delightful Canadian couple from Vancouver, BC and their three sons, sailing *Bagheera*, a Beneteau 38. We first met Liza and Andy Copeland in Bora Bora. They too were entered in the Tall Ships event. Denise particularly enjoyed the children, Duncan, 12 years old, Colin, 8 and Jamie, age 5. The lads visited *Endymion* daily, mostly because Denise served them Crystal Light lemonade. One day little Jamie shyly said, "This is for you," handing Denise a lovely yellow flower, as kids have done through the ages when struck by a lovely lady's presence. It motivated Denise to write home:

Jamie is adorable and only five, but such presence. Today he gave me a yellow wildflower for our salon table. He said he liked the flowers Skip brings me, like the yellow rose yesterday, and he wanted to see me smile. Am I spoiled or what? Duncan, the oldest, brought me a headless fish. Do you suppose that tells a different story? An hour ago all three were banging on the hull wanting me to help a seagull they had wrapped in newspaper. It had broken its leg or maybe was just old. They wanted "the nurse" to splint its leg but I just couldn't. All I know about mortally wounded birds is to give them an eye dropper of whisky, but I couldn't do that either because we drank it all with the quarantine people. The boys were sure it was hungry so we fed it some crumbled crackers and set it on the dock. It was gone last time I looked. Skip says probably stray Marina cats.

December was on us. The days sped by. We had only weeks to prepare ourselves and *Endymion* to participate in Australia's Bicentenary Tall Ships Race. As mentioned in *Leg One* of *No Return Ticket*, a race regulation required fifty percent of our crew to be "Australian youth in training," generally meaning with no experience, though heaps of desire to learn. They wanted to be proud, to be involved in the nautical heritage of their motherland.

As a bicentenary gift to Australia, the British built *Young Endeavour*, a modern day replica of Captain Cook's original flagship. Seven thousand Australian teens had competed for only a dozen positions as crew. Over a thousand who missed the opportunity applied for positions aboard participating yachts from other nations, including ours. We received thirty-two well-written, polite requests from youth all across Australia. Denise and I worked for four days, sun-up to bottoms-up, attempting to reach every kid who had hopefully entrusted us with their dreams. We selected ten for further interviews; all lived three hundred miles south in the Sydney area. Time was fleeting. We knew the coastline heading south had challenges. It was rugged and dangerous, with shifting sandbars at most harbor entrances, so we rented a car from the only agency in Coffs Harbor to scout the coast in advance of our sail south to meet the kids.

CHAPTER 2

CHICKEN! YOU'RE GETTING CHICKEN, SO SHUT UP!

An Australian entrepreneur, Gary Wolfe, operated the only car rental agency in town. As luck would have it he was out of vehicles, having just rented his last car to "the most beautiful Polynesian lady" he had ever seen. So beautiful in fact, he told us, he hadn't bothered to get her driver's license.

Dope!

We gave Gary our IDs and he rented us his private brand new VW Bug. 100 km out of Coffs we discovered the gas cap was one of those locking gadgets. We had no key. Thus began our strange and humorous relationship with Gary Wolfe. We abandoned the idea of a look-see drive south, deciding instead to just sail. We could handle the rugged coastline. We've done it before. No problem.

Gary, the town's entrepreneur, also had a souvenir shop near the harbor—a good one. Additionally he was opening a spanking new bistro restaurant the following weekend.

"I'm going to call it *Happiness Hour,*" Gary proudly told us.

"Yeah, that's cute," commented Denise, "I get the play on words."

Larry and Mike had been with us since Fiji in August. They were set to fly home to America and offered to sponsor Denise and me to a dinner on opening night at Gary's new digs. The place was packed! We waited an hour to be seated and twenty minutes more before we could order. I chose lamb shank. Larry opted for a monster Angus steak. Mike went for cordon bleu and Denise, ever mindful of health and figure went for a cheese and fruit plate. We waited for our food—a long time.

"I didn't order chicken!" We heard a loud angry female voice.

"Well, chicken is what you get."

"Hey mister," from a different direction, "I didn't order chicken either ... and I don't want it. Take it back."

"You heard my wife," the first man bellowed, "she ordered lamb, not chicken! What the hell are you pulling? We didn't order this. Take this crap back."

Clearly the man was not happy.

"Uh ohh. Trouble afoot," said Denise.

"Happiness Hour is over," Larry agreed.

The place erupted in shouting. Every person in the place was being served chicken. Only chicken. Gary had run out of everything else, substituting chicken for the entire menu but not telling anyone.

"Chicken it is—you're going to love it. Special recipe." Gary had the hype, trying to convince everyone, but people were furious. Some started to leave but Gary pushed in front of them, bolting the door. Sirens filled the air. The police came. They sorted it out in time, but these were Gary's neighbors in a small town, so it will take time. We caught a burger on the way back to *Endymion*. Mike and Larry saved some money on our dinner expense and flew out as expected the next day with Mike promising (threatening) to return.

Denise and I sailed the following day for Sydney, gunkholing our way safely down the Australian coast, yielding to the persuasion of an occasional beach barbeque. We sailed close to shore on days so beautiful and clear it seemed we could touch the sky. We ghosted along on dying zephyrs of evening breeze and anchored in small coves as dusk became dark. We drank boxed wine with fellow wanderers. We were indeed drifting and blending. Life simply could not be better!

And, by the way, Gary's "so beautiful" Polynesian girl? She turned out to be a he, and had stolen Gary's car.

Way to go, Gary!

CHAPTER 3

SELECTING OUR YOUTH IN TRAINING

Sydney town for Christmas holidays was a welcome change for Denise and me. As our lives together gradually melded we thought more about people close to us. Our letters home, and those from home, intensified our love for family and friends who sailed vicariously with us. We spent a lot of time corresponding, putting to words how lucky we felt for the pure magic, the joy we experienced being able to cruise.

We listened attentively to tales from other sailors, especially those who faced rather than avoided challenges. We learned to separate fakes and boasters from like-minded vagabonds who had broken free of life's routine shackles to wander the world with zest. Sometimes their experiences were difficult, but they were grounded people with big hearts. Denise and I considered ourselves among those who said not "can we afford to go," but "can we afford not to go." Our skills had surely been challenged and like others we worried about finances, or living within 43 feet of space. It tested relationships. We occasionally made mistakes or got unnecessarily angry. But where, we asked ourselves, would we be if we had not followed the dream? We knew our lives were enriched because of the chances, adventure and beauty we have seen in the last year. We learned laughter and forgiveness are far more powerful than a booming voice, especially mine. We believed in our hearts that our souls would never perish; that surely there is a God, for all the harmony of nature we have experienced could not have been orchestrated by accident.

Denise and I were in high spirits setting about our final *Youth In Training* crew selection. It wasn't easy. Sitting at the salon table one wretchedly rainy day we combed through the stack of applications. We didn't have a phone. Some applicants' letters listed only a local number and no area code. We didn't have a clue where in Australia many of these towns were located. We narrowed our search to candidates from New South Wales and Queensland. Next we carefully constructed rejection letters to each inquiry beyond those two areas. Each was hand written, attempting to be kind, respecting the youngsters' enthusiasm. We encouraged their determination and admired their commitment. Then we hit the pay phones with a sack of coins, eventually selecting Kylie and Caetlin Jopson, perky strawberry blonde teen-age sisters from Sydney, partly because we were close enough to meet them.

Caetlin Jopson

Caetlin Jopson

As sisters, if necessary they could share one of our limited bunks. They also had experience getting along with each other, having shared a bedroom growing up. They appeared to like each other and had athletic abilities. Like most other applicants though, they totally lacked experience. I felt we could count on their boundless enthusiasm. Denise was more skeptical.

"How, after all we've been through," she asked, "can we consider, in race conditions, taking inexperienced kids across the Bass Straits, keep them safe and unhurt, and have our boat in good condition?"

"We'll have to be good coaches. Probably lose a ton of sleep," I answered.

"That sounds stupid, Skip. How can you have a 'ton' of sleep.

"Same way you refer to a ton of ants I suppose."

We solved the experience issue in part, by inviting the girls to sail to Hobart with us. That gave us six hundred and fifty nautical miles (nm) to teach what we could, observe their judgment, endurance and fear levels. They each contributed $10.00 a day toward food and the privilege of being verbally abused by the captain if they messed up. In turn, I gave both sisters a written agreement stating either party could cancel if they wished, once we reached Hobart. The Bass Straits separating South Australia and Tasmania can be a savage experience with gale force winds close to 40% of the time. We all agreed that if they couldn't handle it, the whole deal could be called off with no hard feelings.

Kylie's boyfriend, Jordain, was our third selection. A square jawed, muscular youth, he had sailing experience, including some spinnaker work and a crossing of the Tasman Sea from Australia to New Zealand. I heartily welcomed that experience. Our fourth choice, Jamie Whittleson, would come aboard in Hobart. Jamie was in law school and unable to make the voyage south with us.

With crew selected we staggered through a barley-soaked Christmas, partying with other drifters, new shore-side friends and the sisters' parents. Kevin Jopson, the girls' father, had been an Australian heritage artist. His art was on display in banks, fine homes and institutions nation-wide. He gave Denise and me a handsome original oil painting of *Endymion* sailing in the Pittwater area north of Sydney.

We learned to admire Kevin as a true 'Aussie,' always carrying an artist's brush, and an 'eskie' (cooler) containing a cold six-pack.

The final Tall Ships Race roster published just before Christmas listed 185 competitors for the first ever such race in the Southern Hemisphere. At forty-three feet, we were the smallest of four American entries, including the three-hundred-foot-long *Eagle,* the U.S. Coast Guard's official Tall Ship. *Vadura,* a stately classic wooden yacht from Delaware checked in at a hundred and four feet, and *The Rachel B. Jackson,* an eighty-foot schooner from Boston, rounded out the US entries. Of the one hundred eighty-five entries we were rated eighty-fifth, meaning we had to beat all one hundred of the boats between our 85 and the total 185. They were considered slower, according to ratings.

"So, do you think it's fair?" Denise asked.

"Tell ya what, pretty lady. It's fair if you beat 'em and totally unfair, even rigged, if you don't beat the damn rating. Been that way since mankind first paddled on a log."

Case settled.

Excited as we were for Tall Ships I also harbored a personal sadness thinking about my son Tony who had sailed with me from Los Angeles. We hadn't seen it coming, or happening, when he got involved with drugs while we were in Tahiti. He later left *Endymion* in Raratonga following a trivial and unnecessary argument with me. We learned two weeks ago, in a letter from my dad that Tony is in jail on drug charges in California.

"It breaks my heart," I told Denise, "Tony would so enjoy the kids we're meeting, and can you imagine the experience for him to sail with the Tall Ships, especially in a race?"

Denise saw tears welling in my eyes; "I feel your hurt, Skip. Your long face says it all—but my captain, it's done. Finished. You can't put life in reverse. I love Tony too and miss him terribly. I've seen a lot of drugs as a nurse, and if Tony was smoking, or snorting, or doing whatever and was at the stage of stoniness I suspect he was, then there isn't *anything* you could have done to prevent this. Tony made his own poor choices. Now—snap out of it. We have a race to prepare for."

"And race we will." I promised Denise with a hug, while wiping away the tears. At least my dad's letter had answered questions nagging me the last few months. And sadly I knew where Tony was.

Race Committee literature suggested we would be participants in the "largest armada of vessels ever to be seen in the Southern Hemisphere." That sounded good to me—like 'Woodstock' on the water. Four Australian war ships and two cruise liners would be in Hobart as well. We would be tied as many as six abreast with yachts from around the world at Tasmania's Constitution Dock in central Hobart. An ambitious agenda of social events, structured toward the trainees, had been planned and we were invited to attend as adults, if we wished.

"Whadda ya say Denise?"

"Wouldn't miss it for anything."

CHAPTER 4

CHRISTMAS IN SYDNEY TOWN – AUSSIE STYLE

We were berthed during the Christmas Holidays at Sydney's Birkenhead Point Marina because we couldn't get space at the Cruising Yacht Club of Australia. The club was packed with maxi ocean racing yacht teams from around the world preparing for the Southern Cross series—and the toughest of all yacht races, the Sydney to Hobart International Yacht Race—that six hundred forty nm sprint across the Bass Straits from Sydney to Hobart. It's known globally as a gear buster. We felt humbled, heck—we felt thrilled just to be berthed in the neighborhood of these serious warriors.

On the lighter side, we found Australians to have varsity letters in party endurance. Had Denise and I not said 'no' graciously, we would not have drawn a sober breath during Christmas holidays.

With laughter and coaching we learned to speak "Stralian," meaning we tried to speak as our Aussie mates did. Chicken was 'chook' and a shopping cart was a 'trolley.' Denise jotted down her favorite

Stralian expressions: *Giddy Mate, havin a barbie? Fair dinkum. You're buggerin good blokes* and *my shout I believe, if we can wear ya for supper.*

On the unpleasant side, there was work to be done and—we had roaches, a serious mob of them. Every voyaging yacht has them. They're lying if they deny it. We tried everything known to mankind to go one up on the freeloaders. Written material informed us one American or Mexican (yes there are national varieties) can produce eight hundred offspring annually, and I'm here to confirm that's an understatement.

From the day we left California we carefully washed fruits and veggies coming aboard. We've also immediately discarded cardboard boxes, paper bags, even plastic egg cartons. Still they find a way to get aboard, perhaps racing up a dock line when our heads are turned, though we had not used rat guards on lines at some questionable docks we tie to.

Regardless of our cautions we were aware well hidden roaches boarded illegally as we prepared for the Pacific crossing in Mexico. By mid-Pacific the more hearty began to appear in daylight hours. At Bora Bora they invaded the aft head and dined regularly in the galley. Finally, in Australia we reluctantly shared our bed with an occasional Viking roach. We had tried everything possible, from obsessive cleanliness to illegal sprays. The situation was desperate.

We won the battle with Zoro Zoro, a wonderful product with results like fly paper. I got a demonstration one morning. Sitting at the chart table sipping my first cuppa joe I watched an emboldened gorilla cockroach, one that could surely survive fifty megatons at ground zero, swagger across my chart table—right in front of me. I laid out a Band-Aid size strip of Zoro Zoro. Got him! Another time a strip of Zoro Zoro had a female roach in its grip. I watched as the product prevented 26 babies from becoming shipmates. I didn't feel at all bad—it wasn't like a love-fest litter of puppies. At last we were ahead of the problem. After months of hesitation I knew again that when I felt a faint whisper of a touch on my skin as I lay sleeping, it was human, hopefully a mating call.

CHAPTER 5

MAINTENANCE IN THE PRETZEL POSITION

Serious maintenance chores needed attention. By now readers know I'm a doofus when it comes to mechanical issues—but have become reasonably self sufficient by necessity. An example was our freezer pulling the batteries down. I spent the better part of a hot sticky afternoon cranked into a pretzel position in the engine room, a wrench in each sweat slickened hand, a flashlight in my teeth working on a compressor that could only have been placed there by a deranged monkey who resented seafarers. Amazingly it worked. I solved the problem.

Some days were twenty-four carat joy, and a few rather frustrating. Birkenhead Point was under development, meaning noisy construction and services we needed not yet available. One day my chore list included:

Pick up and send mail from Sydney

Take my typewriter for repairs

Buy oil & filters (Don't forget to bring specifics).

For the filters and oil I walked a mile to an automotive supply store. No problem except for the overwhelming aroma of fish & chips from a neighborhood shop, resulting in a pit stop. The typewriter repair wasn't so easy. I carried it a half mile, in its case, to a ferry that ran on a semi-firm schedule to Circular Quay in downtown Sydney. From there I hoofed it a mile along streets teeming with people to the post office where I tasted and pasted stamps, attaching them to thirty-eight outgoing letters.

Eventually I found "Typewriter City," a business that was not pleased to see me.

A dope with a crew cut and soiled bow-tie said they couldn't fix my machine. In fact he flat refused, but seriously wanted to sell me a new one. I explained, "I'm a cruising sailor. Can't you tell by my long hair and hard earned tan. I don't have the money for a new one. Help me a little here."

"Junk. It's pure junk." they said of my user friendly, light keyboard, magic screen, (pre-computer days) 2k memory, battery-powered marvel that had served me famously well crossing vast oceans.

Typestar 6 on desk in Endymion's *aft cabin*

"It's the very same junk as that one!" I pointed to the display window. "Yeah, the one with the $600.00 price tag." (I wanted to add, "asshole.")

"I told you. It can't be repaired, mister—it's junk."

"How do you know? You haven't even plugged it in."

"Tell you what," he said, "I'll offer you $20.00 trade in."

We were getting nowhere. I congratulated him for his communication skills, his several million misfiring brain cells, told him to kiss my ass and said, "Watch this."

Directly in front of his store was a waste can encouraging citizens to "clean up." Into it I firmly deposited my "*Typestar 6*" miracle machine. Next I savored a quarter pounder with cheese, fries, and a large coke before dashing for the return ferry to Birkenhead. A want ad soon solved the typewriter problem for $50.00.

CHAPTER 6

THE DUNALLEY BANDIT

December 26th, Boxing Day, was sunny, warm and blessed with a steady warm breeze. Along with over 1,000 other spectator vessels we gathered to watch one hundred sixty-eight of the world's fastest maxi yachts disappear beyond Sydney Heads (the harbor entrance) en route to Tasmania. It was the start of the Sydney-Hobart Yacht Race, one of the most grueling sailing competitions in the world. It tested gear, boats and sailors who in turn tempted and tested their limits against a plethora of weather conditions. The start and weather was favorable.

Two days later we followed, the Jobson sisters, Jordain, Denise and me, all getting acquainted on a leisurely sail to Hobart. When we ducked into the coastal port of Eden, near the southern tip of mainland Australia, it was a windy day, blowing straight onshore. We sighted a large concrete municipal pier giving modest protection to numerous boats anchored or moored in its lee. Vessels not sheltered by the pier were subject to considerable bouncing. There were plenty of them. We found a convenient spot in the pier's lee and dropped anchor in 20 feet. We laid out enough chain to be certain our anchor wouldn't drag as the water became shallow not far from our stern. We fired up the BBQ, and sat back admiring the cove.

A magnificent Australian flag three-story yacht, looking spanking new and about 100 feet long was heading in from the sea. It had unusual exhausts making it appear a jet-powered vessel. We wondered and joked about what the owner did for a living to enjoy such luxury.

"I'm guessing he owns a professional sports team." I said.

"More loikela a professional brothel I tell ya, n that's fair dinkum," was Jordain's contribution in Stralian. "Didja see the sheilas up forward. Gimme the glasses."

"I can tell you," said Denise, "He doesn't make enough for a good captain. That old boy is in trouble."

Indeed he was. The skipper was unable to maneuver alongside the pier. The wind was too brisk. Shortly the yacht was blown into small anchored boats bobbing on harbor waves. Pandemonium broke out aboard as crew struggled to fend off the smaller boats. Uniformed crew had boat hooks while ladies dangled rubber fenders on long lines as they attempted to keep lines from tangling in whatever gear (like rudders) lay below the waterline. All we could do was watch. Two small boats were swamped in the process, boats that were somebody's pride or dream. The magnificent yacht eventually got turned around and headed for the pier, striking it at maybe four knots speed, tearing out a 15-foot strip of concrete. I suspected another want ad before they went to sea again. The captain had failed miserably.

We crossed the Bass Straits and sailed down the East coast of Tasmania over the following days without incident. Before sunrise one morning our radar returned a picture of a large vessel on a course and speed close to ours. It was *Asgard II,* the Irish Tall Ship, also bound for Hobart.

Asgard II *abeam in early morning light*

We were close enough to shout greetings. Maybe it sounds strange but I believed it made all of us feel more a part of the Bicentenary celebration. *Asgard II* would have to sail around Cape Pillar at the southern tip of Tasmania way to the south in order to stay in deep enough water. We could stake a short cut through the Denison Canal, just south of Schouten Island, a faster, easier and potentially more interesting route.

The Denison canal was built in 1905, the same year my granddad's *Endymion* raced across the Atlantic and the first Ford motorcar crawled over Washington State's Cascade Mountains. The Denison, a dirt canal, was narrow and primitive. It didn't get much traffic. Vessel size was limited, and depth at the Blackman Bay entrance was sometimes measured in inches instead of feet because of shifting sand bars. Caution was advised. We took our chances.

The canal had one bridge, the Dunalley swing bridge. It required an operator who saw little action, but accepted gratuities, which were expected.

The Dunalley swing bridge opens for us.

A long, narrow, wooden runway sat atop the dirt/mud bank to port side as vessels approach from Blackman Bay. The operator, when contacted by radio, arranges for the bridge to open. Then he waits until he sees a vessel approaching, when he grabs a forty-foot long pole with a basket on the end. The bridge operator next races along the runway while extending the basket to the transiting vessel. The vessel's crew, us in this case, are boisterously invited to place coins or bills in the basket to reward the keeper. Watching the countryside and children hailing us, as we had been, we were unprepared to gift the athletic operator who was slowly running out of steam chasing us. The girls frantically searched for coins. Denise was having a laughter moment and I, on the wheel, was nervously watching the depth indicator. Jordain, thinking quickly, grabbed a six-pack of Four-X beer and tossed it into the basket a moment before we transited the bridge. Did it please the exhausted gatekeeper? We will never know. The weight of the beer broke his pole, so we hoped so.

CHAPTER 7

HOBART, TASMANIA: PRE-RACE DAY

Constitution dock in Hobart was a scream.
Imagine sixty-six yachts tied to the pier, each other, and a floating fish market/restaurant. We came from multiple countries and spoke various languages. We had a prime berth beside the fish & chips eatery. For five pre race days the people of Hobart turned out to make us welcome. It was a huge undertaking involving over two thousand five hundred captains and crew. Most had come to race. All had come to party. Contestants brought along their customs and traditions from New Zealand, Germany, Canada, Italy, the Soviet Union, United Kingdom, Poland, Holland, Ireland, Oman, Uruguay, America, Spain, Ecuador, Cayman and tiny Andorra. Never once was there a problem, except perhaps a wee bit of intoxication from "overtraining."

Bagheera was also berthed at Constitution dock. Having my morning Joe in the cockpit one day I watched a stream of photographers and journalists practically tripping over each other rushing past *Endymion*, searching for *Bagheera's* youngest crew member, five-year-old Jamie Copeland. They suspected a worthy human-interest news story, and they got one. Race scrutineers had declared *Bagheera* ineligible to compete, claiming Jamie was too young for the rugged environment the race could produce. Jamie's father Andy had been a Benetau yacht broker in Vancouver, Canada, and mom Liza, an educational psychologist. Jamie and his brothers had sailed since birth. They were remarkable children. While others kids went to pre-school and watched Captain Kangaroo, the Copeland lads were meeting new people in distant lands, enjoying (and occasionally heaving) native foods and learning other languages. Before first grade they could take the wheel, plot a course, read the weather and identify the heavenly constellations. For this race they had come all the way from Italy. The press had the youngest Copeland boy circled, but the boy was the hawk. I decided to listen in.

Little Jamie sat casually on *Bagheera's* bow pulpit, one hand wrapped around the forestay. A dozen grown men with cameras and scratch pads leaned in close and listened intently as Jamie described some of the sea conditions and offshore experiences he has been through. I couldn't believe what I was watching. Being polite and Canadian, Jamie didn't shove it down anyone's throat—but it was soon evident his sailing credentials were considerably more impressive than those of Australia's "Youth in Training."

"Sounds good," one reporter remarked, "but can you tie knots or stand a watch?"

"I stand watches with my mom or dad. I take the helm in calm conditions and we are always harnessed. My dad is always talking about safety."

Jamie Copeland answering reporters questions.

A crowd had gathered.

Leaning over to pick up a line lying on deck Jamie continued, "I can tie knots. Watch this." He looked the photographer straight in the eye, put the line behind his back and tied a perfect bowline in less than five seconds.

The journalists and assembled crowd applauded. One journalist put his pad under his arm and whistled. Jamie smiled mischievously.

I saw this as injustice but the scrutineers held firm. In spite of extensive world class experience Jamie and *Bagheera* were not allowed to race.

The Australian-American Club of Tasmania had a barbecue for USA entries and crews at a private home. Our training crew was treated as visiting royalty. Ex-pat Americans asked for the kids' autographs, invitations were extended to visit again post race time and I wouldn't be surprised if a couple of job offerings may have been floated. Exciting as it was, the youngsters begged off early to attend a street dance near race headquarters. Denise and I learned that night, as the girls and Jamie staggered aboard with song on their lips—there was underage drinking in Tasmania. We figured it was likely not the first time our young crew had been a little hammered. Denise and I decided not to make a big deal of it. The kids were happy, having a great time and coming together as a team.

"That," I said to Denise, "is what we want. We are not guidance counselors. We're coaches of an energized small team."

A decision we never regretted.

No festival is complete without a parade. Crews paraded through the streets of Hobart. People lined up to cheer us. It was a hoot. Our youngsters, dressed in *Endymion* crew uniforms, looked sharp and Denise, never one for conformity, wore a multi colored sundress while carrying a banner announcing "*Endymion—USA.*" Pride paraded with us.

Roo carried our flag. Denise refused to wear a team T-shirt.

Denise's letter home captured her feelings:

Mom, I'm tired. We spent all morning cleaning the boat. It looks too beautiful just to race back to Sydney and screw it up again. Oh well, life on a boat! What is so great, is all the admiring people—really good for our egos. Not everyone thinks we are crazy for coming all this way for a race. I'm so tired but feeling really good about the way the boat looks. There is a sister ship, another Amphitrite 43 here—from a country called Andorra, a little place near Spain, and they have all this stuff all over their decks—kinda like parking your car on your yard. We have all our flags up and are lookin good. Makes me proud!

My most poignant moment was getting goose bumps watching the Australian Naval Band strike up the Star Spangled Banner as the US Coast Guard *Eagle* triumphantly approached the official dock, cadets standing tall in every crosstree of lofty rigging and a gigantic American flag flying from *Eagle's* stern.

Denise and I attended dinner at the Governor Generals home. Seated with Tasmania's Attorney General and Captain Brian Wilson, commanding officer of the escort vessel *HRMS Stalwart*, our conversation concerned weather and Australian pride.

There was always talk about weather. Race day was predicted to be windless and dry. Weather concerned everyone from the highest officials to anxious parents. It was a big deal for parents, sending their cherished youngsters to sea on ships they've never seen with captains they've never met. But this was Australia and Australia was strutting! Naval officers, weather pundits and the best of their modern day equipment confirmed it—no wind. But wait a minute ... Denise met a little old lady at a garden party who had a different take on

Denise & Skip dressed for Governor Generals dinner.

things, and disagreed; ants, she explained, had started coming into her kitchen in droves, meaning wind, rain and cold were soon to follow. Denise would later write home:

"Damned if she wasn't right."

CHAPTER 8

AN AGING VESSEL COUGHS UP A DIAMOND

An event that would change our lives began to unfold the afternoon preceding race day. Splicing lines on the aft deck I heard, "Ahoy *Endymion,* is the captain about?"

"That would be me." I said, getting up to address a handsome lad wearing a back pack and carrying a duffel. Though his voice was strong, it carried concern.

"What can I do for you?" I asked.

"Would you happen to have a berth for the race? I'm lookin for a ride to Sydney."

"A bit late isn't it?" I replied, "Our crew was selected a long time back. How come you're wandering the docks with only hours to spare?"

"Capt'n, I had a berth on *Belle Brandon*, but she was disqualified, scrutineers said she couldn't make safety muster."

"Come aboard, tell me more." I felt for the youngster with a long face but twinkling eyes. I had never heard of *Belle Brandon,* but I instantly liked the young man boarding *Endymion*. A more sad and distressing story than his would be hard to find. Eighteen-year-old Andrew Biram, Roo to his friends, had been one of thousands of youngsters to apply unsuccessfully for positions aboard *Young Endeavour*. Turning nineteen and still keen on the race, Roo responded to a television story requesting help restoring a one hundred nine year old former fishing ketch named *Belle Brandon*. The goal was to make her fit to compete in this historic Tall Ships event. The owner's budget was slim and the one hundred four foot vessel, the oldest timber boat in Australia at the time, seriously needed repair.

Belle Brandon late in her life.

Belle Brandon was moored on Tasmania's Huron River. Roo, at his own expense, made several trips from his home in South Australia to assist in making her seaworthy.

"I was too green to know what I was getting into," Roo admitted. "I first realized this wouldn't work when *Belle Brandon* sank at anchor.

I kept at it though, until the official race scrutinizers decided she was not safe for such a passage."

Roo had also paid a stipend in advance for his grub and berth. His money was not refunded. Determined to make passage as a race crew Roo continued, "I put the word out to every contact I had. I've worked hard to find a berth, but no luck. The race is tomorrow. I'm not giving up. I'm walking the docks."

"Here's my position." I reluctantly told Roo, "We're chock-o-block (slang for full). I feel for you and it's a remarkable story. I'll ask my crew to fan out amongst the boats at Constitution Dock, see if we can't help you get a berth."

I called Kylie, Caetlin and Jordain to join us in the cockpit; "Meet Roo Biram. He's on a bit of a downer after a lot of effort to be a part of this event." I asked Roo to repeat what he had told me.

"Bloody hell!" Jordain said. "Leave it to us. We'll find a slot for ya." The girls agreed.

"Great spirit, you guys." I concluded. " I'm proud of you, and Roo, if you don't land a berth, get yourself back here early tomorrow and we'll fit you in somewhere."

Jamie, Kylie and Caetlin took off highly energized, wanting to help, looking for a berth for Roo.

"Skip, that was nice, but are you crazy? What are we gonna do if he shows up tomorrow—have him sleep in a drawer?" Denise spoke from the bean bag cushion she sat upon while listening in. I knew she wasn't serious. She liked him too.

That night, less than 12 hours before we would cast off from Constitution dock I sat alone in the cockpit reveling in the wonder of the moment. The movie *Somewhere in Time* about souls living forever had been one of my all time favorites. I played the musical score at low volume through our deck speakers and sat back with a diet Pepsi. All around me yachts and Tall Ships from around the world were side by side, awaiting the same starting gun. The symphonic sounds of their rigging mesmerizing me. Adrift in the moment I thought; *Why me? What have **I** done to earn this remarkable opportunity? With eight billion people in the world today how do we become one of a few thousand to live this adventure? Tomorrow. Me, the guy from California who said I want a different life, will have one as I lead my crew in a race that will make history. We will compete with ships whose sails rend the sky and massive hulls cleave the oceans—though their day is really past. Like in the movie, we assist each other in living—perhaps forever?*

My last recollection before nodding off was feeling darned humble.

I awoke with rigging around me awash in the sparkle of early morning dew. Roo was on the dock.

"Gidday *Endymion*!" Roo shouted up to me before stepping aboard. He had not found a vessel to take him aboard. Nor had our trainees succeeded.

"Welcome aboard, young man." I said. "Let me show you where to stow your gear."

With those words Denise and I became winners in a lottery of the human race. Roo was expected to be with us for ten days; he stayed for three years. To this day, many years later as I write this, Roo Biram remains one of three best value humans ever to enter our lives—but back to my story.

Roo was a happy lad his first day aboard.

CHAPTER 9

THE GUN GOES BOOM

Race day! January 14th, 1988. The Chamber of Commerce must have struck a deal with God to serve up such a picture perfect seventy degree summer day. Today, on Tasmania's Derwent River a naval ship will fire a deafening salvo signaling the start of the first ever tall ships race in the Southern Hemisphere—and *we* are in it.

Anyone who slept well last night was either not a contestant or not competitive. My mind pushed sleep aside, as it whirled with count-down thoughts. *Is Endymion ready? How about our crew? Will we get a good start when the gun goes boom? Will the weather hold? Dare I think about a trophy?*

We go today regardless of weather. Starting gun fires at 1500. Be there! Gotta have the right provisions. Can't stop in some friendly harbor for lemonade and crackers.

I urged the crew to pack it in early last night. Did they? How many hangovers were housed in sleeping bags sprawled about the cabin as I reviewed final details?

All competitors were to clear Constitution Dock by 0800—sixty boats with anchors tangled in a cobweb of chains, and miles of crisscrossed line connected by endless knots holding each in place.

The Parade of Ships for review by Prince Charles and Princess Diana gets underway at 1000. I wanted to get underway early for the parade line-up, just in case there were problems. Fortunately aside from stubborn hangovers our crew was reasonably alert. We had but one urgent issue. Kylie & Caetlin, our most susceptible to motion sickness, forgot to buy motion sickness preventatives, excusable because of their efforts to secure a berth for Roo, but time was running out. I let them know they won't be much use if they're spewing an hour from the dock should weather should turn sour.

Kylie got the message. She raced off to find an open chemist, returning just as we were to cast off our last line, toting a bag of remedy pills she paid too much for. During her absence I had "borrowed" a half-dozen packets of Dramamine from other yachts close by—just in case.

Shortly after 0800 the same sixty yachts that were confusingly clustered at Constitution Dock were waiting loosely outside of it. We were ready to take our assigned parade of yachts position behind the Dutch tall ship training vessel *Able Tasman*—except she was nowhere to be found. Denise broke out the binoculars. Investigating the shoreline she saw *Able Tasman* still tied to the quay. That was strange. Something was wrong.

"Perhaps her engine wouldn't kick," offered Jamie.

We drifted, waiting for instructions. Parade headquarters told us to take position behind *Aquarius,* the splendiferous 135 foot schooner named for the song and owned by long time Beatle George Harrison. I radioed the committee that it was fine by us, but apparently *Aquarius* didn't get the message—she was headed in the wrong direction. We didn't follow.

So went the best plans, but no worries, the sun was warm and enthusiasm brimming. I couldn't see them of course, but I knew my crew's hearts were beating a little faster. Thousands of folks watched from shore, an equal number no doubt in spectator vessels. Not a soul in Tasmania had ever seen so many sailing ships, such an array of flags, or so much white canvas on one morning.

Able Tasman came on the emergency radio frequency requesting police and an ambulance. A terse announcement followed from her skipper. *Able Tasman* had been involved in a collision with the huge multi mast schooner *Guayos* from Ecuador. They would both miss the contestants' parade.

We were next instructed to take position behind *Asgard II*, the Irish training vessel. They were a fun bunch. We'd tossed some beers with them. As we came close we noticed they had a ten-foot sling shot set up on deck and were heaving water balloons at competitors. We snuck in on their starboard side and gave them a Yankee-style barrage of hand-fired water balloons. Fearing retribution Denise ducked under the canopy to take cover. *Asgard* returned our fire. We escaped a wetting down except poor Denise who took one square on and she wasn't pleased.

The British warship *Endurance* was the review vessel. As we approached to salute Royalty aboard, we were requested to lower our giant pirate flag in respect. We did and turned smartly toward her dipping our ensign as we passed, receiving for our efforts scattered thumbs up and a broad wave from Australia's Prime Minister Hawk.

The parade promptly fizzled so we left to find the starting area about fourteen miles down the Derwent River. Locals called the area

"The Iron Pot" for the big navigation buoys scattered around the many shoals and shallow spots. No big challenge to find it. We just meandered along following the genuine tall ships.

It would have done the city fathers proud had the race start been in front of downtown Hobart but it wasn't possible. The river is narrow. The big square-riggers needed lots of room to maneuver.

Getting closer we took our racing gear out and inspected it. Everything was set long before we arrived at the starting line area. I was confident we were well organized, as we needed to be when nearly two hundred vessels jockey for position along a two-mile long imaginary starting line. *Endymion* was dwarfed by entries such as *Eagle* whose mast towered to sixteen stories. Should they be to windward, the *Eagle* or any other such tall ship would effectively block our wind potentially causing *Endymion*, with our sixty foot mast, to lose steerage way.

The day had gone from pleasingly pleasant to uncomfortably hot. Not good and there was *no* wind—zip! Our wind indicator read 00.0. The gauge didn't move even as the boat rolled, causing the mast to whip from side to side creating its own wind. It was 1300. Two hours until our start. We waited—as did the wind.

Unlike most yacht races, there was no postponement for this start. The big Class-A square-riggers started in a real drifter at 1430. By our starting gun a half hour later it was no better, still no wind. We managed, mostly by luck, to get a great position on the weather end of the line. If you could call either end favorable, we had the right one. We were twenty yards from crossing the line when the starting gun fired.

"Great job," I told the crew in encouraging tones, "We couldn't have a better start."

But in the next half hour we drifted a miserable forty yards—backwards. Eventually a tiny wisp of breeze pushed us forward but the current struggled to move us backward. It would be embarrassing except everyone else had the same issues. Heavier vessels, where more current pushed their massive underbellies, were turning doughnuts. Aboard *Endymion* we all remained perfectly still to keep from negating momentum the boat might achieve. It was frustrating. At 1600, an hour later, we still hadn't crossed the official starting line. The whole fleet drifted aimlessly, in all directions. The weather pundits had been right.

"Jesus, what a mess." Jordain said in a whisper, as if keeping a secret.

"I'll teach you guys a trick." I said.

Using an ancient sailors' method of discovering wind when there was none, I opened my eyes as wide as possible.

"Since eyes are the most sensitive part of our bodies, eyes feel the wind before our skin." I turned my head very slowly. I felt something. Slowly I had my crew back our sails, holding them broadside to the direction my eyes pointed when I felt something against my eyeballs. My crew laughed at me.

"Just do as I say—and wait." I chided, giving them a light-hearted hard time. Shortly we saw tiny ripples of wind on the water called cat's paws, coming our way.

"Stand by." I told the crew as our sails ever so slowly started to fill. We were among the first to get the new breeze. We started to move.

"O.K., let's get the spinnaker set."

Up it went, and though it hung limply, we were ready!

Being almost first to catch the faint breeze was lucky. A good start with clear air was important. Our spinnaker, once limp, filled slowly but steadily like a hot air balloon lifting from ground. We quickly accelerated past some thirty other boats in our class, yet we were still in the midst of slow moving traffic just beginning to catch the wind. We next inched past the stern of the warship *Hobart* and officially crossed the line—intensely exciting.

Chutes (spinnakers) popped open all around us. Ours wasn't pulling right. I didn't like the looks of it; the price perhaps of an inexperienced crew? In total confusion and with yachts fending off each other, we ghosted closely along the side of *Hobart*, doing our best not to touch it as that could be considered hitting a mark—a foul. Bigger boats pushed us closer. I thought we'd be wearing Navy gray. Somehow we missed the ship but next had to worry only about tangling with its massive anchor chain that loomed directly ahead.

"Room at the mark, room at the mark" I yelled, asking other boats to observe the rules and give me the room I deserved at my leeward position. I wasn't positive I truly had the right of way, but calling out helped, especially with a strong authoritative voice. A small hole opened and we scooted within inches of the chain into clear air.

The breeze continued to freshen and veered, shortly increasing to twenty knots so sailing at ninety degrees off the wind was too close for a spinnaker. I ordered it down, but we had trouble. The spinnaker foreguy, the line that pulls spinnaker pole aft, had wrapped around the fitting at the outboard end of the pole. We could work with that, but the halyard, the line that raises the sail, had somehow jumped the sheave at the top of the mast before the spinnaker was all the way up. In the stronger wind the big sail was oscillating dangerously—a situation no sailor wants. Also not helping the situation, half of my young crew began losing recent meals in the freshening breeze.

"We've got a situation—bad one." I half yelled to everyone, wanting them to pay attention. "The spinnaker is jammed at the masthead."

"I'm going up the mast." Denise surprised us all.

"The hell you are—no way! " I said.

"I'll go up." Roo jumped in to no one's surprise.

"Look, Captain" Denise had determined eyes, "I'm the lightest and you can crank me up better 'n any of these guys," she pointed to the crew, "so let's move before we lose that expensive sail."

"No damned way Denise," I shouted back, looking toward the masthead while wrestling with the wheel and watching competitors close by. Denise was one brave young lady who wasn't comfortable any higher than riding my shoulders. "Thanks but you're not strong enough!"

"Bullshit!" Denise fired back. "Come on—lets go," she added, determination in her voice as she turned and clipped her harness closer to the mast. The Jobson sisters were busy throwing up, Roo, Jamie & Jordain were too heavy to winch up and I wasn't prepared to give the wheel to anyone else.

Decision time. Denise was totally into it — involved, living in the moment.

"Roo, Jamie, get the bosun's chair quickly, I'll bear off." I turned the boat downwind.

I didn't like this one bit. We practiced for such a situation at Constitution dock by walking through it as part of our crew orientation and training. That was before Roo joined us. But practicing on a solid dock while joking about what you're doing is enormously different than on a rolling boat in a strong wind. Our situation was challenging. With wind and confused seas we were maneuvering amidst a tightly packed fleet of boats. Each skipper was driving his boat hard, testing them to the max. Anything could happen, and I'm sending the 105 pound person I love most in this world sixty feet up with a knife and pliers. "God help us," I prayed.

Denise was at the mast. There was no stopping her.

Bearing off course I steadied *Endymion* as best I could by riding more with the waves, keeping one eye on each and every wave and the other on my motivated crew. Jamie held the bosun's chair. Roo was attaching it and speaking to Denise over the wind, telling her to wrap her knees around the mast, hold tight and signal with her hands rather than attempt to shout. I knew Denise had to be scared shitless but she didn't hesitate. Shortly she was being hauled to the masthead. Roo cranked the winch. Jamie managed the brake. Wrapping her knees and trying to hang on was difficult for Denise, but up she went—every eye glued to her. Our sky-high rodeo rider was taking a terrific beating. I felt for Denise. I tried to keep the yacht from rolling. I knew at the masthead she was taking a yet to be invented amusement park ride, being rocketed side to side, terrified to look down. Reaching from the tiny platform of the bosun's chair up high, Denise motioned to "Ease the spinnaker sheet. Give me some halyard. More halyard!"

Jamie didn't understand her.

"What?" he yelled skyward

"More! NOW! Let the damn sheet out. Take the pressure off!" screamed Denise, her arm swinging, motioning for less pressure.

I understood, released the sheet with my spare hand and headed dead downwind. Kylie and Caetlin brought the spinnaker pole aft, squaring the sail so it would fall more forward when freed. On Denise's signal Jamie let go the halyard but the wildly thrashing huge spinnaker didn't drop an inch.

"Cut it. Denise, cut the damn halyard." I screamed from the wheel. Hopefully it would land on deck rather than in the water where we might run over it, destroying it, possibly tangling it around our prop or the rudder.

I watched Denise work as if in slow motion. Above her, ragged clouds were tearing themselves to pieces. Bruised, banged up, frightened and hanging on literally for her life Denise knifed through the braided halyard, setting the spinnaker suddenly free. With one hand still on the wheel, I released the spinnaker pole topping lift. The pole dropped to the deck in a frightening crash, helping bring the big sail down orderly before we ran over it.

Roo, Jamie and seasick Kylie and Caetlin pulled furiously, clawing the spinnaker to the deck, and jammed it down the fore hatch. Jordain and Roo then cautiously lowered Denise to the deck. She was shaking violently, nearly uncontrollably, and was unsteady but she was safe. We had been bloody lucky.

"I want a raise," was all Denise said as Roo helped her get below to calm herself. A gratified smile crossed her lips as she looked my way descending the companionway.

We were passed by a bunch of competitors during that incident, but the race went on. We got back on course, upping our speed to eight knots over the bottom—a sleigh ride for a yacht like *Endymion*.

Our four trainees scurried below to repackage the spinnaker with me shouting directions from the wheel. I wasn't prepared to let them do it alone, below decks and out of my sight. The kids were doing well, no slackers and a lot of teamwork.

"Lord—no more fiascos tonight." I prayed aloud.

Next I bore off twenty degrees, and up again went the kite, on a different halyard. Competing again, we gained two knots putting *Endymion* close to hull speed, but the rest of the fleet had inched to weather of us. We headed for our next mark, the jagged rock formation at the very southern end of Tasmania. Once past Cape Pillar there was nothing between that desolate rocky cliff and Antarctica.

I was smiling again. At dusk we rounded the rocky Cape. Seas crashing against the forbidding rock outcropping looked ominous and frightening. Close to this area we had passed the remains of Port Arthur, the first gaol (jail) built in Australia. I couldn't help thinking, *What a lousy place to be a prisoner.*

The wind shifted nor-east packing twenty-five knots. Not our best conditions so we again doused the spinnaker and started beating northward. The motion from entering new currents was extreme. *Endymion* pounded uncomfortably, bashing into oncoming bone-jarring waves that had no rhythm.

I found myself crouching as I held the wheel, just to keep my balance. My crew was terribly sick or very hungry. *Screw the weather pundits* I thought, *these supposed experts with all the latest gear had told us endlessly that there would be little wind the whole race. Dopes!*

Close competition sailing in heavy weather.

We rotated galley duty. Caetlin had it that night and managed to slice one onion, but only in half, before heading for the rail. Thankfully she hurled to the lee side so there was no blow-back. I was amazed later to see her try again, this time barely getting knife in hand before U-turning for the hurling rail.

Denise harnessed herself to the galley bulkhead and took over the cooking. From the wheel I could see bruises on her arms from going aloft. *Damn good mate—amazing woman*, I thought to myself. I knew I owed her one huge debt and needed to tell her so. What she had done took real courage. When the going got tough I could count on Denise.

The night became really rough. Somewhere in the Southern Ocean, a recent good-sized storm had been building—one the weather pundits had missed. It wasn't an exact science in the eighties. In the Tasman Sea, where we were, huge rolling seas passed under us from astern. They were giant rollers we'd read about, born of a distant storm. We would rise on a large sea, wanting to surf down it, but we couldn't. We were also pounding into windborne waves of six to seven feet, running very close, and opposing the huge rollers; one of the most uncomfortable conditions sailors encounter offshore — thankfully infrequently.

I reflected on the aforementioned forecast of light winds and gentle seas. I was standing behind the wheel, drenched by pelting rain, eyes stinging from the assault of salt spray as I tried to see through the darkness ahead. My young crew started this race enthusiastically. No longer keen, they dragged themselves, doing their best to get through a miserable uncomfortable night. What a day. What a first night.

Welcome to the world of offshore racing.

CHAPTER 10

WHAT THE WEATHER GUY DIDN'T TELL US

We heaved and bumped through that first night, uncomfortable and keeping a sharp vigil for other boats. I could see navigation lights of competitors dancing on waves in every direction around us. It was tough to judge distance. We were in fierce winds edging on gale force (34 to 47 knots). Though it was difficult to read in large confused seas we counted heavily on our radar. Often it was on a sharp angle to the ocean surface and difficult to interpret but we never had to alter course.

There's a strange phenomenon that happens when exhausted, sleep-deprived people try to think. I was at that point: cold, wet, hungry, worn down and foggy-headed but optimistic, with a euphoric sense as dawn began to light my world, that all would end well. In the full light of day we were able to identify yachts whose lights we had seen in the darkness hours earlier—yachts I believed should have been well ahead of us.

There was a sister ship to *Endymion*. *Principat De Andorra* was sailed by the Prince himself. We had spoken with the gracious Prince at the Governor General's dinner party and had bet a bottle of rum as to who would win between our sister-ship yachts. One of several distress calls we heard during the night had been from *Principat De Andorra*. In rough seas the Prince radioed that he was dropping out, running back to Hobart, I supposed. I never got my jug of Captain Morgan.

Morning roll call came from *Wayuna*, the radio relay vessel. They forecast moderate southwest winds and two-meter seas. *Good,* I thought, *but where the hell is this—we need a break. We're taking a pounding out here!*

During that same roll call *Hammer of Queensland*, a big powerful racing machine (and eventual corrected time winner) reported a position as only thirty miles ahead of us.

"Hey, this is encouraging," I said to a bevy of crew with bloodshot eyes listening to the report with me.

"She also reported bloody forty knots o' wind across her deck," Roo said flatly, "and that's a far cry from 'moderate southwest with two foot seas.'

City Limits, another pedigreed racing machine, had been dismasted. "Pity those buggers fighting to clean up that mess in these seas," offered Jamie. Next to report was *Aggro*, dismasted only 12 miles from us.

Well into the morning, distress calls and race drop-outs crackled on the radio. Both Australian navy ships, *HRMS Stalwart* and *HRMS Hobart* had their hands full answering calls for help. This had developed into a major storm with potential to become a huge embarrassment to Australia. Scattered across the Tasman Sea were 185 vessels, some old and tired, some big and clumsy, some sleek and fragile—all racing up the east coast of Tasmania, in one of the most dangerous bodies of water on earth, and during storm conditions — downright nasty storm conditions. I kept thinking back to the race rule requiring every boat's crew to be at least fifty percent Australian 'youth in training,' kids who wanted to get a *taste* of the nautical heritage of their country. This was a big gulp more than a taste. It was history in the making with the Navy doing all they could to prevent a national tragedy.

I thought about the five youth aboard *Endymion* flaked out in different spots. Kylie and sister Caetlin huddled together in the cockpit trying to keep warm. Their Sydney department store foul-weather gear had flunked the test. The girls were shivering. Both had been seasick, yet they were always helpful when called. Future barrister Jamie was sleeping below. Let him rest, we need his strength. Jordain, the oldest at 23 was a "punter," meaning he frequently went to the track and probably didn't have a job. Roo was a remarkable young man. We were glad to have him aboard. He turned to for any chore, was never sea sick, and was a natural at the wheel. At the moment he was asleep in the forward V-berth. I sensed they all felt a poke of pride that would increase as they were further tested. They didn't have to wait.

All day and night number two we beat into the same confusion. Monster waves broke over the boat, a few nearly filling the cockpit and knocking people down. We didn't speak much except for,

"Watch out—Duck! Shit, that was close," or "Hold on!"

I knew the kids were frightened. Who wouldn't be, in the dark, far at sea in rough conditions when all you hear on the radio are calls for help from other vessels in the same race. Several were only a mile from us. Fortunately we were harnessed. I thanked God the cockpit self-draining design really worked. It wasn't the first time I said those thanks. I admit too, even though I've been through storms before, each has a personality. Some are killers. Like the radio Comstat fellow had said to Denise when we first approached Australia in another big blow, "It'll be over when it's over."

Comforting.

By day's end nearly a third of the fleet had dropped out. A young man had fallen from the rigging on the Irish tall ship and broken his back. Two boats had lost rudders causing them to drop all sail and heave to. One was said to have struck a whale. Even the lovely *Vadura* had a rigging failure. She had run for safe harbor to make repairs, later returning to the race. They certainly felt the spirit.

The lovely yacht Vadura *in better moments.
Please excuse my fishing pole disrupting the beauty.*

Popping her head up the companionway, Denise shared her summary of the first two days:

"All the books in the aft cabin, remember them? Well, they flew at me, a few at a time like a poltergeist. My crappy little plant I love so much has gone into shock. Damn, I can't wait till racing is a distant memory."

Toward nightfall we had the kind of anxious moment no one expects. A colossal wave broke over the bow submerging our foredeck. A giant roller passing beneath from the stern simultaneously lifted our back end toward the heavens. For a brief moment it felt like the entire yacht was at the top of a wavering unbalanced ladder. *Endymion* pitched crazily. As the yacht struggled to regain her buoyancy it was thrown into a seventy degree forward dive plunging the bow and aft to amidships under a five foot wall of angry sea. Seasoned sailors hang on when this happens. Unseasoned Jamie was halfway up the companionway when he was thrown backwards, crashing painfully onto the galley stove. His fall was partially broken by the stove guardrail, which his twisting body ripped from its foundation. We could handle a damaged stove but broken ribs would have been another matter, likely putting us out of the race.

Denise and Roo lay Jamie down on a wet salon settee. Water had penetrated everywhere. Nurse Denise found no broken bones but Jamie was stunned. We were surprised, having seen the impact, that Jamie wasn't injured except for deep bruises, earning him too much sympathy for his klutz move from Kylie and Caetlin. The stove and oven were inoperable.

Heading into darkness the wind was constant at twenty-five knots and thirty-plus in gusts. Sea spray stung as if peeling skin from my flesh. The seas were big. Thankfully our crew had done well finding their sea legs.

Kylie and Caetlin to my amazement broke into song, hands and arms performing an animated little dance to an out-of-harmony "Jolly Little Spider" song.

When relieved of his watch at 0200, Roo spoke through salt crusted lips; "Golly matey, woaives as beeg as mountains. Me mum, she wouldn't believe it."

Later, in my 0200 to 0400 watch when the boat was quiet I stood at the wheel, alone on deck. I was sailing *Endymion* almost by rote, automatically, without thinking. I drifted into thought about my dad—remembering his encouraging me to follow my heart, live my dreams. Maybe the giant wave triggered my recall of years ago. Dad told me about judging the size of waves by comparing them to the height of the rigging. Dad told me about my granddad and *Endymion*. In 1903 she made her first and fastest Atlantic crossing "to buy Irish linen," as the story went. Sailing from New York, the paid captain doubted his chronometer. He planned to re-check once at sea. Weather began to build, so they abandoned the chronometer check, and sailed on believing they could shoot the sun by sextant making a correction en route. They never had a chance. Laden skies and strong storm winds stayed with them all across the Atlantic. The wind was on the proper quarter for big *Endymion* to show her best speed. The mid ocean seas were fifty to sixty feet high and three quarters of a mile apart, big powerful seas. They judged them by comparing them to the height of their rigging. Breaking seas were measured by how high they towered over the men they temporarily buried on deck. Dad recalled his father saying they would virtually surf the huge schooner down a giant sea at breakneck speed, falling into the trough, until the next wave caught up and hurled them forward again. Their best time was sixty-four nm in one four-hour watch—wouldn't that be fun: sixteen knots on a stately wooden schooner. No winches. No hydraulics. Only muscle to tame nature — and below deck a piano to tame mankind.

Dad also said how that maiden voyage ended. It was the 0200 watch. Grandpa had calculated them to be several hundred miles off the European coast, so he went below for a nap. At first light, the helmsman sensed shortened seas. He looked up and saw towering cliffs in front of him through the morning midst. Acting quickly, he jibed the immense schooner immediately. My granddad was thrown from his bunk. He raced topsides finding a shambles everywhere. Most standing rigging had been ripped out by the sudden jibe. In those days they had only block and tackle, with no turnbuckles or stainless steel fittings.

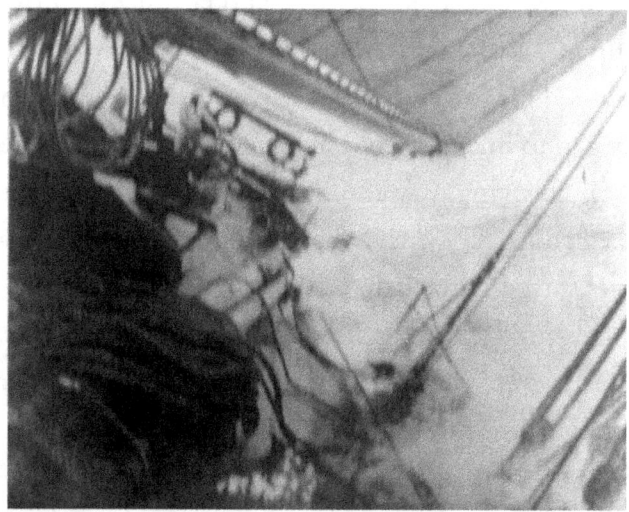

The original Endymion *circa 1905 in similar conditions. I suspect Granddad is in the pea coat to left of helmsman.*

For the entire morning, *Endymion's* crew worked tooth and nail attempting to work out of short choppy seas, the likes of which are always found during big winds near a lee shore. When they finally succeeded, they began to question where they were. It turned out they were off the coast of Ireland, several hundred miles north of their intended course.

While the experience certainly wasn't a testimony for dead reckoning in storm weather, I know they made the record book for fast passages, because I have seen it in my dad's library: eleven days and twenty hours continent to continent, a record now shattered many times.

I never met my granddad. He died before I was born, but racing with the tall ships on that night in the Tasman Sea, as I clutched the wheel and braced my legs, I sensed his comforting presence. It was not the first time. Once we were attending a family reunion at Lake Ontario. The property, still owned by my uncle, was Granddad's old lakefront home, where my dad had come into the world. Something pulled at me; I asked my dad if we could visit Grandpa's grave. Dad drove. It had been years. New roads and new buildings confused him.

"I'm lost,' Dad told me, "I know the cemetery is close, but where?"

"Go another mile, Dad. Turn left at three big trees and it's about a quarter mile to his marker on the left."

My father looked at me in a strange quizzical way. He drove as I had suggested. My intuition (?) was perfect.

I loved my dad intensely. It was hard for me to ask, "Dad, may I be a few minutes alone with Grandpa?"

Dad understood. I don't recall having special sensitivity at the time. The presence was enough. Dad never asked about it. Like I said—he understood.

Roo jolted me back to reality and our own storm, handing me a mug of hot coffee. I said something to Roo about how proud I was of

Dad and his father, and that I was proud to be sailing my own yacht, the original *Endymion*'s namesake. I don't think Roo understood a word. But I did. I felt confident. And about Dad — it's always hard to measure his absence but easy to feel his presence.

CHAPTER 11

MID-SEA APPLE SAUCE CAPER

By dawn of race day three our anemometer had firmly parked itself around thirty knots. Wind howled through the rigging the previous night, making darkness spooky, and breaking waves continued to bash us relentlessly. I was beginning to worry about my crew. They hadn't asked for or expected such continuous punishment. My routine 'crack of daylight' inspection of the decks and fittings showed no damage. "*Old Henry Wauquiez is a damn fine yacht builder,*" I thought to myself.

At 0800 roll call we were abeam of Flinders Island, northbound into one hundred twenty miles of dreaded Bass Straits separating Australia mainland from Tasmania. Here, from west to east a relentless march of waves funnels the Indian Ocean into the Pacific. Shallow depth causes the huge waves to fall over themselves, similar to a surfers dream beach. It's worse when opposing wind driven waves come from the east causing dangerous overfalls (when opposing waves meet, as they did that morning). With a good set of glasses, one can watch the waves come head on into the powerful opposing wind waves in a collision that actually stands them up on end. No place for a yacht. Many a vessel has been torn apart or lost forever in these treacherous waters. I elected not to be the next.

Extreme wind against sea overfalls—we did not see any so severe.

My intention was to sail as close as safely possible, taking advantage of the current, yet staying at least a mile from the overfalls. Our anemometer showed the wind touching forty knots several times. I was about to reduce sail but the wind settled steadily. I held off. By noontime the wind had dropped to a modest twenty knots. We were racing, so up again went our big red white and blue spinnaker. *Endymion* surged ahead in the confused seas. Kylie and Caetlin's seasickness had them excused from helm duty for nearly two days. Feeling improved, they argued for another turn at the wheel and got it. With seas abating, appetites flourished. Moods soared with blood sugar levels. We were about to give the fleet a lesson in Yankee humor and ingenuity.

Afternoon roll call was nil. No emergencies. No rescues. No problems. The weather had calmed across the fleet. It was as if the fleet had an armistice with storms, making the race radio frequency quiet.

"O.K.," I said to my crew, "Stand by for some fun."

I lifted the mike.

"Warship *Stalwart* ... Warship *Stalwart* ...Warship *Stalwart*," said I. "This is *Endymion* ... *Endymion* ... *Endymion*."

A short pause.

"*Endymion*, this is Her Royal Majesty's warship *Stalwart* ... go ahead *Endymion*."

The clear voice was crisp and properly military.

"*Endymion* here. We're having a wee bit of strife this location. Radar puts you thirty two nautical at one hundred seventy degrees. Can you lend a hand please?"

"*Endymion* ... State the nature of your problem."

"*Endymion* back. Sir, we're cooking up tasty center cut pork chops for supper and find we are fresh out of applesauce. We are hoping you blokes could give us a loan, maybe a can or two from your warship larder?"

"Wait one," said the voice from the ship, "I'll have to get my C.O."

The pause was several minutes. We wondered how many yachts were tuned to our frolic, guessing all of them.

A new voice; "*Endymion*, this is Captain Brian Wilson, C.O. her majesty's warship *Stalwart*. Am I speaking to the pride of Southern California?"

"*Endymion* back, yes sir, and about our request. Can you spare some applesauce?"

"*Endymion*," said the Commander, "maintain your course. Warm up supper. We are coming up your stern."

"Roger, and thank you Captain. You're welcome at our table."

"Don't bloody believe it," chirped Jordain. "It won't happen!"

The sisters were excited and animated. They searched constantly behind us.

Twenty minutes later we saw a tiny speck in the distance, which soon became very large. A frightening, threatening looking warship closed on our stern.

"Bugger me," Roo commented, "How many times in one's life do they have a battleship coming at them?"

"Not many."

The mighty *Stalwart* came alongside to leeward, carefully not taking our wind but totally blocking the horizon and sun, cover to cover. Standing off one hundred and fifty feet she looked elephantine, and we would be the mouse. Intimidating. I was thankful not to be the enemy.

"Bet it's a comfortable ride, too" said Caetlin.

Denise just smiled; a curious mischievous little grin crossed her face causing me to wonder if she had known Navy men before me. Sailors aboard *Stalwart* lined the rails and looked down at the small yacht sloshing through the seas ten stories below them.

Jordain was at the helm concentrating to keep us apart though the temptation to turn and watch must have been powerful.

"Attention—attention." We turned toward to voice coming from a loud hailer (electric megaphone). Standing on the bridge of *HRMS Stalwart* Commander Wilson once again lifted the load hailer.

"*Endymion*—have all hands take cover. Hold your course properly. We are going to fire a gun line across your foredeck."

"A whaat?" Denise cried out.

The shot was perfect. It soared right across our spinnaker lines. Jamie, still having trouble bending from his recent fight with the stove, joined me gathering in a thin poly line with a two foot orange heavy plastic fixture at the end.

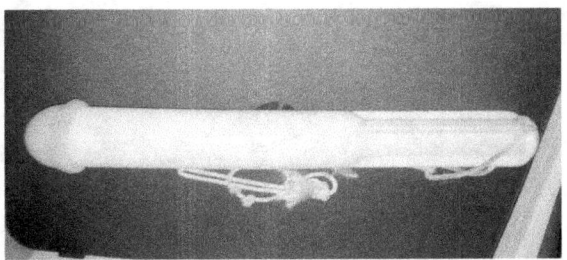

Drone fired from HRMS Stalwart.

We pulled and heaved on the thin line. It was spliced to a heavier one attached at the warship end. Clipped to the line, a canvas bag appeared over the rail of *Stalwart* and bounced in the waves as we heaved pulled it toward us. In short order the "booty" was transferred from one nation's warship to another nation's small ship.

We dragged it aboard.

A container of applesauce had made a mid-sea transfer.

"Thank you *Stalwart*." I said by radio as our crew whooped and waved.

"You are welcome, *Endymion*. Hold your course. We will circle you for pictures. See you in Sidney. *Stalwart* out"

The applesauce was generic.

Warship Stalwart *as we saw it from* Endymion. *(left)*
Endymion *from the bridge of* HRMS Stalwart. *(right)*

CHAPTER 12

ABC TELEVISION—CHOPPER BUFFOONS

No sooner had *Stalwart* disappeared from sight than the weather tanked again. I found it hard to believe weather could so constantly and quickly turn sour. It required us to dump the spinnaker, replacing it with a very small jib to punch through fresh gale force eight winds. (34-40 knots with 15-20 foot waves)

"What the hell did we do to deserve this?" asked Jordain.

"Not we, brother!" said Kylie "Don't make me a part of this charade!"

"At least we at last have sun."

Life in the Bass Straits. Not for everyone—hardly for anyone.

Below decks everything not bolted down was in a heap or scattered: books, plates, clothing, tools, cameras, cosmetics, boots, flashlights, pillows, food—everything!

I watched Denise move from the settee to the pile on the cabin sole (floor). Dressed in yellow foul weather gear she sat in the middle of the mess and looked slowly around. I could tell she was heartbroken. She looked up toward me standing behind the wheel. I'd been there most of the past forty-eight hours. I probably looked as battered as the mess around her. Suddenly a river of tears flowed from her weary eyes. I could feel her heart reaching out to me. My courageous best friend wept.

"This is our home, Skip," She sobbed. "Why are you letting this happen? I can't take much more." Grief tumbled with her troubled words, "Everything—everything's a horrible soupy, messy shambles, and for what—for a lousy name on a stupid trophy we probably won't win anyway?"

She hid her head and continued sobbing. My heart ached for Denise. She was right. I knew it and wanted to comfort her. But it wasn't just a trophy; it's competition, doing my best, beating nature, not giving up and yes, of course winning if possible. I couldn't throw in the towel and resign from the race as long as we could sail, and where else could we go right now anyway?

Denise chose that moment to speak up, as if reading my mind, to let me know she understood and I loved her more for it. Looking up she forced a smile said, "Like the guy said, it'll be over when it's over, right? I know you will bring us back safely."

What an "atta boy" that was. Denise standing strong meant the world to me. I needed approval. I had my own problems topsides trying to dodge stinging salt spray in bright sunlight though it was part of the game. It was everywhere, starting in fact to cake on my eyebrows, lips, beard, yellow slicker, even on the wheel and my hands guiding it. The entire race had become an ordeal, a test of endurance.

Late in the afternoon the weather bordered on downright violent. *Thank you again you clever weather pundits.* The radio sparked once more with navy rescues as the fleet got smaller. I decided to replace the small jib with a storm jib, barely big enough to help us maintain control. Some call it a 'hanky' sail.

I ordered all "all hands" for the jib change. I half expected calamity due to fatigue. But the kids did well in spite of the sisters' weakened, near frail conditions and the boys being rightfully exhausted. *Where, I thought, are we getting the stamina? Thank you God.*

During the next 24 hours the wind eased, the sun poked out and the forever promised southerly filled in. Up again went the big chute. We sprinted across the last of the straits toward Gabo Island at 8.5 knots.

Kylie offered her thought, "Yes, God of the sea, there is such a thing as perfect weather."

I just smiled.

Alongside and sailing close was another yacht. We checked her sail number against the race entries. I was surprised to learn the European yacht was in a non-spinnaker class because all day long she flew two different spinnakers—my first ever experience with obvious cheating at sea.

We held Gabo Island off Australia's southeastern tip abeam shortly after dark on our fourth night. Again competitors' lights were close by. Yachts that had followed different meridians across the straits converged on the southernmost point of mainland Australia. Our not-so-secret tactic was to hug the shore, along with everyone else, all bunched together. We tried but couldn't identify which boats were close in the darkness.

Around 2200 the wind shifted from southeast to west. It happened in less than a minute. Australians call these phenomena "busters." Roo was at the helm. He bore off sharply to avoid tearing sails and called "All hands." Once again we took down the spinnaker. There was enough moon to make out an unfortunate competitor behind us. The yacht had wrapped her spinnaker hopelessly around the head stay. Certainly they would need to send someone aloft.

"Been there, done that," Denise said, "I pray no one gets hurt, even if they are competition. It's a tough break."

"Yeah, well I hope it's the cheater." Kylie announced. "Serve' em right."

We hadn't seen *any* of the genuine tall ships in three days. They're fast when the wind is pushing them but suffer badly when trying to sail upwind. We figured they had sailed way off course to maintain speed and would try to make it up on a wind shift, if one came. In tall ship races there is an arbitrary finishing time deadline to enable all boats to be in port for post race ceremonies. Our deadline was 1830 on Tuesday, January 19th. If not finished we were to report our latitude and longitude to be properly handicapped by the race committee.

When the "buster" hit, *Endymion* needed to average 5.6 knots to finish in time limits. We were making 8 knots and were pumped with new adrenalin. Only two things could mess us up: another wind shift or light air, and both were predicted. Clouds rolled in through the night. Daylight dragged slowly.

We were densely fogged in by mid morning. We knew *Young Endeavor* was nearby because we could hear the ABC television helicopter whizzing around looking for her. Interview time—Captain Skip was ready!

By radio I asked the chopper if they might like to do a story about *Endymion*. "Not interested" was their empty reply. This ruffled my feathers and I thought to myself:

Hey ABC. There's a damn good story here about five Australian youth crewing on a US flag vessel in the only tall ships race ever held down-under. Your government calls it a 'sail training' exercise in your water-surrounded continent, but sailing isn't a school sport because it's too dangerous. What's with this?

Yet we take your children around the southern tip of Tasmania, as close as one can get to Antarctica, up two hundred miles of the roaring 40s rugged east coast, across the dreaded Bass Straits, and up the New South Wales coast where opposing currents raise vicious overfalls and fifty knot 'busters' occur with virtually no warning. Whaddaya mean no story?

In five days these kids have tasted a real sailor's life. They managed gale force winds, struggled through flat calms, set spinnakers on unsteady decks, felt the sting of wind-whipped spray and the bite of a barking skipper. Our youngsters sailed in thick fog, knew hunger, had been sick and so tired they could drop. Still, they remain enthusiastic and happy (I think). They even composed a silly crew song for our Parade in Sidney. Yes, ABC, there is a story and you buffoons are missing a great opportunity."

I kept those thoughts to myself. On we went through the fog and night using sound signals to announce our position, always keeping our ears tuned for sounds of other boats. No radios, no songs, very little talk. To avoid collision or rocky coast the prudent rule sailing in fog is to be able to stop in half the distance you can see. Not easy in fog at night. But we managed.

CHAPTER 13

NON TRIUMPHANT FINISH

Could anything more happen on this race? We learned shortly: yes. I awoke to the sound of distant waves crashing. Our sails luffing (flapping) indicated the wind had taken a day off. Poking my noggin through the aft cabin hatch I saw Point Perpendicular indicating the entrance to Jarvis Bay was close—a mile away. The southeast swell, left over from previous wind, was pushing us toward the beach. A 50-foot ketch, not a racer, was abandoned and breaking up on the beach. I knew we didn't have enough wind to sail away from shore safely. Checking our Brooks & Gatehouse instruments I saw zero wind and twenty feet of depth. Not enough depth. Not enough wind. All it would take is scraping bottom once on one wave heading to shore, and *Endymion* might easily be lost. I made a tough decision.

"Denise, fire up the Perkins, we're going to motor around the point to a safe distance and declare our motoring time to the Race Committee. It's legal but not a feel-good maneuver."

"Aye aye Capt'n" she responded, putting her toast on the settee while she reached over to start the engine.

As we powered into safe water further from shore a chilling metallic rattle sounded from the engine room, tripping the engine overheat alarm. Denise shut it down immediately.

Taking stock of our position, I was comfortable with our distance from shore, more than three nm. A light easterly was developing, enabling us to concentrate on sailing to weather even though against the current. There was little chance of making race deadline with nearly 90 nm still to go. Denise ordered sails set accordingly.

Roo and I assessed the engine problem, concluding we had a raw water problem where seawater that cools the engine wasn't circulating. We had tackled a similar problem the previous day, to a lesser extent. Apparently we hadn't done enough.

Sailing north against the southerly current was bumpy. Being a dope, I told Roo to put the engine problem aside. We could handle it in port, only ninety nm away.

Throughout the day the wind continued to build. At about 1400 our world came apart—again. We were beating into twenty-five knot headwinds with reefed sails and a heavy running sea. A monster wave, reminding us again of the power of the oceans, broke over the bow smashing into the jib with tons of force. That jib, one of my favorite sails, literally exploded. It sounded like a cannon. The clew had torn cleanly away and both the luff and leach ripped full length.

"All hands" was called to haul in the remains of our supposedly "bullet proof" storm jib. Taking the forward position, wedged into the bow pulpit and hanging on as waves submerged me, I made another troubling discovery. The aluminum extrusion surrounding the head stay (on which the jib roller-reefs) had been ripped to shreds—jagged all 360 degrees around. It was now useless.

Out came our sail of last resort, a postage stamp sized storm jib. Bone tired, we carefully led the luff up the forestay, by hand, inch after inch. There would be no reefing this sail. We were dejected, burned out, starting to feel indifferent. Like the ninth inning, two out and your team is down six runs. There is always hope. Hope is good. Then there is reality. Your team probably won't win. For us the reality against hope was that there was no chance, even an outside chance that we could finish before deadline.

But I still had hope, eternal hope—I had been taught to always do something positive in times of despair. So Roo, Jamie and I tossed aside some of the mess on the salon floor and set about repairing the jib. Using a marlinspike to punch holes in the tough sailcloth to replace and relocate the clew, we jury-rigged the rest with whipping twine and seizing wire. It was slow work in heavy pitching seas. Six non-stop hours later, the damaged sail was ready to serve us again.

Alas though, when the race deadline passed we were thirty-two nm from the finish line. We had logged over eight hundred nm in the crappiest conditions imaginable. It was a huge disappointment to an already disheartened crew. The kids, Denise—all of us had all tried so hard. Bummed out as our team was, there was no grumbling or whining. I thought privately about Denise, the way she had looked at me through tears, asking why we did this. That was a tough question to answer.

At least the wind moderated as we sailed into our last night—dark with heavy clouds and dark with our heavy spirit.

"It's time," I announced as the bells chimed midnight, "to get plastered! Good sailing everyone—no more singing the blues."

Those still awake watched with smiles as Denise popped a bottle of champagne, initiating a quasi celebration. I thought of Grandpa off the cliffs of Dover, having to turn back. He wasn't racing at the time, and we were not a 130 footer crewed by heavily muscled men, yet we had a commonality. We had won over nature and danger at sea. Caetlin passed out paper cups.

"Hold a sec, Caetlin. I'll make this better. Open the cupboard behind you," I directed, "yeah, the one below the TV."

Caetlin opened the cupboard.

"Great, now bring out six glasses."

"These?"

"Yes. Faithful crew gathered round, you are about to sip champagne from glasses that were aboard the original *Endymion* close to ninety years ago. What you are holding in this distant corner of the world is genuine *Tiffany* glassware from their original 1800's store in New York City. Let us drink."

"Hear, hear," said Jordain, "let us also be careful handling history."

That wiped the edge from our gloom, at least temporarily. Progress was slow in the soft wind. In the last forty hours we had progressed thirty nm toward Sidney. In the last six hours we had given up six of them by current pushing us backwards.

Finally at 0800 on January 21st came the ultimate embarrassment. We fired up the engine—but it wouldn't start. Less than three nm offshore of Sydney Heads we radioed for a tow. A police launch pulled us to our pre-assigned berth in Sydney's Darling Harbor where we received an unexpectedly warm reception.

Endymion, the smallest of the four yachts from America, including the US Coastguard tall ship *Eagle,* had at least arrived safely.

Final count: seven dismasted, two lost rudders, *Winston Churchill* from England sank (her crew were rescued). Across the fleet there were many injuries, some serious. Another forty yachts had dropped out. No tall ship finished before the deadline. On corrected time we placed 32nd of a possible 185 starters. No trophies.

Denise and I were, and remain, intensely proud of the youngsters who raced aboard *Endymion* with us. We believe they felt our pride in them. Those friendships, carved in the moods of nature and born under thunderous conditions, will understandably last our lifetime. More about that later.

Tied up in Darling harbor, we looked for a shower.

CHAPTER 14

THANK YOU, AUSTRALIA

Sydney town's entire waterfront, from the Opera House to Birkenhead, was packed with race yachts. It appeared all of Australia's citizens had come to visit the fleet. For hours on end our young crew happily signed autographs and posed for photos with endless admirers. They deserved every ounce of admiration showered upon them. Many who came for the festivities had small souvenir books with a brief write-up about each competing yacht. It was heady stuff. Australian pride was rampant as the nation celebrated its 200th birthday.

We visited until wee hours with yachts from other nations. The skipper and crew of the forty-three foot sloop *Kommander Bering* joined us aboard *Endymion* for "Big Macs" and vodka. None of us understood a word spoken by either team but it didn't matter. The evening was rich with understanding and camaraderie. She was the first and only yacht we had seen from the Soviet Union. Believe me, we solved all differences between our nations that evening. Every yacht and all crew from every country behaved impeccably.

"Ya know Skip," Denise pointed out one evening as we cuddled in the cockpit, "You're right. I know you were kidding before but if leaders of countries represented here were like the yachtsmen representing them, there would be no trouble in the world."

I so agreed, and still do years later as I remember her words.

An amazing visit for Denise and me was to *Shabab Oman,* owned by the absolute monarch of Oman in the Arabian Sea. Built in 1971, *Shabab* was the world's oldest surviving wooden tall ship, sailed by British X-Pat Captain Christopher Biggens and crew. Following a glass of wine aboard *Endymion,* he invited us for breakfast the following day in the Sultan's suite. Considering its tropical homeport environment *Shabab Oman,* with exquisite gold trim in abundance, was in pristine condition. Uniformed orderlies elegantly presented breakfast, including caviar, calamari and duck eggs. Denise will remember it fondly, as I do my first Big Mac.

We participated in a parade through Sydney, finishing at the Opera House for a raucous awards ceremony. Three thousand exuberant young and old from around the world gathered in the famous building to receive their honors. Even *Endymion* received an armful of plaques, engraved silver cups, tee shirts, posters, badges and pins.

At one point Prime Minister Bob Hawke was about to speak into a microphone. The crowd screamed for the Navy band to play "La Bamba." At first the bandleader refused, then acquiesced causing the Opera House to erupt in spontaneous song. Flags were waving wildly—not as one would expect in an opera house. On stage even the normally prim Governor General's wife was slapping her knees to the rhythm—causing the crowd to cheer wildly. I felt goose bumps. People shouted and waved. They wouldn't stop. It was infectious pandemonium. Just when it couldn't become more raucous virtually everyone in the packed house stood for the unofficial anthem, Waltzing Matilda—Australia's most coveted tune. It was lifetime unforgettable, wild, exhausting fun!

And that wasn't all. Like many other skippers, I lingered after the ceremony to be interviewed by media, which I relished, as readers of my first book know. Interviews would take about a half hour. I had promised to meet Denise in front of the famous structure.

"Take a short cut, right ober dere Captain," said a worker pointing to a stairway in the corner of the pressroom. I took it. The door at the bottom opened to the outside. Being in a hurry I swung it hard, practically bumping into Princess Di and Prince Charles. There was no security. None. In fact no other people at all. They were awaiting their transport. I was alone with cherished royalty. Flustered and caught without words, I gave a quick salute and ran off to meet Denise, never giving it another thought.

The official Australian two hundred year birthdate was January 26th, celebrating the first settlement at Port Jackson in 1788. A colossal parade of boats through Sydney Harbor was scheduled for that night. It would culminate with a spectacular fireworks display from the Harbor Bridge next to the Opera House. We challenged our crew to invite their Sydney-sider friends aboard *Endymion* for the evening. Denise and I would supply food if they would bring their beverage. Man, were we asking for it.

Friday, January 23rd I went to the bank to secure some extra cash. I asked for $200.00 in tens.

"Would ya like some Bicentenary tens?" the smiling clerk asked. "They're being introduced this morning, and have a hologram. Here, take a sticky-beak (look)," she said, handing me one for inspection. (Never see that in a US bank!)

"Those are great." I said, thinking the notes, picturing a tall ship on one side and an aboriginal person on the other, would make great gifts to friends back home. "I'll take twenty of them please."

By noon that day the Royal Bank of Australia suspended distribution and recalled all the notes. Rushed into production for the bicentennial, they contained the world's first sophisticated optically variable device (hologram) intended to discourage counterfeiting. But they scratched, and the ink could smear. Alarmed at the public's negative opinion, the bank asked the bills be returned. I still have mine.

$10.00 notes issued on Bicentenary day.

Throughout the afternoon friends of our crew began arriving. When we tossed off our dock lines and headed for the harbor party, we had thirty-eight guests and their twenty-eight eskies aboard. *Endymion* was seriously overloaded.

Denise approached me at the wheel; "We have trouble below. There's water over the floorboard."

"What! You mean *on* the floorboards or *over* them?'"

"Over, and Skip, I can't tell where it's coming from."

"And I can't leave the wheel, unless you take it. Everything that floats must be out here. Not many are sober either."

"Not me tonight. No thanks. I'll grab Roo, have him take a look."

I heard Denise getting Roo's attention as I maneuvered to avoid another overzealous party bunch in a small motor launch. Roo was back shortly.

"Skip, I closed all the thru-hull stop cocks for the sinks and both heads. Pump is on. We need to keep an eye on it. Otherwise — party as she goes."

Sure, easy for you to say, I thought. Then re-thought it. Roo was a responsible person so I stopped worrying. This was celebration time. Times Square on New Year's Eve couldn't be more crowded than Sydney Harbor on Birthday Night. All of the tall ships along with every competitor yacht still in Australia was on the water, as was just about any object capable of supporting an Aussie and his eskie. We took position at the stern of *Juan Sebastian Elcano,* the massive frigate from Spain.

Sydney harbor celebration.

Every yacht with a mast had people hanging in the rigging, including us. Boats were going in every direction, some under command and others free spinning in a scene of mass confusion. We averted collisions and created a night never to be forgotten by any of the enthusiastic and socially engaged (drunk) persons aboard *Endymion*. The last of whom departed at the crack of noon the following day.

The whole Bicentenary celebration had been spectacular.

Thank you, Australia. You are a marvelous nation.

CHAPTER 15

BEYOND SYDNEY

Kylie and Caetlin left to continue their educations, Kylie to someday be a vet working with big animals and Caetlin to be a flying doctor. Somehow I couldn't grasp a life-size picture of either but best of wished the best to both. They were great young people to know.

Denise believed they would both succeed but added, "I had some vet training. Not for big animals like Kylie wants. She's too sweet to be stickin her arm up the butt of some cow."

Roo hadn't had enough and remained aboard.

In February we sailed to the Hawkesbury, a vast network of bays and small rivers surrounded by national parks. Alone again, we were bathing under waterfalls surrounded by abundant parkland wildlife. I thought of Australia's 200 years and bet myself this spot hadn't changed since the first settlers. A troubled iguana, and a big one at over three feet had tangled with a plastic shopping bag and lost. The bag was stuck around the iguana's neck. It seemed to '*hiiiissss*' when I looked its way.

Denise kept one foot in the inflatable and one on land in case she had to make a hasty retreat. "OK, my captain," she remarked, "How are you going to handle this one?"

"Pass the buck. I won't. Roo will."

Roo shot back, "I thought I'd ask you Denise, you're the vet trainee. Got a plan?"

"To watch Skip herd it up that tree with a stick," she said, pointing out a flimsy sapling just beyond the creature, "Then he'll beat the tree with the stick, the iguana will fall and you catch it in a trash bag."

"No damn way fair maiden," Roo said.

Skip already had the iguana treed. Roo walked to the tree. Denise kept her distance.

"Aww, don't fret skipper—it's probably not poisonous."

Roo shot a hand out faster than a professional boxer, grabbing the ugly beast behind its neck. Carefully he removed the confining plastic, then jumped back, setting his new friend free.

"Gotta tell ya Denise, that scared the piss outa me but I wasn't half as fearless as you were climbin' the mast in Tall Ships."

If he was fishing for praise he didn't get any.

Mostly in the Hawkesbury we worked on our tans, bathed beneath a favorite waterfall and relaxed—the way we should when life is all about drifting and blending. Our race crew and their families came to visit. We bathed some more and BBQ'd on the tiny beach below the waterfall until we couldn't eat anymore. One evening a mega yacht flying the colors of Singapore anchored close by. They radioed an invitation for cocktails and dinner aboard. I've been asked not to repeat the owners' name. I'll say only he was a Chinese gentleman who owned an Asian publishing empire. His vessel was elegant. We felt privileged to have been aboard and were even offered showers in any of seven lavish bathrooms. He gave me a business card saying; "If you ever write about these adventures you're having, let me see it first." I lost the card.

Our visitors and Roo all left shortly thereafter. Roo promised to rejoin us further up the Australian coast, in a year or so. He would always be welcome.

Returning to reality Denise had a rapidly growing plethora of ducks she enjoyed feeding. Seagulls discovered the free chow and circled *Endymion* patiently waiting for crumbs Denise would toss overboard. The gulls then swooped in snatching the crumbs in mid-air, depriving the poor ducks of their chow.

"Crapola," uttered frustrated Denise, returning from the galley with more bread slices. "I'm running out of duck fuel."

"I believe I have a solution. Be right back," I said sliding below to the galley.

"Here, try these crumbs Denise" I said returning, passing her a handful of moist breadcrumbs.

"Why are they wet?"

"Don't ask questions, Babe. Just toss 'em, OK?"

Denise lofted a handful. The seagulls swooped in, grabbed every one, and flew away, never to return.

"Damn, that was easy. What'd you do, Skip."

"Tabasco."

Charlie Conlen, a close friend from California, and his lady friend Miriam came to visit. It's important, I believe, to understand Charlie enjoyed a cocktail more than Miriam and occasionally sipped from a vodka-laden diet Pepsi can. Charlie wasn't an alcoholic. He simply enjoyed an occasional "pop" for which Miriam did not share his enthusiasm. Charlie replenished his diet Pepsi can from a Grey Goose bottle hidden in our 'black hole' storage compartment. Generally speaking Charlie enjoyed everything, except a little black cloud that followed him.

Charlie handles BBQ one of few evenings it didn't rain.

Charlie was a handsome, generous individual. He offered to sponsor dinner at the Pittwater's Royal Prince Alfred Yacht Club, with a typical expensive private club menu. We took advantage of his generosity.

What unexpectedly followed the next morning was a remarkable example of Australian humility and hospitality.

Denise and Miriam loved animals. A trip to Australia's famous Taronga Zoo was to be a highlight of their visit. We planned to go there by bus. I went to the club early in the morning seeking directions to a bus stop, but the doors were locked. Turning to leave, out of the corner of my eye I saw someone inside coming toward the door. The man who opened it slightly was grey haired, semi distinguished in appearance with an open collar, loose tie with a club burgee on it, no jacket and black trousers — obviously the uniform of a watchman. His shirt was slightly wrinkled; he wore a paging beeper on his side and carried a black umbrella. No doubt an employee getting off duty.

"Pardon me," I asked looking past him into the empty clubhouse, "is there a nearby bus stop?"

"Who are you, and where do you want to go?"

"Four of us are aboard *Endymion,* the America ketch registered at your guest dock and we hope to go to the zoo."

"Taronga zoo?" he inquired. "It's at least two hours from here."

"Thus we're looking for a bus, is there a stop nearby?"

"About two kilometers." he said. "I can draw you a map. When do you want to go? Service is rather bodgy."

"Anytime. We're ready now," I fibbed. The girls are never ready.

"I'm about to leave myself. Give me fifteen to wrap'er up here. I'll come down the hill here in a bluish colored ride," he said pointing past a small boathouse, " I'll take you on right here and drop you at the bus stop."

"Great, and thank you, I'll fetch my friends."

Gathered at the clubs front entrance we waited but a few minutes before sighting a metallic-blue Mercedes, long as a hearse, approach from the hill. Mister security was at the wheel. We piled in with me up front as company for the watchman cum chauffeur.

We had yakked for twenty minutes when I commented, " it's a long way to the bus. I was thinking you said 2 kilometers."

"Slack morning," said the driver. "We like Yanks, so I'm taking you directly to the zoo."

"Thanks. Good stuff, but your boss, will he be good with that?" I asked.

"I am the boss," he laughed heartily, "and it's my car. Don't be embarrassed, it's happened before."

During the remaining drive we learned our car pilot's name was George and that he made coffee for a living.

"George, I'm guessing the sport fisher we walked past this morning with the name *Coffee* something is your boat?"

"Right-ee-oh. *Coffee Time* is her proper name. She's a good boat and where I taught my kids basic skills and values."

"Tell me about them."

"Skills or kids?"

"Both."

"My daughter's a "jillaroo' (ranch hand) on a station (ranch). My son works in my warehouse, learning the business ropes. They both handle ropes." He chuckled at his joke.

George seemed a typically humble Australian. We carried on a lively discussion about securing shelf space in grocery or big box stores, as that had been my skill in the manufacturer's rep business.

Parting at the zoo I told George he likely had a future in the coffee business if he decided to stay with it, and I wished him luck. George handed me his business card, which I pocketed without examining as we shook hands.

Taronga Zoo was complex. We hired a guide to aid us in understanding the zoo's nocturnal exhibits. I told her about the remarkable guy and the stretch Mercedes who had given us a long ride from the Pittwater.

"Did you get his name?" she asked.

"George."

"OK, but did you get his surname?"

"No, he never—Hey, wait a sec. I've got his card," I said, fishing in my pocket. "Andronicus, George Andronicus, sounds rather Greek."

"Oh ... my ... God!" Our excited guide practically fell over herself, "He's Australia's coffee magnate. He's one of our country's most wealthy men—his father was the Greek Consul in Australia—and *he* drove you here *himself?*" she asked.

We were as amazed as our guide.

But back to Charlie's little black cloud. It bothered him when Captain Skip shook the gondola riding high above the gorillas. Frightened me too. It concerned him, as would be expected, when a Doberman chased him onto the bonnet of a parked BMW (with a driver inside)—and pissed him off when Denise held a brown bag to his nostrils helping him breathe during a modest panic attack. Charlie thought he was dying. I don't recall what caused the panic attack. I know I was standing by asking, "Hey Charlie, can I have your Jaguar?" Writing home about it Denise said;

I think both of our men packed away too much wine & vodka. It may have affected Charlie more because of the drag long distance travel sleep deprivation puts on a person.

I agreed. Charlie and Miriam packed a lot into their two weeks with us. We had fun.

CHAPTER 16

BEFORE MOOLOOLABA

Denise and I gunk-holed up the Australian east coast anchoring most every night. By now we were well acquainted with the Australian fantasy called weather forecasting—more of a scientific wild-assed guess. The term "fine" was supposedly akin to "sunny and warm" as would be said in America. We learned to interpret "fine" to occasionally mean pissing down rain, high winds and rough seas. Denise and I operated well as a team. Anchoring had become second nature and I trusted Denise implicitly. But mistakes occur.

Port Stephens lies along a thirty-kilometer plus stretch of sandy beaches. Slipping into Port Stephens at dusk and quite tired from a "fine" day we found the anchorage shallow, small and tightly packed with smaller boats—mostly day sailors or cuddy cabin models. The breeze was strong. Bobbing anchored boats faced into it. We were large for this small harbor and sensed many eyes on us. To find a slot we needed to circle behind those already anchored, putting us broadside to the wind and dangerously close to the beach. I would have to pass close to the stern of anchored boats and "crab" a bit to windward to keep from going aground. Denise went forward to handle the anchor.

I passed ten feet from the stern of an anchored catamaran. These boats tend to swing more on anchor than a monohull. This dope, unlike any other boat in the anchorage, had a stern line running to the beach. The line was slack and underwater. I didn't see it. *Endymion* suddenly jerked to port and nearly stopped.

Denise lost her balance, nearly fell and yelled from up forward, "What are you doing Skip?"

"I caught the stupid catamaran's stern anchor. Hang on! I'm in neutral."

"Crapola Skip, you're gonna sink that 20 footer. Slow down."

"I'm *in* neutral damn it."

We were being blown into a boat with no one on board. We could do it serious damage. I took a chance throwing the helm to starboard and giving us half forward throttle. *Endymion's* prop was powerful enough to cut the light line of the catamaran. We broke free and found a spot. Denise handled the anchor perfectly, even shouting out for me to give depths so she could judge scope as we backed to set the hook. We settled in for the night with our only damage being pride.

Denise had come a long way from her earliest experiences with me as skipper. I thought back to a time shortly after we started dating a few years back. We were spending a weekend at Catalina Island aboard my thirty-six-foot "cigarette" type boat named *E-Ticket*. At one time an 'E-Ticket' bought the best rides in Disneyland—thus the name.

We anchored in a small cove for a naked swim. Our anchor was "stern to" encouraging our lying in the sun or making love on the swim platform while cooling gentle waves lapped around our California

E Ticket *as seen from my bedroom on Naples Island.*

tanned bodies. It was a superb slice of life day. But a strong afternoon wind set in, making the cove uncomfortable. I *carefully* explained to Denise how to take in the anchor line:

"Hand over hand. Hold it high, like this." I instructed, holding the line in both hands high over my head. "You have to keep it out of the water so it won't get caught in the props."

"OK. OK!" Denise had become a little impatient with my over-coaching. "I can do it."

It didn't work. She either paused to sip champagne from an unfinished glass or got interested in nearby seagulls. The line wrapped solidly around our port prop. I had to dive to clear it. I have never enjoyed working under water but I dove to clear the line and to impress my girlfriend. *E-Ticket* was rocking enough at this point that I took a couple of uncomfortable whacks on the head from the swim step above my work area. Not so silently cursing, I gave up. After climbing aboard I cut the line and surrendered the anchor to the ocean bed.

Now we had only one engine to get us 10 nm south to Avalon where I might find a diver. The going was slow. We spotted a small sail boat with no sails up. Someone was waving a paddle. We went to investigate.

"Can you tow us into Avalon?" the skipper yelled across 100 feet separating us.

"We could," I hailed in return, "but I've got a line wrapped around a prop and have only one engine. Be slow going."

""I'm a diver," he shouted.

"Yea!" said Denise.

"OK. Good stuff. I'll toss you a line. Maybe we can help each other."

Denise's job was to steer us close enough for me to heave a line by which we could connect both boats. I gathered an appropriate line and went to the pitching foredeck to toss it.

"Gotta get us a little closer." I told Denise, "Another 20 feet will do it."

In her joy for the day or whatever other nonsense went through her mind Denise decided she wanted to give her new friends a bottle of my champagne. Maneuvering close, so she could hand pass the bubbly, she got into trouble. In an instant we were broadside to the bow of the sailboat. A second later the sailboat punched a good size hole into our port side.

Fortunately the hole, though expensive to repair, was above our waterline. We all got to Avalon and eventually shared the champagne. *Incredible*, I thought to myself, *how far Denise has come since those early dating days.*

Back in reality, I decided to move on from Port Stephens. We found a diver to fetch the catamaran's anchor, paid his fee and pointed our bow north again in mostly "fine" weather. Denise described it in another of her letters:

Well we're back in the "fine weather." It poured all day with wind again, lots of it along with rolling seas. We were trying to go north against a southerly current for nearly 18 hours making us well familiar with the lights of Port Macquarie on shore. Exhausted, about 24 hours later we pulled into a small anchorage called Trial Bay. We made it to Coffs Harbor, the place where we had first arrived in Australia, the next day.

Eventually the "fine" weather turned fine and we had a fine time at Coffs Harbor playing cards, munching fresh seafood or sleeping for a change on a boat that didn't move or make strange noises because we were tied to a dock. I also worked on a private top-secret project involving a couple of pipe cleaners. I always carried a few in our toolbox for odd jobs. Superb weather conditions lasted three days before "fine" became foul. Sitting under the awning Denise and I pondered alternatives. I'd had an idea up my sleeve for a while and turning to Denise said, "Remember Barry Manilow? He sang the McDonalds commercial *You Deserve a Break Today*. Well, maybe we need one too. Let's go to New Zealand!"

"When?"

"Now!"

"You mean like *right now?* Today?"

"Exactly!"

"OK."

Simple as that—the joy of schedule free drifting and blending.

CHAPTER 17

THE AMAZING PIPE CLEANER STORY

We left the following day for Sydney where we transferred to Air New Zealand for a flight to Christchurch on New Zealand's southern island. Only Business Class was available. We splurged.

Crossing the Tasman Sea at 30,000 feet was a lot different than sailing across. Denise was yakking with a stewardess about our experiences. The stewardess asked Denise to "wait one" and disappeared forward. Returning shortly and wearing a huge smile she said, "The captain invites you to join him in the cockpit."

"You're kidding. Us—really?"

"Yes. Follow me please."

Denise and I were offered jump seats behind the pilot and co-pilot. The pilot was a sailor. We had a lot in common. We stayed forward the remainder of the crossing including the approach over the Southern Alps and until the flight was docked in Christchurch.

A debate that had percolated in my mind several times recently was taking shape again. It involved the pipe cleaners. Decision time was close. More shortly.

This was holiday time for Denise and me, as lovers, friends and shipmates. We took in the tourist sites of Christchurch, rented a car and drove a coastal road south to Queensland—a superb highway with almost no traffic. I made a mistake by whizzing past glow worm caves Denise was anxious to see. I made a second mistake trying to convince her it was "by accident." Our drive included revenge for slipping past the glow worms. Denise fed all my favorite cheese and crackers to sheep gathered outside our window while I slept. In the shadows of Mt. Cook on day two she planted a huge kiss on the nose of a beautiful white horse she met in a pasture. We laughed hard thinking of the surprise awaiting some farmer.

Denise about to plant a big red kiss on farmers horse.

On a secondary road to Queenstown we were slowed by hairpin turns offering incredible views and romantic hidden switchbacks. We hid out in one for a picnic and to make love in a forest. We even saw a road sign saying *Please Give Way.* Imagine a sign like *that* in America.

There wasn't a moment where we felt anything less than filled with love and joy — but the private debate in my mind hounded me though our checking in at a secluded Queenstown boutique hotel close to the shores of Lake Wakatipu. Lovely as the lake was, we chose not to take advertised tour boat excursions. We opted to follow the sometimes hazardous, sometimes dirt, and sometimes almost no road leading to the lake's most distant point, Glenorchy.

"What the hell," I told Denise, when she complained about the bumpy ride, "It's a rented car."

"Doesn't mean you can wreck it, or kill us."

The drive was scary along some sections where it appeared the mountain above had crumbled before, and could again—tossing us into the lake between the road and Pig Island. I drove carefully. Denise closed her eyes.

Those who told us Glenorchy was small, spoke not with forked tongue. We found a closed restaurant and a liquor store that was open "just for us"—all we needed. Next stop a romantic waterside picnic and skinny-dip.

"Forget it," I advised Denise after I dove from a rock. "Water has to be 40 degrees Fahrenheit and it's friggin summertime."

"Yeah, damn mosquitos are twin-engine jobs. Ouch!" Denise took a vicious swing at one. "Why I wonder, didn't Noah swat two of them way back when?"

Back in our accommodation Denise lazed away having a "tubbie" (bath) while I worked on my pipe cleaner creation and again struggled with the mental gymnastics of it being near decision time for the idea up my sleeve. I made reservations for dinner at the Stratosfare Skyline Restaurant, a gondola ride up a mountainside overlooking town and lake. A classy dinner was in order.

Denise looked marvelous in a tan and black jacket pant outfit, a snow white blouse and a flower in her hair.

Riding the gondola to mountaintop she turned to me. "You seem nervous Skip. Can't take the height?" she asked with a chuckle.

"No No. I'm fine." I fibbed. I was very nervous, but not because of the gondola.

The lights of Queenstown began to twinkle in fading dusk light. The hostess seated us beside a huge window overlooking all of Queenstown and the lake. Perfect. Truly p-e-r-f-e-c-t.

"What's it going to be for you lovely people?" asked the waiter.

"My lady will have your best local Merlot please, and I will have vodka rocks with cocktail onions. Emphasis on onions, plural."

"It's called a Gibson." Denise regularly reminded me.

We sat. We talked about friends and family, especially Denise's dad and people he had met while he was senior audio engineer for Ed Sullivan, the Beatles and Elvis—she was wishing her folks could be with us. I listened, but was preoccupied. I didn't want Denise to see the little sweat beads I could feel on my forehead. I excused myself, went to the restroom feeling jittery, had a comforting word from the waiter and returned to the table.

"You OK, honey? You seem out of sorts." Denise did worry about me.

"Yup. I'm OK."

"Good. I just love this view. Thanks for bringing me here."

"You know Denise, I was thinking more about your dad ..."

"What about him? Go on."

"If he was here I would have a few questions for him ..."

"About show business? Ed Sullivan?" Denise interrupted.

"No." Reaching out and taking her hand and shaking like a leaf in the wind, I said, " I would ask him for permission to marry you!"

I pulled the ring I had fashioned from pipe cleaners from my pocket and held it before her ring finger. "Denise Wharton—I love you. Will you marry me? Spend your life with me?"

"Ohhh my God! Yes! Yes!"

At the same perfect moment the wait staff arrived with champagne, candles and roses. Denise had come around the table. She was in my arms. People applauded, people we didn't know wished us well—and a long life.

The secret project I had wrestled with was over. The pipe cleaners had been delivered, had done their job.

In our room again Denise couldn't wait to call her mother.

Denise was happy. I was happy. Her mom was thrilled. It was 5:00 am in California. All her dad said was, "She's all yours now, pal."

Wedding arrangements were underway.

CHAPTER 18

UP A NOT SO LAZY RIVER

"How about we do this?" Denise questioned, looking up from her place of comfort in the corner of *Endymion's* cockpit.

Endymion's *cockpit*

"What's this?" I hardly looked up from the log entry I was writing.

"How about we go up a lazy river?"

Denise handed me a chartlet of the Clarence River along with a brochure for the port village of Yamba.

"Looks interesting—fetch me a larger scale chart though. I want to see the river bar. I've read it can be nasty, so let's take a look."

I wiped recent rainwater from the cockpit table to secure a dry spot for the chart. It had been raining constantly for two days.

"We've never been up a river," Denise offered, "I think it would be fun to cruise in farmland, see some critters and sleep without rocking."

Examining the chart and cruising guide I found the Clarence River, second largest in Australia, to be more commercially oriented than for pleasure boats, especially yachts. There were two bridges, one a vertical lift bridge at Harwood about twelve miles in from the coast. The second was a double decker, cars on one level, railroad on the next. That bridge, at Grafton, was forty miles inland. Both opened. The Harwood contraption required a prior appointment because a water main ran across it requiring a four-man work party to close and separate it before the bridge could open. The more complicated Grafton bridge required two years advance notice.

Aussie humor perhaps—but it was in the guidebook.

"The Clarence River," Denise was reading from the guidebook, "pours more volume of water into the ocean than any other river in Australia."

"Really? That's a tad concerning. I suppose it means the river bar could be a dangerous crossing."

"Probably, it says here to exercise 'extreme caution' when attempting this crossing."

"Meaning," I said, "we need to cross on a slack tide in 'fine' weather. Goes without saying we should cross in daylight."

Denise chuckled. We had handled river bars. Australia has plenty of them. With our six-foot keel this one was potentially hazardous.

Our crossing went perfectly. It was mid morning so we powered upstream. We had seen several thousand trawlers since arriving down under. Most were small and crewed by two to four persons. A few larger models may have had ten aboard and cost millions. Several dozen were anchored in the first few miles of the Clarence River, with an equal number either working the river or headed for sea.

Denise, using her sensual voice, radioed for an appointment to have the Harwood Bridge opened. It started raining—hard driving rain. *Endymion* had four hours to make the 1500-hour opening reserved for us. The bridge was less than 10 nm ahead. We throttled back and motored slowly through beautiful, peaceful farm country seeing occasional locals along the banks. Some were youngsters sitting in trees dangling a fishing line. Rain didn't bother them. Shrimping trawlers worked the river's center. Occasionally we would pass a few houses, a small village or deserted barn.

"This," Denise said, "is my kind of cruising—gentle breezes, no seas, interesting scenery. Maybe a touch too much rain."

Arriving at the Harwood Bridge early, we dropped anchor, enjoyed one of Denise's hand crafted sandwiches, and relaxed. At a quarter hour before our scheduled 1500 opening we upped the anchor and moved into position so we would not delay road traffic longer than necessary. But the bridge didn't open. At 1530 we contacted the Coast Guard.

"Sorry mate," the radio voice reported, "they've been blacktopping the road and are running late. Stand by. We'll get straight on it. Fair dinkum." (seriously)

At suppertime sirens howled. Traffic stopped and the center span rose slowly, straight up toward boiling black rain clouds. We passed under, left Harwood (population 120) and tied to the new Municipal Wharf beside a lovely park in the center of MacLean. Population there was around 1600, mostly Scottish. Great bakery.

We were both suffering 'space fatigue' having been below deck so much during rain. It's confining when your entire indoor home is 43 feet by 13 feet and pinched at one end. Denise tended to curl up with a good book while I grumbled and performed chores. She had always been of a more peaceful nature while I sometimes wore an old Los Angeles Rams ball cap, a signal to all in range not to bother me. After two days of this confinement we set off under heavy rainy skies still determined to go up river, at least to Grafton. By midday the river became narrow. It woke me up mentally because it was challenging, requiring real concentration to avoid its many shoals. We passed under two sets of high voltage cables. That clarified for me why tall mast yachts are uncommon on the river—wouldn't want to tangle with that voltage.

"You would certainly be a more electrifying personality," Denise joked.

We set anchor 200 yards south of the Grafton Bridge at dusk, just as the radio announced it was more rain than Australia had experienced in fifty years. It was forecast to continue through Easter, two days away, and there had been serious flooding in a town called Alice Springs. It didn't worry me yet, though I was mildly concerned.

"This is getting tiring."

Denise started a new book.

CHAPTER 19

THE BIG WET

Saturday April 2nd was Easter Eve. Relentless rain continued. It had to be Australia's longest non-stop drenching. During one squall we heard a voice. Someone was hailing us from shore, "*Endymion*—Ahoy there *Endymion*, would ya be hankerin fer a hot shower and tucker (food) ashore. Any interest?"

We about fell over each other accepting the offer from the owner of a stately home perched high on the riverbank. Later that night over coffee and brandy I expressed my concern over the steadily rising level of the river.

"No worries mate," he assured us, so we accepted an invitation to an Easter luncheon.

Easter morning broke looking dark and glum. The river current had quickened its pace. Checking my position fixes I had confidence we hadn't dragged anchor but also saw that the river was even higher. With encouragement we joined our new friends Pam and Ferguson Fysch, and a party of fourteen of their mates. Brunch, the best in

New South Wales, we were told, was only a 30 minute car ride north of the bridge. Pulling into the rustic restaurant parking lot an alarm sounded through the car radio, followed by a terse announcement:

"Following is a flood warning for the Clarence River." The voice was dull and methodical. "Excessive rain in the catchment area has resulted in the following high water warnings for the Clarence River for Monday, April 4th.

"Catmanhurst—11.5 meters by 0300

"Koolkhan—13 meters by 0700

"Grafton—5 meters by 1500"

There would be no lunch today for us. I sat frozen—goose bumps covered me.

"Grafton! Christ! What craziness. The damn river *is* flooding, isn't it?"

"Yes," chorused our new friends. "We've had high water. This much isn't normal. It could be dangerous. Be better we turn around and get you back to your boat. We can do brunch another time but you should head downriver right away—soon as you can!"

There was no panic in anyone's voice, but obvious concern. Denise and I had joked the continuous rain was probably payback from Charlie's little black cloud. The radio guys called it "*The Big Wet.*" Locals had laughed saying, "She's Australia mate—take buckets more than this spit to raise that river." And so it spat. It wasn't funny anymore.

We had promised our new friends that I would whip up some "Yankee Chili" after Easter Sunday. Not to be! The *Big Wet* had changed our calendar.

Back aboard *Endymion* I studied river charts while Denise prepared to weigh anchor. Once more I bailed excessive rainwater from our inflatable and rowed ashore, fighting fields of debris already flowing downriver. Denise bravely waved from *Endymion* as I bid our new friends a hasty goodbye. They understood. They had been watching road closure lists on TV. *Endymion* was in a perilous position.

"Go now!" they said.

Returning to *Endymion* I fought a noticeably stronger river current. Putting the Avon into its davits Denise turned to me, "Here, take this Captain—and this too." She handed me a life jacket and my harness. I wondered if she was a little melodramatic.

"You're taking this pretty seriously?" I questioned.

"Aren't you?" Her eyes were heavy.

I checked my compass reference points again, estimating the river a half meter higher than last night's fix. The radio says another five meters (16.4 feet) higher by noon tomorrow—*Yeah, I'm concerned*. Denise and I have never been in a flood, and want no part of one. I understood the need to get down river ahead of the flood, or risk being grounded or swept away by it—and there were other potential problems like the 10,000-volt cables spanning the river downstream. With a rising river, getting under them could be close, or we may hit them. What then? Navigation buoys and aids may have been swept away or out of place. We could be dealing with a significant unchecked current. The only possible safe refuge I could chart downriver was that sturdy public pier at MacLean. *What if it's already occupied?* I thought, *or worse what if it's under water and we are forced downriver into the Harwood Bridge—a lift bridge that only opens by appointment. Not much chance of an opening appointment on Easter long weekend.*

Denise read my thoughts, "Don't forget that damn bridge was two hours late opening on our way up river. Supposing floodwaters keep the bridge crew them from reaching it? What if we can't power against the current while waiting—or even worse, our engine dies. This isn't good Skip. I'm really scared!"

"Me too. Well, not really scared but motivated to beat the rising river. We have good gear Denise. If it gets really bad we probably have enough anchors and chain to hold us."

"Where?"

"Where ever we need to. Let's get going, OK?"

I looked around. Rain was falling with intensity I'd never seen. Denise had everything ready to get moving. She had the engine running. I thought about the chances, with so much debris, of getting something foreign into the raw water-cooling system—overheating the engine at a critical moment. I didn't share my thought.

"OK Kiddo" I said to Denise, "It's you and me. We'll use sail—ride the current, pray, and use the engine *only* when necessary."

"Like now," said Denise, "to pull our anchor from the mud, and keep us positioned."

At the helm Denise pushed 'up' on the remote for the anchor windlass. Armed with boathook I removed debris from the chain as it rose. I thought half the weeds in the river were clutching our rising chain. I turned momentarily to see a gang of well-wishers gathered on shore waving and snapping pictures. With the anchor free of the bottom *Endymion* began careening downriver. Denise smartly moved her to midstream, cut the engine and settled into dodging floating debris. I set the mizzen and small jib. The mainsail would be too awkward if vicious currents or course required a series of rapid jibes.

Teamwork was paying off.

River clutter was *everywhere,* forcing erratic course maneuvers. I wondered if the depth indicator saw the real bottom. I took time to breathe. I concentrated and got into my two foot zone, and I asked God, if he ever retrofits the human body, to please give us more eyes.

Surprisingly we got into a groove. It wasn't as difficult as I had imagined. Our indicator showed us moving at six knots though it was probably ten since we moved with the current. Denise reported the wheel easy and responsive, indicating we weren't dragging much debris with us. An hour later, and moving rapidly, we saw the first overhead cables. The river appeared wider. The channel markers were gone—washed away but I could see a line where current moved faster, indicating deeper water.

"Go starboard Denise, get into the swift water, away from where those cables hang lowest."

It took both hands on the wheel. Denise clawed us to starboard. *Endymion* lay over on her side as the current became broadside. It was scary but our position was safer. We were coming at the cables fast—too fast to turn around.

"Hang on Denise, take your hand off the wheel when I say *now.*"

I was trying to judge our 60 foot mast against the cable height. 10,000 volts would probably kill us. I didn't want the lady I love touching metal when we passed under or hit the cable.

Closer, closer—*"NOW!"* I screamed to Denise, reaching to pull her from the wheel. We passed cleanly under the cables and gave each other a quick hug.

"I love you, Denise. Nice work." I said, noticing what looked like tears mingling with rain on her face.

Then to my astonishment I saw through the rain the shape of another yacht coming upstream toward us and *into* the flooding waters. Was he nuts? What did he know that I didn't?

Nothing.

The yacht *Hiouchi* (Australian native name), radio off and unaware of flood warnings, thought the going was rough. He was uncertain of his position. We easily convinced them as we rocketed past, to go downriver with us to MacLean. Except for occasional difficulty following the river channel the ride to MacLean was uneventful. Only a charter boat occupied the public pier so we all fit nicely. The water at MacLean was up 2.5 feet from normal.

I couldn't sleep that night. At daybreak I tossed scraps of paper overboard, estimating the current: nearly six knots. At 0700 I radioed Yamba Coast Guard.

"Gotcha mate. No worries. We'll get er up fer ya! She's a bit gritty this morning, this river."

They agreed to a Harwood Bridge opening at 0730 for both *Endymion* and *Hiouchi*.

The rain cleared momentarily. Peeking through black on black clouds, I could see the bridge, 2.5 nm south of MacLean. Also looking at the clouds, Denise commented she would prefer a mountain cabin with a simple blizzard raging outside to this crap.

At 0705 the Coast Guard radioed a "Priority Gale Warning." Approaching the coast we would encounter forty-knot winds southeast to northeast. The vague weather department had struck again. *Damn,* I thought, *is there no mercy?*

I assisted *Hiouchi* casting off, and again into fierce rain we went. Only two minutes off the dock, 35 knot winds hit from the southeast. *Came early,* I thought, *that thirty-five knot wind—how am I supposed to see anything with rain stinging like a thousand bees. I've got to see! What a bitch!*

With wind opposing current we shortly had five-foot dirty brown debris-laden overfalls. This treacherous going required absolute concentration as we barreled toward the bridge and our 0730 appointment, with *Hiouchi* close behind.

Endymion *ripping toward Harwood Bridge in flood waters.*

Our timing was perfect, but the bridge wasn't opening. I was forced to make a circle but there was not enough room. The river pushed us. We were closing fast on the concrete and steel bridge. I slammed the wheel hard over, turning *Endymion* into the current, away from the bridge, and pulled back like a fighter pilot on the throttle.

"There! Look there." Denise shouted, "The bridge! It's going up. I looked quickly astern as *Hiouchi* slid past, nearly taking our paint, and thought, *Good, let her go first. She doesn't need the bridge as high as we do*. I turned, fighting the wheel, and followed to starboard and behind *Hiouchi* when suddenly without warning she turned hard starboard, figuring I guessed that the bridge wasn't open high enough. I was forced to turn again barely missing *Hiouchi* and getting drenched by filthy spray. We again picked up the lead, going momentarily and almost uncontrollably broadside to the chaotic river—me hanging in my two foot zone, concentrating, fighting for control. I had *Endymion* headed up river in a losing battle against the rushing river.

"Crapola. We're gonna crash," Denise shouted as we helplessly were carried backwards toward the bridge, now only 200 meters away. Still screaming she reached for a boathook, as if to fend us off in a collision that would surely sink us. At the last moment I spun my head to look at the bridge towering before us. A flashing green light signaled we are clear for height. My heart was beating staccato.

"I'm going for it!" I yelled to Denise as I turned my most favorite boat ever toward the bridge, giving *Endymion* all power the Perkins could muster—plus some prayers and a heap of body English. The water boiled.

"It's gonna be close," Denise screamed against the wind. She had never looked so brave or so beautiful, clutching a shroud in one hand and boathook in another. "Hope the flashing green's not a stupid mistake!"

We thundered toward the opening. It was surreal, like being in a slow motion movie where I saw and recorded every inch of concrete and steel as we rocketed past a cement piling at a combined power and current speed over eleven knots.

"Jesus—we missed by the length of a fishing pole!" Denise exclaimed.

I throttled back, cut the engine and drifted in the current, trying to grasp what had just happened and what *would* have happened had we been a few seconds or even a few feet different in destiny. The past five minutes had taken all of our skill, a whopping amount of determination and a world of luck. *Hiouchi* came alongside and yelled over the only sensible comment: "That was close."

From there to the coast it was just another gale.

CHAPTER 20

SURFERS PARADISE WAS SPECIAL FOR DENISE

Ten days later we remained captured by the river bar. No vessel had attempted to cross the river bar. The flood crest had moved slowly down river, a giant surge causing immense damage. I thanked God for being on the front end of it. The radio carried so many warning and closure reports we'd be lucky to hear one tune in an hour, and tunes would be welcome. We were completely cut off from the world, except by helicopter or police boat. We had seen neither.

"Yeah, we're adventurers," Denise commented, "but right now I feel a long way from home."

"I'm exhausted. Ripping down a flooding Mississippi River might have been easier."

Our refuge was the Calypso Caravan Park, the furthest spot we could find from mid-river. The docks were flimsy, meant only for small boats launched from a trailer behind a vehicle. Being Easter week, with schools in recess, the campground was packed with families also held prisoner by the elements. Being a large boat by comparison with a big American flag, we drew a lot of attention. We tried always to remember we were guests in this waterlogged world, and these friendly dripping wet, shivering people with their endless questions improved our stay and self worth with their warmth and good nature.

Bad weather, especially long stretches, buttresses the importance of quality shipmates when you coexist in forty-three feet. Denise is congenial. I'm more difficult, more blustery especially when my ball cap is atop my noggin. Denise's smile melted opposition. Sitting below playing gin rummy with rain hammering *Endymion*, we reflected on close-quarters shipboard partnerships, or romances, we had seen come apart. Throw in some 'attitude' from prolonged stretches of inclement weather and it's hard for any peace in close quarters. We had two aphorisms: don't carry a grudge; do have a sense of humor. They worked well.

There were times, especially at sea when I might yell at Denise or she might flare at me (like the dry toast incident off New Caledonia-Leg One). We have to let such things go, not carry a grudge. By having a sense of humor, I don't mean nasty tricks like putting salt in the sugar bowl or closing thru-hull valves on a head. I mean keeping conversation light-hearted, having a twinkle in your eye and being able to chuckle at your own mistakes. These traits are valuable in the unpleasant aspects of cruising, such as weather or repair problems.

In Yamba, speaking of heads, we had a testy trial. Landlubber visitors were often held spellbound by our spirited tales. They also managed to jam our heads—both of them. I got to repair them; clearing toilet clogs in smothering humidity, pounding rain and high temperatures should not be the captain's duty. No way. I never understood why shore dwellers were incapable of understanding our simple signs 'do not throw *anything* you have not eaten into a marine toilet, except toilet tissue.'

The down time in Yamba gave me time to think about my responsibilities. My former business partner Chip Carter once told me he thought we went sailing purely to have fun, to live a simple life. In a sense he was spot on. But since leaving California we had played off-shore 'chicken' with a rogue freighter, had been knocked down in mid Pacific and sailed into a military uprising. We had also crossed the Tasman Sea in the worst weather in over 100 years, taken youngsters aboard in the Tall Ships Race and now narrowly escaped tragedy in a flooding river. I'm the guy held responsible for the outcomes of that simple, fun life. I'll always remember a sign in my high school boys' locker room: "Luck is when opportunity meets preparation!" I asked myself, *Did we get here by skill and confidence, or stupidity and dumb luck?* Both I concluded. You live or can die, literally, by the decisions a captain makes. For me the safety of my crew was my greatest responsibility. I was diligent about being focused. When sudden challenges arose I concentrated. Call it skill or dumb luck, doesn't matter. What does matter is not having luck run out, and that took skill.

Finally, after 22 days captured in the Clarence, we attempted to cross the challenging river bar, notably dangerous considering our six-foot keel. The river bar shifts, the wind blows and flooding changes everything. From high upon a hill we watched a 150 foot supply ship outbound for Lord Howe Island battle breaking seas crossing the bar, seas big enough to push the freighter off course. Soon it would be our turn.

I studied tides, currents and wind for days. I memorized charts. Denise and I knew our assignments. We practiced. We talked them through. We had to cross the bar within ten minutes either side of slack tide.

Finally the flooding had ebbed enough to cast off from the campground dock. With time to spare we threaded our way through what I believed was the channel. Whoops—*Endymion* came to a slow stop, stuck in a mud bank.

"Shit! Damn river. What the fuck!" I fumed. "How could this happen?" I paced, unable to see into the muddy water.

"You said you didn't like the guy who wrote the '100 Magical Miles Cruising Guide.' Now you've got a reason." Denise thought it humorous the book's directions had us aground, never mentioning her suspicion it was my error. Laughing, she hailed a small passing ferryboat. Twenty minutes later the ferry had pulled us free and we approached the bar. We had lost any 'time to spare.' Tide was slack. Heading into the port side of the river bar Denise called out every approaching wave—distance, angle, height—while I concentrated to keep us off the rocky breakwater. One breaking tide-against-river wave pushed us within fifteen feet of breakwater rocks, probably giving hilltop onlookers a collective gasp. Once clear of danger we were on our way to Surfers Paradise, an overnight sail away.

What a relief it was to away from the river. Denise slept with her head on my lap while I piloted *Endymion* through the night. *Lord*, I thought, *I love being at sea.* Lights twinkled from shore as did the stars to seaward, another reminder why we chose to drift and blend. Before dawn we were a few miles offshore of Surfers Paradise and its dazzling lights. We had one more bar to navigate, the narrow but not so threatening entrance to Southport harbor. We could have been approaching Las Vegas by sea. There were so many bright lights. Here, I was certain, I could find a worthy gift for Denise's 36th birthday, April 29th. I wanted to make it extra special for my extra special person. I got my wish though it was a few days early. Denise can make the 12 days of Christmas last an easy 30 days so she didn't mind a preemptive birthday surprise. This is how it happened.

Berthed at the Mariners Cove Marina, Denise and I befriended other cruisers, one was a veterinary doctor. He had a small Cavalier King Charles spaniel aboard, the first live-aboard pet we'd seen since Cheyenne in Bora Bora. Denise, as you know, loves *all* animals and fell hard for little Samantha. The vet told me Samantha adjusted well to sea life. An idea was hatched.

"Doc, would you allow us to babysit Samantha for one night aboard *Endymion*?"

"Sure, I need to get to Brisbane tomorrow. How about tonight? But why?"

"Denise will go bonkers. This will make her incredibly happy and if it goes OK, maybe I can find a little fellow for her."

"Say no more," said the Doc. "Your timing is perfect. A litter was born a few weeks ago about fifty kilometers into the outback. It's too early to adopt one but I'm headed out there next weekend. Maybe you blokes would like to come along."

"Let's see how it goes."

I didn't tell Denise about the dog-sitting gig until I showed up with Samantha in my arms, licking my face. What a happy critter. Denise went berserk with joy over our boarder. I said 'no' to Samantha sharing our bunk, but I lost. I had never seen Denise so happy.

The vet and I arranged the outback trip for Denise's birthday. She had no idea where we were going until she saw the litter of five-week-old spaniels.

"They're adorable! Oh Skip, can we get one—please. They're so cute!"

I guess with animals, one always knows who will be loving caretakers. Both vet and breeder agreed Denise was a match. Because Denise was a nurse, with some animal husbandry training, they agreed she could provide the care, perform the necessary shots and bring a five week old puppy home that night.

And so we came to have a daughter. Brandy Alexandra Rowland, a tiny life that bonded with us, providing love and happiness for years to come. But I'm getting ahead of myself.

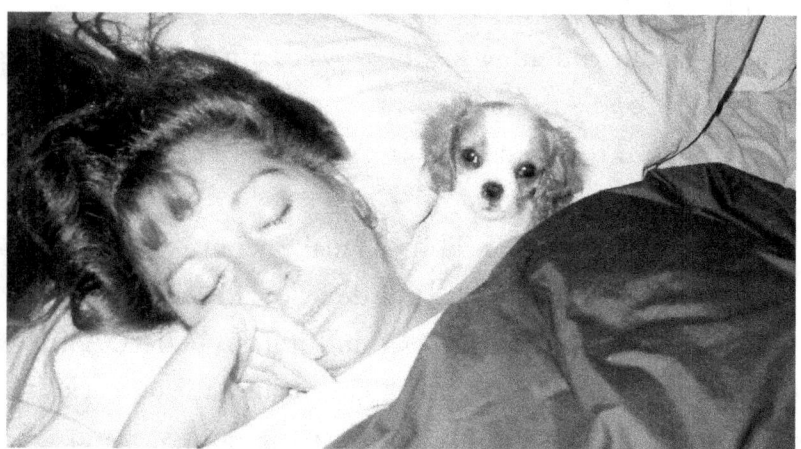

Our New shipmate spends her first night.

CHAPTER 21

SNEAKY PUB—TELL EM TALL PETER SENT YA!

This was our lucky year for major celebrations; first Tall Ships and now world *Expo 88* in Brisbane. Determined to be in the Brisbane River for opening festivities we planned a shortcut, remaining in connecting inland water routes through to Brisbane. That avoided a long sail around North Stradbroke Island and crossing of Moreton Bay to get to the expo area. First we had to pick up stateside friends Tom and Joan West at the Brisbane airport and that required a rental car.

"I want *that* one."

Denise was eyeballing a VW bug convertible. Well, not exactly a true convertible. This bug was seriously modified. The top had been removed, the car painted pink and emblazoned with huge yellow words proclaiming "Go Topless." Denise and I felt it appropriate for our close friends. We rented it, drove to the airport to watch passengers deplane. But no Tom, no Joan.

"Crapola. Hope they didn't miss the flight." Denise said.

"How would we know? Be mighty hard for them to call us."

We were about to turn away but stalled watching and chuckling over a gaggle of Japanese tourists posing for pictures beside the plane's enormous tires, when into the picture appeared two stragglers who had deplaned by the rear stairs. Tom and Joan were toting Tom's three-bottle portable bar.

"We're in trouble now."

Exiting customs, Tom was still fiddling with the latch on the mini bar case when he dropped it. A bottle of Johnny Walker Black became shards of glass mixed with sticky booze on the airport floor.

"Yup—trouble."

To say Tom found the "Go Topless" ride uncomfortable would be an understatement. To say he found the cloud-burst that drenched us distressing would make an understatement of the prior understatement.

Our inland waterway short cut to Brisbane was plagued with shallow muddy areas, narrow channels and multiple opportunities for navigational errors. We stopped frequently to be certain we didn't go up a dead end channel where unrelenting mud would suck us to a standstill. We dropped anchor by Russell Island and went ashore for a look around. Tom wanted to find a restaurant, have a nice meal and a couple of drinks, but we couldn't find even a coffee shop.

"Where does one get a drink around this place?" Tom questioned a man sitting on a bench as we came ashore.

"Nowhere mate. Dry island."

"It's the 20th Century my friend. You tease me, yes?"

"Nope, dry island."

Disappointed, we started walking down a road part blacktop and part former blacktop—in other words, poorly maintained. We were fortunate. Our happy puppy Brandy became our ambassador. Her tail wagged constantly. Denise carried Brandy in her handbag, pleasing onlookers who would see her tiny tail and head viewing the world from her private purse. Tom was walking well ahead of us. A stranger stopped his van to ask Denise;

"Pardon Ma'am, I see the doggie, what breed she be?"

Denise was telling the man who was now out of his van, his hand on Brandy's little head, when Joan interrupted.

"How do we get a drink around this place?"

The man hesitated, looked around as if expecting trouble and quietly said "Sneaky pub. Ya go to da sneaky pub."

"Where. How do we find *da* sneaky pub?"

"Only one. I can take you but we gotta go quick. Ya can't tell anyone—I mean no one. OK?"

We jumped into his truck, picking up a confused Tom on the fly. I sat in front with our driver. There were no floorboards. No springs either as far as I could tell. We jolted down the pot holed road and took a turn onto a dirt road equally as bumpy. I held my feet high to keep them from meeting the road I saw whizzing by through the open space below me. Our driver dumped us on a corner.

"Go down that-a way 'bout a hundred meters, take da path on yer left. That's da sneaky pub. Hey, tell em Tall Peter sent ya."

We cautiously approached the weather-beaten once painted white frame house with six wide stairs to the wood and glass door. They must have been watching.

"Whatcha want?" We heard the voice but the door remained closed.

"Tall Peter says you welcome Americans."

"You American—all a ya?"

"Yup." We chorused.

The door swung open. From the smell it undoubtedly was a pub.

For several hours we drank, laughed and exchanged stories with one of the weirdest, most enjoyable assortment of oddballs I've come across. One, in fact, wrote a poem to Joan suggesting he'd like to marry her. He was gay.

Motoring around the fringe of Moreton Bay and rounding Fisherman's Island we started up the Brisbane River and were struck by the large number of military and police boats present. We were never boarded, stopped or radioed, but rounding a river curve we immediately understood such a presence. Right before us, side tied to a long commercial wharf was *HMY Britannia,* the official yacht of Her Royal Majesty, Queen Elizabeth of England. It took our breath away. I felt amazingly humble. It wasn't that I felt "ordinary" but more that as an ordinary person I got to see this without preamble, as part of everyday drifting and blending—like Denise, Brandy and me meeting other voyagers. But this occasion was special. *How would it be,* I wondered, *to be royalty, to be so closely scrutinized for every move?* Clearly the demands would be high. *Was she aboard? Would I say 'hey your Majesty, I bumped into your son in Sydney last year,'* I wondered? She hadn't waved.

As I write this years later I'm pleased the Queen is still with us though the lovely and stately *HMY Britannia* was decommissioned in 1997.

We were fortunate further upriver to get a side-tie position as close to Expo as any vessel might squeeze. We saw the parades, high-power experimental boats, went to many nations' exhibits and even had some Sri Lankan native dishes.

"Watch the hot sauce!" warned Denise

"Babe, no worries. I'm a man with a stomach of steel. I can take anything."

My lips blistered. I was on baby food for a week.

CHAPTER 22

MOOLOOLABA

We continued north from Brisbane to the Mooloolaba Yacht Club on the Sunshine Coast—our kind of place. The club's strict dress code firmly *suggested* footwear was required. Nothing was in the code above ankles. My 'Night of the Red Death Chili' won a visiting yacht cook-off. Brandy had her first romp on a real beach where beer can size waves knocked her over. Denise cuddled a Koala Bear and we partied amidst a hail of black balloons to celebrate my 50th birthday.

We didn't have a topless figurehead like most competitors but placed second in the clubs "Best Dressed Yacht" competition by loading our rigging with flags. We won a bottle of Bundaberg rum, tasty local stuff.

On a fun race with no rules everyone cheated. Some boats started ten to fifteen minutes early. We used our engine and failed to go around several marks except the finish line where bagpipes and a calypso band played for our pleasure.

One member joining me for a beer and relaxing on our coveted beanbags spotted something unusual about our hard cased canister survival raft cradled before him.

"You Yanks," he said addressing me, "are a curious mob. Why is your survival canister stamped 'custom packed'? What's different?"

"You can thank lovely Denise for that. It has non-standard contents. It's more likely to be inspected by authorities, though it's seldom done."

"Why not? Strikes me to be a bloody good place to tuck away a few drugs."

"Indeed. But it wouldn't be easy. Every canister has a specific registered packed weight. If the weight is off it could be the CO_2 cartridge has gone off, changing the weight, and your raft won't inflate when you need it."

"OK," said the clubbie, "but who checks?"

"Every raft has to be certified every few years. That's one check. Customs officials have the right to look as well. We've never been asked." I continued; "So, let me finally answer your original question. Custom packed means we have other than standard survival gear ..."

"Like what?" he interrupted.

"Denise's stuff. You know she always likes to look her best, right?"

"Yeah yeah ..."

" Her female logic wore me down. She wanted our raft to include some makeup, two decks of cards, a score pad, her favorite golfing visor and bottle of champagne."

"What the ... ?"

"She thought if we are forced to take to the raft at sea our rescuers would surely be from a Japanese freighter. Desperate as we may be, she wanted to be sipping champagne and playing cards when they came alongside to rescue us."

"That's crazy."

"Yeah, but that's Denise. Those items change the raft weight enough to have it indicated in the manifest and the certified contents are declared at every port entry we make. It's a pain in the ass."

"Like I said," he stated, "you yanks are whack-a-doodle."

During a club fun day tug-o-war Denise and I shared an inglorious mud bath with James and Nancy Tiddy, part owners of a recently launched state-of-the-art prawn trawler about to go on her first expedition. James, a big pure Aussie fellow was not the man you would want as an enemy. James's wife Nancy was a lovely wisp of beauty from the small Pacific atolls comprising Vanuatu. They invited us to their place for a surf & turf "barbie."

Before getting into their car James opened the door and out leapt a ferocious looking Australian Blue Heeler. Denise was thankfully holding Brandy.

"Back Up. Sit!" commanded James. The heeler obeyed.

"I'm not feeling good about this," said Denise clutching Brandy closer.

"No worries—in, boy," James again ordered his dog (named Back Up), this time into the boot (trunk) of his sedan, adding, "He's used to it. Just a short ride."

We thought it strange.

Over a scrumptious "barbie" Denise and Nancy quickly bonded. James told me his dreams of treasure hunting off Australia's northern coast and spoke of his contributions to the construction of *Valkyrie Voyager*, a newly launched 75 foot high-tech prawn trawler. He had my interest. I related my curiosity about trawlers —why they frequently don't give right-of-way to sailing vessels, don't use radios properly and too often run dark at night, adding "I'd sure love to get a taste of a prawner's life."

"I'm an offsider in *Valkyrie Voyager* so I'm not the captain," James told me, "but I suspect I've enough juice to get you a working berth if you'd like to sign on. Her maiden voyage is next week. You'll be joining with a bunch of real rag bags."

I got the call. We left on Wednesday, June 29th. I'd be a deckie (common deck hand) working for wages, doing "dirty work." We would be at sea for a month. Denise would stay aboard *Endymion* in our guest berth at the club docks. She had chores to do and wanted a break. There were plenty of willing folks, mostly men, who would look out for her safety.

CHAPTER 23

WANTED FOR MURDER

It was official. I started at 0700 June 29th as a deckie on Queensland's newest, best-equipped prawn trawler. My first assignment—unload six tons of snap frozen shrimp into 6.5 kilo boxes. I did this by hand, in an assembly line with the other deckies. Next fun chore was scrubbing metal decks with an acid bath. Before day's end I helped stow our provisions in the snap freezer. At minus 34 degrees Celsius I would have been snap frozen myself except for heavy thermal garments. At dusk I was given a whole hour off. I raced back to see Denise, took my last shower ashore and returned to duty totally worn out! At last we went to sea, a place that to me meant peace, calm and beauty. Not any longer.

Allow me to introduce the granola bowl mixture of 'rag bag' screwballs that were my shipmates.

The captain, Phil Jolly, had his 30th birthday at sea last week. He appeared an educated man, up from South Australia for the assignment. I liked him but didn't sense much command ability. My counterparts, other low life deckies, clearly didn't like him. They said he didn't know these waters, and will have us in the wrong place about half the time. However, he had the ticket (license). That gave him command, and the better quarters. His was a comfortable stateroom just aft of the bridge.

The mate was James Tiddy, 24% owner and my friend. He couldn't be captain because he lacked the ticket. James was a good organizer with a sense of responsibility. His problem was lack of motivation and little interest in work. James wanted to pursue his treasure-hunting dreams. Prawning was strictly a money event for James.

Another casual acquaintance from the yacht club was Paddy Brighton, the engineer. The guy knew his stuff. He kept everything but his personal life running smoothly. Paddy was up tight—tighter than a piano wire. The police were actively looking for him, and it wasn't just for his multiple previous drunk driving charges—on which he had skipped. The day before we left port there had been a shocking hit and run accident. Paddy had been involved, and not as the victim. A trip to the Graybar hotel was pretty well assured for Paddy when he made port again. He sensed the cops were aware of our schedule, and openly expressed his desire on our return from sea, to duck into to port early, when we wouldn't be expected. Paddy's popularity with lawmen was a hot subject around the galley table, in fact everywhere aboard. Part of the issue was that Paddy worked on salary. The rest of us were on percentage, so everybody except Paddy wanted to remain at sea until the catch was complete. Resentment festered. It was a recipe for trouble.

Marilyn, our cook, was once a high school home economics teacher. She tired of the teaching grind and wanting to add a new dimension to her life decided to take a shot at life at sea. She was sturdy stock, strong but not fat, had a winning smile and easygoing manner. Chef Marilyn occupied a semi-secluded berth halfway between the captain and we low-life deckies, a good thing for her safety and unlikely virginity.

Aside from myself there were three other deckies, the lowest form of life outside of the catch. Bruce, in his twenties, maintained a perfectly trimmed beard and had impeccable manners making him the antithesis of what I expected as "ragtag" shipmates. Bruce could repair a torn net or tie a sheet bend faster than I could say the words.

Tim was a kid. At 17 he was at sea for first time. Fact was, he'd never seen an ocean or been away from home. He was teased a lot. Tim worked hard, had unlimited energy and a stomach that failed in high seas.

Then there was Lurch. His true name was Ian. At 6 foot 3 and 230 pounds Lurch had a scarred face and quick temper. He was the guy you avoided. I found he had a softer, less terrifying side; Lurch liked to write poetry. It was rumored he was the son of a prominent doctor, though he often spoke in guttural tones and claimed to have won 42 consecutive fights—none of them in the ring. It was also rumored he was wanted for murder in Western Australia. Rumor? Fact? No one knew. There were no background checks for deck hands. I could visualize all of it. Fortunately Lurch liked me.

These were my shipmates. Lucky me. The photo on next page with Lurch in shadow is only shipmate picture I have.

Allow me to describe the NOISE!

Valkyrie Voyager worked a 24-hour day with the emphasis on night catches. Night is best and a full moon is better than no moon, or a quarter moon.

Lurch munching live lobster, Bruce in center and Paddy to right.

The engine ran around the clock. Its constant rumble was the base of our orchestra, actually comforting in some perverse manner, as the noise became a familiar component of our environment. Were it to have stopped we all would have awakened suddenly.

Two huge generators, 70 KVA each, serviced the ship. Since everything on board was either electrical or hydraulic, demand was immense and one generator operated constantly. The noise, slightly higher in pitch, was the tenor section and it never stopped.

The sopranos were the hydraulic pumps when engaged. The music they created varied in pitch and resonance, depending on duty: relatively quiet for steering, but screaming like a banshee in despair when straining to haul in 2.2 miles of four ton cable plus the weight of nets attached.

And there were human noises, if certain crew could be considered "human".

First, let me explain. The sleeping quarters semi-surround the crew's galley and lounge. Doors are fixed to the various sleeping compartments, but to close them would surely cause death by slow suffocation. There were no vents or ports of any kind. Each compartment had a heavy curtain to keep out light, enabling crew to sleep in daytime. The curtains have little effect on noise. The layout was like this:

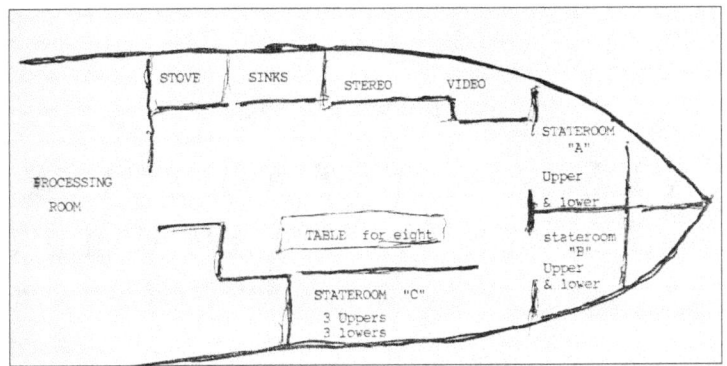

Rough sketch of Voyagers interior. I shared "A" with Paddy.

Most of the crew likely lost their hearing months or years ago. The stereo was always at full blast! A video was normally playing a small collection of last centuries movies; we saw them all at least twelve, maybe twenty times.

For flavor, stir in a minimum of four people at the large table—all talking at the same time (35% profanity) and at a level necessary to be heard above the orchestra.

Next mix in sounds of refrigerator, compressor, various communications radios, stabilizers, autopilot, galley noises and farts.

You now have the *Valkyrie Voyager* orchestra. Those were living conditions. Believe it or not when you're tired enough the orchestra fades and sleep, heavy dream laden sleep, creeps into your bunk. During earlier passages aboard *Endymion* Denise had often reminded me, "No one ever died from lack from sleep." I finally believed her.

CHAPTER 24

A DECKIE'S LIFE ABOARD A MODERN PRAWN TRAWLER

At 0400 our first morning at sea, hydraulics wailed, the captain barked orders, and a mile plus of cable screamed from giant spools headed for the bottom to make us rich. All day and night the nets came up, went down, came up again and went down again in an endless routine. It was tiring work. It drained every muscle. Teamwork and trust in each other was required despite our vast differences. For all the effort, that first twenty-four hours we captured enough prawns to earn us a couple of cents north of $10.00 per deckie for the long days work.

"This sucks." mumbled Bruce.

"Fookin A," agreed the alleged murderer.

Before Captain Jolly could find another place to drop nets we scrambled to our quarters for a few winks and to escape the orchestra. The cramped bunks, either forward as V-berths or near the galley, were an echo chamber for non-stop varsity cursing or off color jokes.

Layers of cigarette smoke added to the misery for me. I was the only non-smoker.

By end of day two we'd had only a couple of nets with good catches. At 0030 on our third day, the captain declared the tide too strong to prawn.

We were hunting prawns in the "Swains" area, well outside the Great Barrier Reef. The depth could be 2,000 feet. The hope, and rumor again, was prawns there would be larger and fetch higher prices. They were known as U-10's, meaning ten or fewer would weigh a kilo (2.2 pounds). The depth is also why it took a half hour to get the nets to the bottom, and almost an hour to get them up. To further tantalize the seabed dwelling crustaceans we rigged tickler chains to the nets. These were two foot long pieces of chain sewed into the leading edges of net. When at depth the chain would stir the muddy bottom, hopefully causing prawns to jump into our nets.

"This dumb-ass captain couldn't find a prawn with a hundred mile net." mused Lurch, going into a slow boil. "No fookin way to make a fooking living on this shit tank. Dumb shit!"

"Give'im a break mate." said Bruce.

"You're a fookin dope, mate. Capt'n is whacko sayin tide's too strong. Do ya think the stinking prawns 2000 feet down sense the fookin tide? Fookin captain is off his bloody rocker! You can tell'im Lurch said so."

Nobody did.

At 0300 the captain called "nets down". It's a lot of work and we did it two more times, bringing up a miserable 96 prawns. At least they were large. Captain Jolly spoke to the crew, "We're going to steam south a few hours and try a new location. Prawns here seem to have gone off."

"Gone off," argued Lurch. "What the fook is gone off? Does the dope mean off to church or taking a vacation. Dumb shit."

It was clear trouble was brewing. Lurch was stirring up us deckies.

As nets came up they were guided over the hopper, a large catchment area centerline of the vessel. Two deckies then grabbed a "quick release" line on the lower portion of net. A pull in the right direction opened the net and dumped the catch. Prawns and by-catch, usually unhappy fish still alive, moved along a conveyor belt to the sorting area. Tim, the youngest, and I, the oldest, were on opposite sides of the conveyor. Our job was to separate prawns from other species and drop them into pails. It was simple when the nets yielded small quantities. If the nets were full we were like Lucille Ball in her famous chocolatier sketch, frantically trying to keep pace with a moving conveyer belt full of product needing to be sorted. When our pails were full they were lowered immediately into a 35 degree below zero snap freezer, where the critters' lives ended quickly, their meat preserved for some Frenchman's palate in far away Europe. It sounds simple, but hold on—things didn't always go as planned.

Our fourth day out, the catch was still low—miserable in fact. We were working in areas that allegedly had never been prawned. We could expect the unexpected, and we got it. Working our second scrape of the seabed the bottom dropped suddenly, like going over an under the sea cliff. Captain Jolly was playing fancy with chef Marilyn and didn't see the bottom's irregularity on his instruments. The weighted nets plunged into a deep but short diameter hole, hanging up on the far wall as we passed over it. All 70 feet of *Valkyrie Voyager* jerked violently, almost pulling her stern below the surface and sending the bow toward the sky. Bruce and I both lost balance and fell. Thankfully James was at the wheel and put the engines in neutral quickly enough to prevent the cable from snapping. We recovered the nets; they needed substantial repairs. Once again almost no prawns. Stock in the captain declined. Grumbling increased.

Stormy weather was closing in. I found sleeping in the forward V-berth impossible. Noise of seas pounding the hull combined with the orchestra was too much. There was no ventilation, only air laden with noxious diesel odors. Visible layers of stale cigarette smoke stung my eyes. With boots, gloves and full wet-weather gear I sought a few winks lying in the sometimes partially flooded hallway leading to the aft sorting deck. I'd never slept in such miserable conditions.

Our seventh day out was the third day of gale force winds. Prawning had been impossible. It would have been for any boat or any skipper. We were eight souls well offshore in a wildly pitching fishing vessel. With violent wind and high seas all ports within 200 miles along the East Coast of Australia had been declared unsafe for entry, so we made the best of it.

We gathered in the galley/dining area, smoking the majority of time and hanging on as *Valkyrie Voyager* bashed into oncoming seas. Life inside the cabin's protection was confining and downright lousy. I spent as much time as possible on the bridge. Our skipper showed his experience keeping the bow to the seas, taking tons of water in wave after endless wave—I estimated to be 20 to 25 footers. They would break across the plunging bow, sending torrents of water against the bridge safety-glass windshield, the wipers working double time. Outriggers with stabilizers deployed were out both port and starboard helping to keep the vessel from rolling. Aside from Tim and me, the crew knew how to work the boards to keep them from being torn apart. Everyone stayed inside either the bridge or galley area except Lurch. He went onto the foredeck, working his way to the very bow, putting his head into breaking waves that often buried him in seawater. Somehow, after the seas swept the deck, Lurch could still be found. Nut case or death wish? He never told us.

About this ship in that situation—I was glad not to have been in charge.

When the storm died the next day we dug again into hard dangerous work, laying out nets on miles of cable that tickled the bottom, hopefully motivating prawns to take a journey with us. Four hours into the trawl I was assigned a crappy job: go into the snap freezer to count boxes. My fingers numb inside insulated gloves, I counted 425 three kilo boxes totaling 1275 kilos of product. At $8.00 per kilo (anticipated value) our catch was worth $10,200. My cut at 3% amounted $306 for the entire trip thus far. No wonder, is it, that I preferred sailing?

Eighteen exhausting days after departure we were back in port for one day to fuel, unload our lousy catch and take on provisions. I made $450 or $1.56 per hour working round the clock in occasionally treacherous conditions. I never worked so hard or so long for so little money. I had sympathetic feelings for the men and few women who make their living from the sea. It's a tough, demanding life.

Enough whimpering. On our one day in port, I worked alongside Lurch for twelve straight hours cleaning the snap freezers. I managed a brief conjugal visit with the lady I love and we put to sea again on the next high tide. If the fishing and weather didn't improve, none aboard would see the upper end of poverty. More catch means more $$$. The second half, we were promised, would be better. I prayed. Maybe it was a hard life, but I was happy living the adventure compared to droning days of business in California. I never doubted my decision to exchange executive privilege and money for drifting and blending. There simply is no way however to understand the challenging lifestyle of offshore fishermen, other than to live in their boots.

CHAPTER 25

SURPRISES IN THE CORAL SEA

July 18th, 1988. We were again 120 nautical miles east of the Great Barrier Reef in search of elusive prawns that have as many ways of avoiding us as we have devices for capturing them.

Paddy somehow avoided the law during our brief shore visit. The cops came to the boat asking a lot of questions but didn't search the vessel. I have no idea where Paddy was at the time but noticed that Lurch stayed in the freezer during their hour of questions.

So far, fishing on the voyage's second leg has been roughly as bad as during the first leg. I earned a whopping $280.00 Australian in the last seven days—a tough way to gain passage anywhere, or even buy a round for thirsty mates on a pub-crawl.

My mates had theories about why the yield has been thin. Some were:

* We have a substitute captain. He doesn't know the waters.
* We're going too fast.
* We're going to slow.

* We're too deep.
* We're too shallow.
* Wrong nets.
* Water's too warm.
* Water's too cold ... and of course—The prawn have gone off.

I put my theoretical money on the phases of the moon. It made the most sense. We are coming into a new moon. The catch has been gradually improving. Maybe by the time we come ashore again in early August, short of a breakdown, a decent catch may earn worthwhile wampum. Money talk amongst us unprivileged deckies became encouraging discussion.

Marilyn kept us well fed and helped with sorting when needed. Her attitude was generally positive, except when she was up against it with Paddy. There was no love lost between them. Paddy had watched her tip-toeing into the captain's chambers, almost daily, he suspected for some extracurricular training. Paddy generously shared the information among all shipmates, and over the radio. It pissed off Marilyn. But after a few days she and the skipper stopped pretending. Chef Marilyn moved her scant belongings to the captain's quarters. I had a feeling Bruce may have been dipping his pen, or wished he were, in company ink as well. He seemed disheartened. I kept my suspicions to myself. I knew these things happen. I didn't see a problem. The quality of our chow continued to be very good.

Engineer Paddy though, had a different attitude, wanting to emerge as superior. No one understood why. It made him appear an empty suit. He'd been in a foul mood the entire voyage, bringing the rest of us down. After Marilyn's shifting he became downright miserable, arguing with everyone. Policy was to work in teams, mostly for safety reasons. Paddy didn't fit the team picture, even for washing dishes. Paddy flatly refused to do galley duty. He was convinced his engineer status put him above the task. We had to pick up his slack, and no matter who said what, Paddy always told them they were wrong. Then he would correct them. I saw venom building in Lurch.

On July 21st I learned why our gaff was designed not to have a barb. The boards connected by chain to the forward end of the nets are large, often weighing 800 pounds and are similar to sail boards. When they hit the water the boards "sail" to each side, spreading the net. It's ingenious. During a mishap bringing in the nets the boards went awry and crossed each other. Lurch scrambled over the stern onto the wildly swinging boards—riding them over and across the stern's whitewater like a rodeo rider on a bucking bronco. He took the gaff with him to snare the line and pass it back to apprehensive me, also leaning over the stern wanting to help. Without harness lines we hung by one hand over the extreme outer edge of the boat's stern with a gaggle of hungry sharks in close pursuit. It was *insanely* dangerous.

"Catch it Skip. NOOO—not that way you fookin dumb ass. Lean out. Like *me*! Further man. Lean out. Get some guts, pussy sailor boy, and catch this!"

Leaning and praying I hung on. Lurch swung the gaff and let it fly to catch the line I was holding.

"Got it!" I yelled. The gaff gripped my line. I gave an all-my-strength thrust to slide it out of my way—but I didn't move quickly enough. Like so many accidents, it happened so quickly I didn't realize I was injured. I felt a numbing thud when the point of the gaff dug solidly into my palm between thumb and forefinger.

I didn't want to, but I looked. The gaff was embedded in my hand. *Can't panic now*, I thought, *does it have a barb?* Nausea was creeping in, blood oozing out. *Probably a puncture wound. How much rust is there? Can't be much. It's all new equipment. At least I think it is—worry about that later. I gotta get the gaff out before I go overboard, before anyone sees what's happening!*

I still had to connect the two lazy lines for Lurch. Somehow I clipped them together with the gaff still in my hand—pushed to the limit to stay calm. My mind was in overdrive. *No way I'm gonna scream ... there's only bravery in this macho crew. Gotta man-up now Skip. Damn this hurts!*

I looked for a more secure position. I was still too far over the stern, but now connected to Lurch by the grappling hook line. Nausea was inching toward control.

I could either pull it or cut it out, but I had nothing for cutting and the idea was repulsive. *I'm a gentleman sailor, not a barbarian,* so I pulled—slowly. It seemed forever, but I got it out. *Thank God no barb!* Blood was everywhere. My knees were jelly. Squeamishly I stumbled toward the First Aid cabinet, wondering, *when was my last tetanus shot?*

Not one shipmate had noticed. I got little sympathy when they later saw my injury. Things like that are not unusual. They are expected.

CHAPTER 26

WHALE BONES, WHALES AND BOMBS

An old seafaring superstition is having whale bones aboard your vessel is an omen of bad luck. The next day we raised the partial vertebra of what was once a large whale.

Our luck went south.

Whale bone & odd catch on sorting table.

First, the hydraulics, by which nearly everything aboard except the dunny is operated, failed to operate. Paddy fixed it.

Then a big generator wouldn't shut down.

Repairing this, Paddy dropped a much-needed spring into the bilge. There was no spare. Lurch suspected he dropped it purposely. Paddy eventually managed to jury-rig a system far too involved for me to explain.

Then, at 0450 the following morning, one of deep-sea fishing's most feared mishaps took place—the main cable holding *all* over-side gear and nets parted. Just plain snapped. I was in the processing room, slipping prawns into their new long-term sleeping quarters when I heard the snap. Not knowing what it was, I didn't do anything. From the shouting though, I knew there was more bad news.

$10,000 worth of gear had settled half a mile below us with no line, wire, cable, string or anything else connecting it to us. Boards, nets, ticklers, cable were gone, along with any possibility of continuing our work.

How the hell did that happen, I wondered, *another screw-up on a new ship. Doesn't make sense.* Then, I looked at the frayed cable. What a mess! I was no expert but it was apparent the alleged spanking new cable had considerable rust. Either it was old and polished to look new or the quality of stainless steel was seriously lacking.

Our choices were to give up and steam to port some 200 miles distant, or to rig a grappling hook and go looking for the gear, a needle in the haystack situation if ever there was one.

Returning to port was out. We'd been experiencing poor catches and poor money for huge effort. To go home would end it, taking weeks to replace the gear. So we decided to drop a grapple. But we didn't have one.

Captain Jolly made a radio call to competitors fishing 50 miles away. Two hooks were volunteered. We dropped a buoy to mark our place and steamed off to borrow the hooks. Once they were aboard, Paddy used his torch to refashion one, making it more effective. Nearing where we believed the gear to lie we started a criss-cross grid pattern. GPS was years to come. We dragged the hook across the predominately muddy bottom nearly half a mile below and a full mile astern. Standing on the winch deck looking over the vast, empty ocean, it seemed a hopeless course. Spirits were low. We cursed two convenient targets, Paddy and the captain.

Captain Jolly pierced our eardrums by announcing through the load hailer mounted directly above us; "We will do this for 48 hours. If no hook-up we're returning to port."

"Fuck you!" chorused the crew.

Amazingly, after only four hours of dragging we had a hook-up. Perched in various observation points we anxiously watched the long slow process of screaming hydraulics bringing in the cable. We cursed, cheered and made bets that would never be honored. At approximately the one-third mark, the cable went slack. We lost whatever we had hooked.

This same process was repeated eight times in the next twelve hours. Each time, we lost our hook up, but continued to wind in the grapple looking for traces of net to indicate we had located our prize. No luck.

Lurch and James were big men. Bored men. They used the torch to fashion an enormous fish hook (with a barb). They attached it to six feet of chain followed by braided half-inch line. The two took turns swinging it, sending it over the rail to lure and catch shark. When that failed they created a bag from fish net. It was 12 feet at the opening. Loading it with chum they crawled out the starboard boom and lowered it into the calm deep blue water. Within seconds several sharks frenzied for the chum. The bag was pulled tight and three irritated sharks, six to eight foot man-eaters, were dropped into the hopper and shot. It was illegal of course but nobody cared. Kind of like being a "dry" ship but I seldom saw Paddy sober.

As dusk fell we had a solid hook-up. An hour later our nets were again on the surface. Under floodlights we slaved non-stop another ten hours to straighten out the mess, replace the cable and repair or replace the damaged nets. Remember my comment about teamwork? Even Paddy pitched in on this one. But Captain Jolly (Bligh) stood with a warm cuppa, just watching. His approval rating had rocketed up to thirty percent range with the hookup. It was sliding again. We were worn out but fishing again by daylight. Income for that day: $0.

At 12 days out scuttlebutt, most often pure fiction, was that we will be heading back to Mooloolaba on the 30th—the day after the full moon.

Last night was Friday, the day (or evening) of the week Denise and I most enjoy going to someplace for a drink or having friends aboard. I thought a lot about her as I always do, and was hoping she and Brandy were coping okay. I had confidence. Laid back as Denise normally was, she could also be resourceful when necessary.

Denise and I had a radio schedule set up, by which we could talk every couple of days.

"Crapola, Skip," she told me, "I've been pestered with the flu bug."

"Not good," I replied, "You make a far better nurse than you do a patient."

At that point, for the small amount of prawns we are capturing and minimal earnings resulting, most crew wanted to head home early. It wasn't worth the effort staying out there some 300 plus miles away. But an ocean going expensive prawn trawler is not a democracy. Nobody votes except the captain. So we just waited to see.

We had another foul-up. Seemed there was one every night. One of the nets came up twisted like a pretzel. Somehow chain got wrapped into the mess as well. Instead of being able to empty it into the hopper we were ordered to empty into a giant plastic tub. A stupid idea and I'll never know why. Cook Marilyn and I had then to shovel, lift, tip or carry it by whatever means possible to the conveyer while Lurch, Tim and Bruce repaired the damage to get the net back into the sea. It was tough physical work for about an hour, starting at 0300.

We handled the chore without losing any precious time. It's always a race to get nets aboard quickly. A sizable convoy of scavenger sharks follows the boat. When a net-full of flopping future food neared the surface, sharks attacked the contents, doing considerable net damage in seconds. Again our catch was a poor one. I made about $40.00 for the last 24 hours effort.

As a follow-up regarding noise, the daytime sounds of stereo and video combined with the orchestra became so unbearable for the captain that he was losing his ability to concentrate. From listening to him I knew he was a radio novice. I was not impressed either, with his navigating—particularly important skills anywhere near the Great Barrier Reef.

Skipper Jolly initiated daytime "*Quiet hour*" from 1000 to 1500. I made the first announcement.

"Attention on deck—attention on deck. It is now 1000 hours. Cease all videos, personal stereos, dishwashing, and vibrators. Quiet hour follows, by order of the Skipper."

Laughter, hoots and cursing followed but it worked—for about an hour. Fishermen who spend their lives at sea are not easily disciplined. They do pretty much as they please unless under orders involving ship's business or safety, when they do what the boss wishes—maybe.

We hardly ever see the cook any more. Since the captain "bedded her down" nearly a fortnight ago, it had blossomed into true romance. She moved her swag (pack) to "officer country." Rumor had it they will share a roof when the long journey's over. More fiction?

Lurch was our strong man. When a job required bravery like climbing out on the gear astern while moving through choppy seas, Lurch volunteered. We all agreed; "Yeah, you go Lurch. It's OK." Lurch dominated most crew-quarters conversations. I was surprised to learn he rumor was true, he was private school educated. His talking points mostly involved fights he had been in, or would be in, plus sex and drugs. To keep pace with his macho image we peppered our tales with profanities. It was a conversational wasteland.

Paddy's disposition was constantly nasty. The chip on his shoulder was enormous. If the worst could be made of this voyage, Paddy made it so. He actually threatened to sabotage the boat so it will be necessary to return to port.

While working on a solenoid for the hydraulics, he dropped a precious small fitting into the bilge, too far and too tight to reach. Paddy fashioned retrieval by taking apart a deck speaker and tying the speaker's magnets to a long stick.

Pretty clever, I thought, but it didn't work. Perhaps the submerged part was stainless steel. Anyway, Paddy took the flooring out, and fished by hand for his prize. It was stinking hot down there. I admired him for that but loathed him for not taking a shower. A dead fish smelled better. Paddy looked the picture of a "grease monkey" covered in sweat, oil and bilge grime. It was personal to me because we shared a claustrophobic V-berth room. I mentioned his BO to him, casually and carefully on several occasions, but with no results. I took a more direct approach. I was in my bunk when Paddy entered the confined compartment. I aimed and sprayed aerosol room freshener directly on him. Not subtle.

On July 28th, at roughly 0345 Lurch and James released the catch from nets. Two ominous metallic thuds where among sounds of squishy sea life hitting the metal deck. James jumped down for a sticky beak.

"Stand back! *Shit. All hands back away*! Looks like a fuckin bomb."

"A *what?*" shouted Captain Jolly.

"Bomb you asshole," shouted Lurch, running to it instead of away.

"Can't be," was my offering.

In the hopper were two unexploded World War Two bombs encrusted in barnacles and sea life. I had read about such things and joined James in carefully rolling them over nets we spread on the metal surface. Our plan was to lift them by crane and return them to Davy Jones. First though, James and I carefully scraped the bombs being careful to stay away from warheads. We found the inscriptions "*W-AIF-1943, No.24200 II and N9, BRII-1943.*" I have since searched for these serial numbers with no success. My guess is they were under 500 pounds, perhaps six feet long.

Anyone missing a bomb?

Working the nets was flat out dangerous. On one occasion Bruce was seconds from releasing the catch of a 52-foot bulging net stretched high above him.

"Twist the net. Bruce, twist the fucking net! *Twist!*"

All eyes went immediately to the net. Thrashing wildly at the net opening was a very angry, much alive fully mature tiger shark. Against the orchestra of trawler machinery, Bruce had not heard Phil Jolly's call. The shark was two feet from Bruce's head. He hadn't looked up.

Lurch leapt from the winch deck to the hopper with the suddenness of a crazy man and sureness of a ballerina, grabbing the net chute from Bruce just as the shark was breaking free. Lurch spun the giant net, trapping the angry shark only inches from Bruce's head. James, also throwing caution to the wind, bashed the shark with a massive sledgehammer. It took ten minutes for the sharks jaw to become motionless. Just another night in a different world, far from home.

Once in wee morning hours, Bruce was about to release the catch from a net appearing to have an abundant catch.

"Jeezus," he said, "Will you look at this? Bout time. Gotta be our biggest catch ever."

"Stand clear." Tim shouted. The net was bulging in every direction. Tim jerked the release line and an 800-pound basking shark tumbled from the net with the other miscellaneous catch. Basking sharks are plankton eaters, mostly blubber and not good eating. They can weigh several tons. This guy was small.

"I seen it a shark movie," said Tim in semi perfect English. "Them basking sharks are the second largest fish in the ocean and they have the smallest brain."

"Kinda like Lurch!"

"Yeah, but they don't hurt no-one. We gotta get this one back into the ocean."

"OK, get some line." Shouted James.

Lurch was attempting to lift the shark's huge tail. It lay on the deck, gasping. Hardly moving.

"Sailor boy, (me) you're the knot guy. Tie something around its tail."

"I'm on the winch," hollered Captain Jolly.

I secured the tail feeling sorrow for the poor thing. It wasn't the whale's fault. I tied a quick release knot to insure we could free the monster when it returned to sea.

"Better get something around the head too."

"What for?" I questioned.

"Can't pick up 800 fookin pounds by the bloody tail. Break the fookin thing clean off dere, sailor boy."

But said too late. Captain Jolly was already winching the monster off the deck.

The shark's tail came off! The blubbery body slammed into the deck causing *Valkyrie Voyager* to lurch.

"What the fook!" Lurch was nearly crushed. "Scum bag skipper. Shoulda listened. Dumb ass, go drive a maggot barge in the bloody billabong. Stupid sonabitch..."

In the end we had to kill the gentle giant. No fish can survive without a tail. It may have had a pea size brain but I've felt terrible about the outcome, even to this day as I recall the incident.

Spirits tanked. Jolly's approval rating hovered in the mid teens. His hasty winch action to raise the whale had been thoughtless. Even the most hardened felt some compassion for the gentle giant.

We turned toward port that night. I was content. We would shortly be home. No more "winch up" commands or screaming hydraulics releasing wire cable. All was well until:

"Put it down fooker or I'll make ya one sorry sumbitch." No mistaking Lurch.

"Yeah, says you. Come'n get me ass hole." Paddy was taunting Lurch, a sizeable wrench in his hand.

In moments the crew was on the upper deck watching the blow-up below. We didn't know how it started but this was an ugly situation. A fight for-keeps. Paddy threatening with the wrench, Lurch in a crouch moving in a circle, his extended menacing hands giving the "come here" signal.

Paddy dove forward. Lurch danced sideways, the wrench glancing off his right shoulder. Paddy was absorbing the recoil when Lurch dove into his mid section knocking the air out of Paddy. The wrench fell in a clatter to the steel deck. Calls from the crew were brisk, sharp and vicious:

"Kill the fucker. Get'im Paddy man!"

"Kick'im in the aggots!"

"Nail da skinny little prick."

Somebody, I thought it was Marilyn, threw a kitchen knife to the deck. Paddy reached for it. Lurch kicked it away and started pummeling Paddy. It was over in seconds. Paddy was a bloody sight when James and Captain Jolly decisively pulled Lurch, still relentlessly punching, from Paddy's motionless body. I've seen fights—been in a few, but none like that one. Lurch had the audacity to give a victory sign before moving into the cabin. The captain and James carried Paddy.

On August 2nd we returned to port, slipping in an hour before we were expected because our steely-eyed captain/navigator had miscalculated the tide tables, so Denise and other expected ladies were not dockside. Nor were the police there for Paddy. But there was an ambulance.

The rest of the crew including me were below in the lounge a little later when Denise came charging in and threw her arms around me with a big hug. I loved it.

We were a total of 34 days at sea. We unloaded the catch the morning after our return. It weighed 4.1 tons. That is about two tons short of a normal four week catch at that time of year.

When the catch was received in Adelaide we got paid. I took home just shy of $1,000 Australian—not much for the effort. But money wasn't solely important. I learned what a gamble it is to be a commercial fisherman. I learned to work with people I may have once feared or thought not deserving, no matter their backgrounds. Can it get more unruly than a suspected murderer, hit and run driver, wannabe treasure hunter, and poet? I don't think so. I thank them all for adding color and bounty to my life.

CHAPTER 27

RETURN ENGAGEMENT IN MOOLOOLABA

We needed to haul *Endymion*. She hadn't been out of the water since leaving California and was due some bottom service. And Denise's parents were coming to visit. We wanted our home pristine so we set to work. It was a non-event except Brandy's incredible timing to be below a small can that accidentally fell from the deck above her. She was bathed in toxic bottom paint. The boat yard ground to a halt. Kind natured Australians rushed to help, hearing cries from a puppy in distress. Denise, clutching Brandy, and I piled into a worker's van to rush Brandy to a critical care vet. The little dog handled it better than the anxious adults—and Brandy had her first taste of ice cream.

Denise's folks arrived as advertised. Her dad Bob had show business stories on top of stories to relate. It would have been nice to hear them, but he couldn't get a word in sideways. Denise and her mom left only milliseconds, if any, between words or sentences. Bob and I devised a plan. We would get our time for man talk and a beer. I phoned Binkey. He owned the local chandlery (nautical supply store). With a plan, I sent the ladies to Binkey for some much needed nautical items.

Denise was to purchase 20 feet of shore line. She returned visibly upset. We made up. Then I sent her for a gallon of striped paint. This time she came back clearly angry. Bob and I retired to the yacht club taproom, and dinner alone. We all won.

For the finale, since her dad and I enjoyed our devious fun I shouted "Awww CRAP!" loudly enough to interrupt the ladies' jaw dropping conversation about handbag zippers.

"What's the matter?" Denise questioned.

"I'm trying to plumb a line for the boot stripe and I don't have a long weight."

"What's a long weight?"

You get 'em at Binkey's. Kinda hard to explain."

"No way Skip. I'm not falling for that crapola again."

"Well I'll get one for you." Denise's mom was lending a hand.

"Yeah, would you. That'd be great. Just tell Binkey to give you one long wait and have him put it on my account."

The ladies left. Bob and I cracked a brew.

Denise and her mom found Binkey behind the charts counter.

"Skip says he needs a long weight."

"Right-ee-oh. He phoned me. Be right with you," answered Binkey with a knowing smile.

Twenty minutes later a now impatient Denise approached Binkey. "Hey Binkey, where's my long wait?"

"You just had it!" Binkey chuckled, pointing to a nearby clock.

Denise's parents were not sea faring people, however it was good to have them around, and for them to see how we were living. They were proud of their daughter, and rightly so. I was too. Bob, a social guy, enjoyed meeting people.

Bob Miller. Do you think sea dog Brandy was fond of Bob?

At the club bar one evening he met a reporter who had worked with Edward R. Murrow in the 1940's. Bob had also worked with Mr. Murrow. That encounter made his trip.

We took them sailing on a calm day because Bob was concerned he might get seasick. He was right and never left the dock again.

After her folks left, Denise and I met what we considered a nice couple with a young daughter. Jock, an experienced sailor, had recently sold a number of gas stations. His partner Linda was charming and her four-year-old daughter well mannered. They, like us, had no fixed schedule. Jock was flush with gas station money and liked our concept of "drifting and blending." We agreed to meet later in the Whitsundays where they would sail with us for a month or so. We didn't know it then, but Jock would cause trouble.

CHAPTER 28

WHITSUNDAYS AND THE GREAT BARRIER REEF

Compared to harsh living on a prawn trawler, guiding *Endymion* as we pushed north was easy in light winds favoring calm seas. We entered the Great Barrier Reef north of Fraser Island and partied nightly with Aussies cruising the reef aboard their own yachts. Proud Australians all, they let us know in short order that *their* Great Barrier Reef was not only the world's longest barrier reef, but also the world's largest living structure. That's still true. The 2,000 kilometer body of shoals, lagoons and channels lies 25 to 44 nm offshore and contains nearly 700 tiny islands, many of which we found.

Airlie Beach became headquarters for some of the best months of our lives. It's a gateway to the 74 islands making up the Whitsundays, a massive coral stretch of the Great Barrier Reef teaming with marine life and islands to delight us. Hamilton, Hook, Daydream and Hayman Islands became our playground.

We first tied up at Abell Point Marina, under construction at the time. It lacked amenities but had abundant people, warmth and hospitality. Our first contact was at the post office, an immaculate and tastefully decorated building. Checking in, Denise was wearing a T-shirt from the Tall Ships race. It read *Endymion—USA.*

A postal lady greeted Denise, "May I assist you?"

"Yes please, I was wondering if you have any mail for...."

"I believe this is for you. Welcome to the Whitsundays, Ms. Denise."

Denise hadn't finished her question. The smiling lady handed her an envelope.

It was addressed:

Ms. Denise Rowland

USA Yacht Endymion

Australia

"Thank you, thank you, thank you!" Denise said, each thanks slightly more enthusiastic. Someone in the extensive postal service, we were told, recognized the name *Endymion* from Tall Ships coverage and had tracked us all the way from Tasmania. Imagine that in any other country!

Anchored one night in the serene lee of Dent Island with only one other boat in sight, we listened to endless songs from seemingly millions of collected happy shorebirds—so tranquil as night fell over the hills. Later, cuddled together with a glass of wine we savored the piano artistry of Roger Williams with *La Mer* (Beyond the Sea) playing through our deck speakers.

Awash in the splendor of it all Denise mused, "This is *wonderful* Skippy. Good as it gets. It won't stay this way, will it? Makes me sad to think how this will change when people discover this area. I'm happy for other people who will get to see this beauty, but we're lucky aren't we, to see it now?"

"Yes." We were, and it had only started.

CHAPTER 29

RAINBOW BRIDGE

Jock and Linda arrived early October in the Whitsundays. We liked them. Jock was strong and Linda a delight. We participated in the Airlie Beach fun race with half the crews sailing naked, followed the next day in a 'Hair of the Dog' race to Hook Island. Afterwards we took short casual sails during the day, concentrated on shipboard BBQ seafood dinners and getting good sleep at night.

Jock played continually with Brandy, tossing a ball or floating on rafts with her when they weren't fishing together. Little Brandy, nearly eight months old now, had never had a bad day. She loved every human she met and bonded easily with Jock. We invited the couple to sail north to Townsville with us. We planned to put *Endymion* on the hard (in shipyard) once again so we could return to America for Thanksgiving, intending to stay through Christmas.

Townsville Yacht club was a crazy pleasurable stop. We were given a prime berth close in to the club. When the kitchen staff discovered we were American they made me the world's biggest hamburger. It must have weighed three pounds, and was delicious for a week.

Theft, we were told, had been on the rise. We were cautioned about boatyard security for *Endymion*. After hauling the yacht out, Denise and I hid a few precious items before lingering to write a note. We affixed the following directly inside the companionway:

ATTENTION THIEVES: This is an American yacht. Everything aboard is NTSC electrical system. **NOTHING** *will work in Australia. There is warm beer in the fridge and scotch in the locker below the TV. Help yourselves. Have a good time—sleep over if need be—then go rob someone else.*

Linda offered to care for Brandy during our absence. We accepted, thinking Brandy would be in a good home. Linda lived with her parents.

Denise and I flew to Los Angeles from Brisbane, carefree as anyone ever was. Culture shock slapped us in California. We had to pump our own gas, and didn't know how. Credit card gobbling pumps were new to us. Crowds were disturbing and freeway traffic a nightmare. I found it amazing, the difference a few years can make.

In Pasadena Denise and her mom were in perfect sync. Yak yak yak. I thrived listening to US news for the first time in years. I should have paid attention to Denise and her mom; before thanksgiving rolled around they had clandestinely planned to forever change my life. Rather than my desired romantic wedding on distant Easter Island I had so yearned for, we were to walk the aisle Sunday, December 18th at Trinity Presbyterian church in Pasadena. It wasn't exactly a shock. I sort of expected it.

From a spur of the moment bachelor party (of which I will report nothing), to tossing rice on a departing car, getting married was as Denise told friends, "It was a good gig!"

Funny what stands out about one's own wedding. Touring the church our minister pointed out candelabras. Denise blurted. "Oh,

I had those the last time"—so I asked if she was also responsible for the ruts in the carpet. One friend gave us a dozen video tapes. I figured they were blank, awaiting our recorded memories, but no, the benefactor advised they were selected for our private viewing pleasure—porno tapes. When I got around to cracking the wrapping I found all twelve had been previewed. I presumed Denise's parents viewed them while we were honeymooning.

"No need," I said to my now father-in-law Bob, "to jam them into a few days viewing. We'll leave them with you. Not the souvenirs we want foreign authorities inspecting, even if they can't play them."

Arriving in Brisbane early January 1989 we were excited to see little Brandy. Linda met us, but without Brandy, because of some rule about dogs and airports. Next we were delayed by one crummy piece of paperwork for ship's equipment we carried with us, meaning a night in a motel that didn't take dogs. We were to meet Linda and Brandy the next afternoon at one of Jock's service stations. It was a hard night for us; we were love-starved for Brandy. I also had a twinge of jealousy.

Jock's service station turned out to be a certified dump—a gloomy run down decaying place on a busy highway. We arrived and were startled to find Linda pumping gas and Jock barking orders like a hard-helmet German general. But he called for assistance and invited us to their home to chat and pick up Brandy. I was blown away when I saw the dilapidated shambles they lived in—two ancient trolley cars linked sideways.

"They left the line in 1954," Jock proudly declared as we approached, bumping along a dirt road built across a muddy field surrounded by swamp. *Jesus*, I thought to myself, *those trolleys don't look like they've been washed or painted since ...* calculating mentally, *maybe 35 years ago.*

"Oh ... my... GOD." Denise gasped, then cried out in anguish. Brandy was chained to the trolley, covered in fleas and dirt. She went berserk when she saw us, her tail wagging with happiness. There would be time for explanations. For now tears, hugs and love flowed intensely.

We sat on old wood chairs around a cluttered metal kitchen table while Jock bragged about his business acumen. I wanted to challenge him but chose the high road instead, excusing ourselves as soon as possible to go to the motel to change for dinner. Linda asked to keep Brandy one more night because strict Queensland regulations forbid animals in accommodations. We didn't like it but had no choice since we were visitors in their country. We couldn't risk authorities taking Brandy from us. Denise had been picking ticks, ants and dirt from our puppy since arriving. We vowed to return early in the morning to rescue her, a term I didn't use lightly. And poor little Brandy—she didn't understand. She only wanted to be with us.

Linda went with us to our motel. We would meet Jock for dinner and he solemnly promised Brandy, well fed, would spend the night inside, dilapidated as the joint was.

We checked in, changed to cooler clothing and Linda called Jock. He didn't answer so we went to the restaurant. Jock never showed. Linda continued calling. Jock didn't answer. Linda had no car so she came back to the motel with us, constantly dialing Jock. She was agitated and nervous. I worried about Brandy. Something seemed terribly "off."

"Linda, what's going on here? I gotta tell ya, something seems really amiss."

"Anything you want to share?" added Denise.

Linda broke down, sobbing uncontrollably; "I feel *so* bad about Brandy."

"Thanks, but forget Brandy for the moment." Denise broke in. "Is he beating you?"

"Not—not yet. Denise, I'm so scared ... he's been drinking, a lot, and has scruffy friends." More sobs.

Denise reached out to hand Linda a tissue. At this inopportune moment Jock burst through the motel room door screaming at Linda, "Get the hell outside, bitch. We need to talk!"

Linda went willingly outside. Denise and I reluctantly chose not to get involved. We heard arguing, then convulsive crying. Linda let fly a bone-chilling scream. We raced outside. Linda lay in a motionless lump across the curb. Jock had knocked her out and disappeared.

Denise checked Linda for wounds or anything broken. She asked questions, checking for signs of concussion as Linda slowly regained consciousness. We half led, half carried Linda carefully back into the room.

"Here, hold this my friend." Denise said, applying a cool damp cloth. Linda's right cheek was turning dark purple. A small trickle of blood ran down below her right ear where Jock's ring had apparently struck her.

"Look, honey," Denise said, "There's an extra bed here. You're staying the night. No arguments."

"Thanks." Linda whimpered through a river of tears.

"Bastard."

The ladies stayed up talking, with Denise continuing to comfort Linda. I tried to catch a few winks. Trouble was, my mind percolated, though my body was weary from our long flight and following the torment of both Brandy and then Linda. Eventually I faded away, drifting off to sounds of ladies' soft voices.

Impact awoke me. Jock had burst through the locked door, knocked Denise to the floor and was savagely punching me. I pulled to rid the sheet covering my body. *Has this asshole gone NUTS?* As he punched at me Jock repeated in a hostile half-crazed tone, "I killed your dog. *I snapped your stupid dog's neck.* Your dog is gone."

That sent 'Once a Marine always a Marine' Skip over the edge—crazy.

Screaming "Ohhrah" I lunged for Jock as he turned to run outside. He didn't make it. I had him on the floor, striking and kicking in a rage. Linda had called the police. Denise hovered with a flashlight, looking, if she could, to land a blow on Jock.

The police arrived. They broke us apart, both bleeding, me from the mouth and Jock from the nose.

"Hey scumbag, I hope I broke it."

"That's enough. No more. Steady, boys," said the calm cop, further separating us to get both sides of the story.

They heard mine, with support from Linda and Denise, so I was genuinely surprised when they let Jock go—free to walk, which he did. Aussie law, I was told. "Can't hold'im for fighting unless one of youze is in 'ospital."

I had been keen to put him there and protested until Linda reminded me of being guests in their country. Best to leave it be. She even quipped, "Don't suppose that makes you blood brothers, do ya?"

"Whatcha *can* do mate," said the Constable, is press charges on the bloke in the morning for assault and killin yer bitzer (dog) if that comes to happen."

"Denise, Linda, let's go find Brandy *right now!* O.K. with you Constable?" I asked, turning to face him.

"Yer a Seppo (American). Go fer it. She'll be right happy to see ya I suspect!"

We drove to Jock's place, arriving around 0100. Using flashlights and car lights we searched his shambles. We looked everywhere, even poking in the swampy areas while keeping an eye for snakes, rats or other vermin. We patrolled along the forest edge, yelling for Brandy, but with no result. We couldn't find or hear her.

Denise was sobbing, overwhelmed with grief. It broke my heart to see her like that. I gave her an Ativan pill to calm her. Raw energy kept us searching until nearly 0400 when we were ready to drop and covered with mosquito bites that began to itch. In my two foot zone I had a mental picture of Brandy, chained and bitten by multiple hungry insects. We reluctantly agreed to give up temporarily.

Sitting on a log beside the car, her torch still combing the darkness Denise kept calling for Brandy. Tears rolled down her sweat-glazed, dust-covered cheeks. Her voice hollow and empty, Denise looked up to me; "Why? What have we done to Jock? My little Brandy—so full of love—she couldn't have done anything to that bastard Jock."

Denise put her head in my lap and through tears continued, "She is the victim Skip—I mean, isn't she?" Her voice momentarily stronger, "the victim of a sick, sick person. And where is she? Did she die? How did she die? Oh my God! I feel so traumatized, so deeply hurt."

Denise broke down completely.

When morning came we shared an awful breakfast and the ladies took a rest. I was solidly in my two-foot zone, wired for revenge. Screw the high road. I *wanted* Jock. I found the police barrack and pressed formal charges against him. He could go to jail for this. Trouble was, we would have to testify and we were already overdue in Townsville, far to the north.

Captain Skip Rowland

I rejoined Denise and Linda around noon.

"I'm not giving up!" said Denise. "We need to look again."

We headed back to Jock's property. We parked and started looking for Brandy. 100 yards away Jock was standing by his truck. He turned as if he hadn't seen us.

Denise called out, "Where's my dog. Where's Brandy, Jock. Tell us."

Jock looked at Denise. Deliberately holding his arms up he gestured the motion of breaking a twig, signaling to Denise he had broken Brandy's neck. Then he jumped into his truck and sped off. We had left our rental car to search. It wasn't possible to scramble back into it fast enough to catch him.

Kind neighbors joined us combing the wooded areas. No luck. I searched again inside the dump Jock called home. What an implausible mess, but not a trace of Brandy. I noticed the chain that once held her and outraged me, was missing. It wasn't broken, but totally missing, causing me to wonder, *Is there hope?*

Later, standing at the edge of the swamp Denise took my hand, "I'm so afraid she's at the bottom, isn't she Skip, the bottom of this horrible place. But, where? Why?"

I didn't say so, but I agreed. It was so senseless.

We put ads in local papers, questioned anyone who would listen, without results. Nothing. With defeat all but confirmed we loaded the car for the lonely drive back to Townsville.

Denise, in her grief and in pain, turned and put her hands up to God. "Please Lord, let her be at the Rainbow Bridge."

"The what?" I softly asked, not knowing the expression.

"Rainbow Bridge. It's a place in heaven where animals we love go when they die.

There are meadows and hills where they can play. There's plenty of water and food, and lots of sunshine, and they live happily forever, like your people in 'Somewhere in Time,' the movie you love." Denise was weeping openly.

"Yes honey, I believe Brandy is at the Rainbow Bridge." I gathered Denise and held her close. Her sorrow losing Brandy was overwhelming.

"Will we will see her again, do you think?"

"Yes. I do. Someday, I really do."

Brandy Alexandra Rowland

CHAPTER 30

JOY, LOVE AND PRAYERS

To reach Townsville in our rental car we passed again through Mooloolaba. We decided a couple of days hanging at the Mooloolaba Yacht Club could be soul food for our damaged spirits. We saw James and Nancy Tiddy sitting in lounge chairs, looking over the marina. Nancy immediately noticed our sidekick Brandy was absent.

"Where's the pooch?"

We related the story, ending with a wish for Jock to rot in hell.

"And you tried everywhere?" asked James.

"Even newspaper ads with pictures and contact numbers in Townsville."

"What about the pound?"

"Huh, hadn't thought about that one. What pound?"

"Not sure exactly," Nancy replied, " but there has to be one around Surfer›s Paradise or Beenleigh. Wait a sec, I'll grab a phone book."

Nancy darted off.

"That's nice of Nancy to care so much," Denise said to James, "but I would hardly expect Brandy to be in a pound. Jock's a mean bastard. He intended to kill her."

"Me either," said James referring to the pound, "from what you say, but you know my wife. She's giving it a go."

Nancy made a list of pound phone numbers in the greater Brisbane area. We went to their house for "roo-burgers" as James called them, and to make calls.

After several unsuccessful calls Denise and I were ready to quit.

"One more try. OK? Just one." Nancy dialed the Beenleigh animal shelter and handed me the phone; "Better when you talk."

The phone rang many times. Discouraged I muttered, "It's Sunday and suppertime. There won't be anyone … "

"This is the Beenleigh animal shelter. Hello, hello."

"Hi, my name is Skip Rowland. I'm calling from Mooloolaba. Our dog is missing. We were in your …."

"Describe your dog for me."

"She's a Blenheim Cavalier King Charles Spaniel puppy."

"Yes, we have one here."

"You DO?" I practically screamed. The room went silent.

"Yes," said the lady casually. "She's so loveable I have her in the house."

"Ohhh my God. Is she in the room with you now?"

"She is."

"Our doggy's name is Brandy. Call her please and see if she answers."

A slight pause. "She's your dog."

The pound lady's voice practically smiled through the phone. They agreed we could ring her doorbell late so Denise and I left immediately.

We drove five joyful hours to be reunited once and forever with the wondrous small creature that had become the love of our lives.

The Dog Pound people—Hearts of platinum.

If I were to write ten books I could not adequately express the love and joy Brandy brought to our lives—the roller-coaster emotions: anticipating seeing her when we arrived in Australia from America, or the despair of believing she was dead, to the joy of the pound reunion.

The Rainbow Bridge will have to wait.

Denise wrote home:

Mom, I will never understand the venomous mean streak in some people. We learned Jock had chained Brandy to a gas pump at a closed service station along Coast Highway.

She was there all night. Wild dogs called dingoes and all sorts of other predators live around there. Honestly, it still makes me cry and still gives me shivers. A crew inspecting the station's pump found her near dawn, trembling and crying. The pound lady told Skip the inspector said she nearly licked him to death. I'm happy again.

CHAPTER 31

THE RICH LADY AT HAMILTON ISLAND RACE WEEK

Because Australia is a place everyone should visit our friends lined up to come sail with Denise and me, and Brandy.

Next up in terms of important events was the Hamilton Island Race Week. Hamilton was the only Whitsunday island with an airport. Keith Williams, an Aussie bloke, developed the island claiming the property as cattle lease land. I never saw hay or a cow but I expect it meant a better tax rate. Everything about the island screamed development, development and more development. Hotels, condos, restaurants, a church, a petting zoo, even a museum—the whole nine yards was brand spanking new construction, built for tourism, not bovines.

Our dear friend Shirley Rich, a diamond broker and astonishing personality worth a book of her own arrived at 'Hotel *Endymion*' for the event.

Denise and Shirley—note Denise's cup says "slave."

Nearing 50, Shirley was a statuesque platinum blonde endowed by God and nature with significant twin mounts on her foredeck. She dressed to the nines wherever she went, attracting men to follow like children to the Pied Piper. Shirley was nobody's fool. She flew her own plane, was a black belt in several disciplines and had been married so many times she had rice marks. Better not to mess with Shirley. Example: after she tied down her plane in Burbank, California, following an out of state diamond showing, a thief stuck a revolver through her car window. Shirley raised the glass and drove off dragging the frightened man until he dropped his gun (which landed in her lap). Only then did she lower the glass. The guy fell to the ground and Shirley drove away. By choice she met clients in crowded restaurants where her open cases of loose diamonds were surely a temptation. With a crowd of gawkers looking on she'd depart the eatery in her Rolls Royce displaying her vanity license plate *Hep Mama*. Shirley was a hoot to know and have aboard.

Race week attracted over 200 yachts and crews, plus spectators. Shirley, being momentarily single, found "the next man I'm going to marry." We didn't see her for five days.

1989's first race on a Sunday was fun. Then the weather went bad. Hurricane Aviva, it was announced Sunday evening, was due to visit on Tuesday. Races and events were cancelled. Winds were expected at 70 knots with higher gusts, accompanied by torrential rain lasting up to eight hours. Denise was worried and didn't keep it a secret.

"Crapola Skip, we're packed in this marina like sardines. What's your thinking?"

"To listen to the radio, make a decision in the morning. It's not like we have a lot of options."

"OK, how many then, and what are they?"

"Two, as I see it, because we can't get to a mainland marina in time. That might not be better shelter anyway, plus they are probably full."

"Or will be ... so what's the first one?"

"We could leave here, sail into a mangrove mud bank and ride it out."

"You're kidding me!"

"Not really, mangroves will break up the seas. The mud will hold our anchors, no worries there, then we'd just have to wait on a high tide or get dug out." It didn't sound bright even as I said it.

"What's your other brain buster?"

"Stay where we are, batten down and tie down."

"That sounds better if you ask me. Being around people—I find it comforting."

"Yeah Honey, I getcha. What I'm looking for from the radio is how high above normal high tide they believe the water will rise. The pilings holding the docks in place have to be tall enough that the docks won't float off the tops, get blown down on each other and crush us all."

"That could happen?"

"Comforting huh? Probably not. Don't worry so much. Wanna go grab a burger? Everything might be closed tomorrow."

"Let's go—and a good glass of red. Might as well enjoy our misery."

Walking up the gangway it was hard to believe a storm was approaching. Temperature was 74 degrees and the wind soft like the music that floated over the marina from dockside eateries, but there was no laughter. People spoke in sober tones. Our dinner was great, as if the restaurant knew they would lose refrigeration and were heaping food on plates.

Denise and I stayed up late, playing cards. We had the radio on but heard nothing more. Monday morning's 0800 weather broadcast forecast wind at 70 mph, pegging 90 in short bursts with a rising sea level within safe measure to feel the pilings would hold us.

We set about preparing. Denise cleared the decks, so to speak. We both worked to deflate our Avon and stow it below. In torrential afternoon rain we had help from Allain, a Swedish fellow who crewed the first race with us. Between him, Denise and me we took in both mizzen and jib sails, stowing them in the forepeak below deck.

Our radio reported that places in Queensland had received more rain in six hours than they had in the last four years. Damage was extensive. I worried about a massive high freeboard 52-foot wooden sloop rafted to us, with *Endymion* sandwiched between it and the dock. Marina authorities kindly moved it, to where I knew not.

My Swedish crewman Allain and I huddled over strong coffee in a rising wind. I didn't want my yacht being bashed against the docks by savage winds. Allain carried two spare 45-pound anchors to the next dock finger to weather of us. Dropping them to the muddy bottom he next swam the lines back to *Endymion* where I took a turn around a winch on both lines, cranking them tight. That pulled *Endymion* a short but comfortable distance from the dock and gave us additional stability.

Then we waited, but not quietly. It seemed everyone on the island took to the streets that night to dance and sing-along with the haunting sounds of didgeridoos played by the 'Gunnadoo' Aussie bush band. I fell hard for the resonant, earthy timbre of didgeridoo music—never expecting we would again hear it again a few days later.

The storm hit hard on Tuesday morning. Wind howled and shrieked through our rigging but it was below advertised velocity. We fared well, except for Denise getting "a bit of a rash," as she liked to say. It could have been worse had the whole marina not come together to help each other. By evening the awning was again over the cockpit, shrimp was on the barbie and cocktails served. Denise asked and answered her own question; "Isn't yachting fun? Now where in hell have I heard that before?"

With the storm past we got back to racing on a gloriously sunny day. The wind was under twenty knots with a few 'rain areas' forecast 'at times.' Well, those clowns prognosticating weather blew it again. The wind piped to thirty knots and it poured buckets all afternoon. We were short crewed. Allain was excellent, a strong young fellow who cranked a winch with power. We also had two 'pick up' crew who lacked sailing skills but made up for it with personality and appearance. One was a striking 19-year-old, the daughter of the island's chief security officer. At better than six feet tall she and Denise were the Mutt & Jeff of the fleet that day. And I can promise, no one would mess with the security chief's daughter, because they would be messing with him—a gorilla of a man. The rest fell to Denise and me. Racing short-handed wasn't dangerous or hard on a well-built yacht like *Endymion*, but it was tiring. We called it our 'fun day' and enjoyed a long spinnaker run on a flat but choppy sea with plenty of wind.

Hamilton Island Race Week

The last day's race took us to Whitehaven beach, famous for brilliant white sand made feather-soft by its high silica content. Soft sand with a good anchor grip is an oxymoron, so we anchored with caution. There was zip wind, so little concern. Lying in the soft silica sand I looked seaward. The sight of *Endymion,* with maybe another sixty multi colored yachts anchored head to wind, took my breath away. Denise was in the water playing with Brandy. Fetching a stick was their game. The race committee threw a barbie after which Denise, Brandy and I lay again in the feathery sand. Life was grand. I was a contented man.

"Having fun?" I asked Denise.

"You know racing isn't my favorite, right?" Not waiting for a reply she continued "But this, this is incredible. I'm *sooo* glad you brought me here, Skippy."

"Yup. Me too."

Brandy 'yipped' and wagged her tail. Aside from Jock-ass she's been making the most of life—island hopping, hiking with her parents, chasing crabs on beaches, being the center of attention and standing anchor watch. Young as she was, Brandy learned to stay in the cockpit until she heard the anchor chain going down. She then took to the deck.

Race week ended, but not the magic. We sailed to a small island. Expecting to be alone we found one yacht already at anchor. *Music* by name was a ragged-looking tired old vessel. Her skipper hailed us by radio:

"Welcome *Endymion* ... Beach barbie tonight. You blokes are welcome, in fact more than welcome. See ya ashore."

"I don't know." Denise was skeptical. "Remember the druggie boat at Huahine?" (*Leg One, chapter 32*)

"Yeah, well *Music* isn't a proper yacht, that's for sure. We've seen plenty that don't look too keen but had great people. Besides, we've never said 'no' to an Aussie invite so I say— let'er rip—let's go."

Denise did her usual, looking radiant. With Brandy poised on the inflatable's bow we motored ashore to an amazing surprise. The skipper and crew of *Music* was the bush band "Gunnadoo." Far into wee hours, in flickering firelight of native wood burning on a distant island shore, we were treated to songs played only for us by some of Australia's most talented didgeridoo artists. That night, filled with the crew of ragged yacht *Music,* spoke volumes about not judging a book by its cover.

With late morning sun behind us Denise went to the rigging to guide me slowly through dubious uncharted patches of the barrier reef. We anchored in a tiny circular lagoon about 200 feet in diameter. Twelve feet of crystal-clear blue-green water was below us. Exposed portions of the reef no more than a foot high nearly surrounded us just two boat lengths away. Tight quarters, but weather was calm and tides slight, generally two feet or less. We felt secure in that isolated spot on our planet, yet we were not alone. A goliath grouper fish I guessed to be one hundred pounds swam lazy circles around us for fifteen minutes. Huge sea turtles scoured the reef for snacks. Boundless multi-colored reef fish darted in all directions. Famished pelicans hung out watching for mistakes.

We dug into our music library for the soundtrack from *Somewhere in Time*. Denise and I, in love, anchored in the Great Barrier Reef. Kissing tenderly we lay under millions of stars, tiny wavelets lapped gently on the reef adding to the romance. With sounds and scents of nature swaddling us Denise quietly asked;

"What do you think right now, this very moment, my captain?"

"I think at this moment we are probably the most fortunate people on earth. And I believe this proves above all else that there is a God, a higher power. All that we've seen so perfectly balanced, so in harmony can't possibly be an accident. Agreed?"

"I love you Skippy."

Kisses became serious.

Remember *HMRS Stalwart*, our escort vessel in the Tall Ships Race? A couple of weeks later, anchored in a quiet island cove, I was working on gear. Denise and Shirley (who had rejoined us) were sunbathing on the foredeck. Neil Diamond's *The Jazz Singer* wafted from our deck speakers. Fishing lines hung limp in noonday sun. I spotted something seaward and lifted my binoculars. Steaming by fifteen miles distant was *HMRS Stalwart*.

I stifled Neil and grabbed the radio; "*Stalwart, Stalwart, Stalwart*—this is *Endymion, Endymion, Endymion*—come in *Stalwart*."

Within seconds Captain Wilson was on the radio. "Nice to hear from you, *Endymion*. What's your 'QTH'?" (position).

"We're in a secret cove and we're not sharing it." I said with a smile.

"You think so—really hidden huh? Fat chance. We'll find you."

"I doubt it Captain. Your ship won't fit where we are. We're remaining reclusive."

"Stand by." Captain Wilson went quiet.

Maybe seven minutes later a deafening 'whomp-whomp-whomp' sound came from behind our anchorage and a massive navy helicopter swooped over the hill and hesitated over us.

"Gotcha!" came through our radio.

The women scrambled for their bathing suit tops.

CHAPTER 32

HOOK ISLAND OVERFALLS

Overfalls are experienced by most long distance sailors. We had witnessed the phenomenon near the Bass Straits. (*Chapter 11*)
In mid February Tom Gates, another statesider came to visit. Tom was a former competitor to my business in California. He segued to a demonstration company. Most ladies serving samples in Costco stores worked for Tom. He couldn't cook water himself. Tom owned an Islander 36 sloop and was a good sailor. Shirley was still aboard. We anchored in the lee of Gloucester Island in a building nor'easter. We sailed the following morning in blowy conditions, planning to anchor at Hook Islands Underwater Observatory in the Whitsundays. A seven-foot swell was running, well above average for inside the barrier reef.

Tom and Shirley snoozed while Denise and I guided *Endymion* around the south end of Hook Island, before turning east toward the Observatory. The nor'easter by then was fully developed to a steady force 6 (twenty five knots) with large waves and nasty spray. With opposing current against the wind It created an overfall condition requiring total concentration, though it was a short sail to the small semi-protected anchorage by the Observatory, a great spot close to, but safe from, the overfalls. We shared it with only a prawn trawler, anchored a hundred yards from us.

Leaving Brandy to guard *Endymion* we went ashore for a swim, sandwich and sticky beak. As we sat on the beach with toes in the water I looked out at the two boats at anchor, their bows pointed toward the wind. *Endymion,* streamlined and modern had carried us safely over 18,000 nm since her birth. With the huge American flag hanging from her stern she looked downright regal. The trawler "*Esperance*" was more rugged, fitted with heavy gear used by professionals to carve a living from these waters.

Later, sitting on the Observatory deck with coffee and a sandwich I watched Brandy on deck keeping a vigil toward shore where she had last seen us disappear. Something though, was wrong with the picture. It took a moment. Then I realized *Endymion,* with its streamlined shape and deep keel was still heading to wind. The trawler, with its massive bulk below the waterline was surrendering to the current. The rule about anchored boats and drifting birds flashed in my mind; *both will always face into the wind or the current, whichever is greatest.*

What could be making the trawler change direction? Looking more intently I saw the overfalls had moved closer inshore. Currents do that. They move as tides or conditions change. Barely 100 yards wide, the current was taking the trawler firmly in its grip—right before my eyes.

"Hey guys, it's time we got back to mother ship." I didn't want to sound alarmed. We paid our tab and headed for the Avon.

"Hang on folks, I gotta pee."

"There's a facility room over there." Denise pointed it out for Tom.

Tom took more time to relieve himself than it took to build Rome. I was getting nervous. Motoring the Avon back to *Endymion* we saw she was pitching—tugging harshly on her chain. The overfall current had moved ashore enough that both boats were in the midst of its sharp, steep 4-foot waves. *Endymion* started to sail on her chain (move swiftly in one direction). She'd come up hard at the end of her leash, then move in the other direction. Getting aboard would be difficult.

I noticed our swim ladder jerking in its brackets as waves hit it. If it popped free and hung by its tether line it would be a bitch to get back in place. Worse could happen if the inflatable got under it, pushed it up and caused one of us to get hit by it. The swim ladder was made of stainless and heavy teak.

"Hang on!" I yelled as we crossed the line from calm water into the sharp overfalls.

"Damn—damn again." Shirley half shouted. She was grabbing at her straps. Bouncing seas had caused her aforementioned considerable twin mounts to nearly break free of her swimsuit. Not to worry, only Tom took a wide-eyed sticky beak.

This was going to be treacherous. *Endymion* was pitching, rocking and sailing wildly on her chain. When she cinched the chain tight her stern would rise from the water, then slam down burying the stern to the swim step.

"Take off your backpacks. Stow 'em low, on the floorboards."

"Glad it was a wine free lunch," added Denise.

"Yeah." My eyes darted between waves, trying to keep from being swamped, or losing someone overboard. I flashed to Brandy. She had sturdy sea legs. I couldn't see her and suspected she was lying low, safe on the cockpit floor.

"Shirley, you're in the bow. You'll be first up. Tom, you and I will grab the lines hanging from the davits to steady us—see 'em?"

"Yup, gotcha."

"Shirley." She turned the other way.

"Shirley, look at me dammit!"

"OK." She looked frightened.

"Step *firmly* on the ladder Shirley—*do not* let the dingy get under the ladder and knock it out."

"OK, Capt'n, I get it."

"Important, Shirley, the ladder could seriously hurt you. If you don't think you can make it, back off. We can make another try."

"What do I do when I get onboard?"

"Make sure Brandy is OK!" Denise yelled, interrupting.

"Stay low. If you can, help Denise up next."

Shirley looked at me momentarily—an intense look. I knew exactly what she was thinking. She was truly afraid. Shirley had lost a daughter overboard from her family yacht during a storm in the Catalina Channel maybe ten years ago. They had been adjusting a towline to an inflatable when her daughter lost balance on an unsteady deck, a situation with components mirroring this one. Miraculously her daughter was saved. I sensed rekindled private fears none of us could ever comprehend.

Back in my two-foot zone I was judging waves, looking for the best final approach to *Endymion*. A new problem loomed. The Trawler *Esperance* and my yacht, one controlled by wind the other by current, were rapidly nearing each other.

A collision, not a light kiss, was imminent. Shit!

Where's her crew? I wondered. *Probably in the bar.* It made me angry but no time for negative thoughts. We were alongside.

"*NOW*, Shirley!"

Shirley planted herself on the ladder as a wave swept the inflatable away. Tom missed the davit lines and fell back into the Avon. Shirley scrambled to *Endymion's* deck. The instant her foot left the ladder the inflatable pushed against it, breaking the ladder free. From the corner of my eye I saw Brandy. Overjoyed at our return she happily licked Shirley, hampering her movement on deck. But holding Brandy she lay prone and managed to place the ladder back in its brackets.

S-m-a-s-h, there was a loud metallic crash, sounding like an auto accident. The trawler's outrigger, with its 400-pound swinging stabilizer board, careened into our mizzenmast. If it hooked while the boats rolled in opposite directions it would rip out the mast, possibly even sever the backstay to the mainmast. If it broke or fell to deck it could kill anyone beneath it.

I agonized to be on deck myself but needed to board the others first. Tom had grabbed the davit lines, helping to steady us.

"Up you go, Denise."

She positioned herself.

"Denise, start the engine! Stay clear of the trawler board—and let out chain if you can. Understand?"

"*OK, OK*" Denise shouted back as she stretched for the ladder. The dingy lurched forward and up. The ladder broke free, and swung crazily. Denise, clinging to the bottom step, went into the turbulent water up to her neck. *Endymion* pitched. Denise went under and came up yelling, "a little help over here." Tom grabbed her arm. Denise let go the ladder. Leaning over, Tom and I pulled Denise over the edge of the pitching Avon. Tom lost his balance. Denise gagging, went into the water again. I barely held onto her. She cried for help. Tom regained his footing, enabling the two of us to pull her trembling body fully into the Avon.

As suddenly as the two larger boats had come together they separated, flooding me with relief. The board and outrigger were still dangerously close, but not tangled.

Shirley held the ladder from above. Tom boosted Denise and she got to love her doggy again—after starting the engine. Next, Tom went up the ladder. He secured the painter for the Avon and I followed him onto the safe platform of *Endymion's* aft deck.

It had been a team effort. Denise had the Perkins purring. I went forward, released the safety on the anchor chain and let out another 100 feet of scope as insurance.

Battle report:

Injuries—none.

Damage—badly scarred mizzenmast.

Elapsed time: maybe six minutes.

CHAPTER 33

ROO RETURNS

Checking the Post Office in Airlie Beach a few days hence I found a letter from my dad expressing concern that I may be working Denise too hard, particularly in heavy weather. Denise may agree. I responded in a letter home:

> *Yes Dad, sometimes I take Denise's watch, and others as well when conditions are violent enough that I feel they might do wrong or become frightened. If you recall I was at the wheel almost 46 hours straight crossing the stormy Tasman Sea. (Leg One, Chapter 45). Denise has gained confidence, partly because I don't force her to take the wheel in conditions beyond her ability. To her credit, big credit Dad, she can handle steady winds at 25 knots and seas at ten to twelve feet and that's remarkable for a 110 pounder, soaking wet. On passages Denise follows my watch. I help her if needed and the next most experienced follows Denise for the same reason. Sailing the coast has been easy excepting a wild ride down the Clarence River and recent overfalls at Hook*

Island. I'll leave that story to Denise. We work well together, Dad. Roo returns shortly and we have no long passages until we skirt northern Australia from Cape York to Darwin. That passage is over 800 nm.

I was messaging Dad, telling him I'm lucky, that I couldn't have a better mate than Denise. Besides, her perfume keeps Brandy and me interested. Were Brandy a male dog she'd probably hump the perfume bottle.

We had been corresponding with Roo. He wanted another bash at Denise and Skip and we needed another "Roo fix." Roo took mechanical courses during our time apart, and though his parents weren't thrilled with his jaunting off with a couple of "Yanks" for an unknown slice of time they seemed to semi accept it.

Denise and I had a pleasant easy sail north, tying to a worn and rather battered dock at an equally battered Cairns Yacht Club. The joint was about to be leveled in favor of a high rise. They called it 'progress.' What we saw was a tourist trap, motivating Denise to write jointly to our parents:

Well, we are in Cairns. I'm glad you didn't break your necks to get here. Mooloolaba is far superior. Roo arrives tomorrow. We really look forward to that. He is bringing his dad, I suppose to look us over before letting his son wander away with us. He will be here three days and then it's "outta here." This place just seems to want our money. We are getting anxious to leave civilization anyway, see Indonesia and get back to the adventures of island life and pleasantries of native people.

I was surprised Denise's letter made no mention of our trials at Hook Island. Women, I guessed, think differently than men.

So I added a postscript:

We're off next for Port Douglas and Cooktown, the only two stops before rounding Cape York at Australia's northern tip. Then we tackle 1200 miles of close-in reef and mangrove type coastline bringing us to Darwin. It's said to be crock infested, not where we will take Brandy or ourselves ashore. Except for a short note from Cooktown please don't expect more mail until Darwin.

Meeting parents of young people who crewed with us was never a problem. Roo's dad was a pleasure. Sure, he was giving us the eye; what else could be expected. He stayed with us until we reached Port Douglas on the far north Queensland coast. I was confident he departed knowing the people and vessel carrying his son were capable and trustworthy.

Prior to leaving Port Douglas Denise posted a letter home with her thoughts about the community and the return of Roo;

Mom, it's a really quaint, pretty place. Skip thought so too. We could live here except for mosquitoes and sandflies. Honestly, well almost honestly, they are so big a dozen could fill a foot locker.

It was great to see Roo and meet his dad. A nice bloke, as they say here. Roo is back with us permanently. Mothers hold your daughters ... he's tall, handsome, talks funny like an Australian, and is well mannered.

Sailing was fun with Roo lending a hand and entertaining us with his humorous Australian jargon.

Off the Low Islands Roo hooked an unfriendly a six-foot tiger shark. He let it go. Smart fellow.

One afternoon we dropped a day pick (a small anchor) in a shallow exposed area by Cape Tribulation. The name alone telegraphed adversity. I wasn't comfortable. I had an odd feeling; a sense of foreboding.

We went ashore anyway to water Brandy and have a 'boo.' Just before nightfall the wind shifted, becoming blustery in moments. We upped anchor and headed back toward the Low Islands.

Roo—happy to be at sea again.

CHAPTER 34

AN INCONVENIENT THEFT

Denise smartly brought *Endymion* head to wind. Roo called out "let 'er rip." Denise remotely lowered the anchor and reversed the Perkins, assisting the anchor to grip the hard sand bottom. About to cut the engine Denise heard an unfamiliar *Ssshhhiiissh* sort of sound. New noises usually signal new troubles.

"Roo, you took a mechanics course at home?"

"Sure did Missy Denise. What's up?"

Denise tried to explain the noise, but she couldn't. There was no hope. Roo had no more idea what she was saying than she did, but he found the problem straight away. A broken hose clamp, easily fixed.

We were the only yacht anchored among a dozen trawlers in the Low Island area near Mossman, Northern Queensland. Half the trawlers were rust buckets on their last legs and used only in coastal waters. We took comfort though, knowing trawler skippers knew the best holding and most protected areas for anchoring. A substantial fuel barge was permanently moored here. That made sense. It's a few days' run to Cooktown and nothing more until Darwin, over 1,000 nm distant.

On our fourth night reunited, we barbecued fresh fish, had a glass of Australian boxed wine and celebrated another sunset. Denise retired around 2100. Roo and I played backgammon on the inlaid teak and holly cockpit table until nearly midnight. I was keen to keep an eye on the trawlers, not that we expected trouble or for them to drag anchor. It was purely personal, having lived a spell with the crude characters prawn boats collect. I also monitored the wind, steady at around 12 knots, just enough to create white caps and a swell over the long fetch from shore to our anchored position.

Asleep below at 0100 I was beckoned awake by Roo. "Cap'n Skip. Something strange going on. Come on up."

I did. The wind was down but the swell still running. Heavy clouds blotted any stars. Voices carry on such a night. From an upwind trawler we clearly heard shouting—screaming actually—and sounds of someone in pain. Roo and I concluded it best we stay out of potentially drunken fishermen's problems. We went back to our bunks.

Frantic pounding on our hull woke us. My watch said 0240. Hastily rolling from our bunk I told Denise, "It's probably nothing but stay below, promise?"

Already topside, Roo was comforting a trawler crewman who had crawled into our Avon and pounded for help.

"This guy's hurtin, Captain."

"How so?" I asked, looking into the Avon.

"He's begging for a lift to the fuel barge."

"Looks a mess."

"Blimey Skip, the bloody guy's soaking wet, shivering, and so frightened he's spooked. The man is too confused to explain much."

"How'd he get here?"

"I dunno, swam I guess."

Denise appeared on deck. She's been watching through the aft cabin ports.

"I'm getting him hot cocoa."

"Hang a moment Denise. The guy's obviously petrified. The whole bizarre incident's way beyond my comfort zone." I didn't want him aboard.

Denise saw it more humanely. "Lower the swim ladder. I'll go down and clean his wounds. Looks like he has a few."

"Not good honey. You could get hurt."

"The man's cut up. We can't just leave him to get infected. What if he's bleeding internally?" she asked.

"OK, OK, I get it Denise. Staying below obviously didn't work. Do what you can."

Rather than us going into the Avon, Roo assisted him to deck while I stood by with a fish bat. I wanted to be humane—but in my two foot zone with caution as well. I'd been with trawler crews. The guy was no problem.

Denise worked her nursing magic. Speaking softly she learned the man was apparently gay. His drunken shipmates had beaten him nearly senseless. He jumped overboard to escape and swam to us, "the only boat that wasn't like the others."

Roo fired up our inflatable and took the man we never saw again, and whose name we never knew, to the fuel barge. In an act of kindness Denise had given him a sandwich, a change of clothes (mine of course) and a simple first aid kit she had thrown together.

Returning to *Endymion* Roo suggested we lift the inflatable into its davits rather than leave it in the water.

"Naw," I said, "unlikely this will happen again. It can't be stolen with the wire tether system, so why worry."

I should have worried. Here's why. At morning light our Avon was gone. The stainless steel cable anti- theft device with a coating designed to make wire cutters ineffective had failed. It hung from the transom in a jagged mess. For a cruising yacht in foreign waters it was a monumental loss. All day we motored slowly, searching coves and inlets with binoculars, even broadcasting a reward—all to no avail.

With failure at hand, at least for finding the thieving jerks, Denise asked a 21st century question; "Didn't you have some guarantee on that locking device, Skip?"

"Yeah, you were with me when I got it. Five years warranty as I remember."

"What's today? Probably five years and a day," Denise guessed.

I had no idea—but out there somewhere that day was an Aussie I didn't like.

Rounding Cape Tribulation with no way to get ashore but swim, we carried on, docking in Cooktown. It was Australia's last port before Cape York and Thursday Island at the country's northern tip. The only replacement we could find for the Avon was a battered up thirteen foot "tinny" (Australian for aluminum) boat that fit poorly on the davits and swung considerably when at sea in spite of our efforts to secure it. We didn't know it then, but the annoying swinging tinny would later contribute to saving our lives.

CHAPTER 35

LIFE GOES ON—TO DARWIN

Sailing north from Cooktown was as laid back as yachting can be. Soft warm breeze, ripples for waves and few other vessels. We did see government spotter planes looking for illegal traffic, we assumed from Indonesia. Twice we were required to identify ourselves. With Cape York and Thursday Island abeam we rounded Australia's most northern point and set off on 860 nm of pure pleasure, sailing across the Gulf of Carpentaria to Darwin. At latitude 12 degrees south, sea conditions were close to those of Grenada Island in the Caribbean.

Shorelines in this chunk of the world are predominantly mangrove swamps, loaded with salt water crocs and sparsely populated, so we stayed offshore, sailing a rhumb line—the most direct course.

About this leg of the voyage Denise wrote home:

Dear Mom & Dad,

If I don't live another day I will have felt the magic. For six days we sailed from one end of Australia to the next in gentle winds that were (yea!) always behind us. We didn't see land for five days. We were between moons but millions of stars looked down on us while yards of greenish white phosphorescence were pushed aside by our bow and ribbons of it streamed from the stern. We always had the best music. Mom, I am surrounded with love and peace.

Remember the guy we saw on the old Indian motorcycle near Monterey, his ponytail and sideburns were blowing in the wind? His jacket said 'Ain't Life Grand?' Well it is! I'm so happy!"

Australia's Darwin Sailing Club was where Mike Mulholland would join us for the leg to Singapore. No space at the club was available so we side tied to a commercial wharf in a 28-foot tide zone. Adjusting spring lines and fenders to keep the yacht floating challenged me. I didn't want to leave *Endymion* hanging no matter how strong our braided lines were. Denise hated climbing up the slimy ladder attached to the wall. It was the only way to get aboard or ashore. She managed.

With Mike aboard we set about the serious business of provisioning for a couple of months sailing in Indonesia. Admiralty sailing directions indicated a country not particularly hospitable to yachts. A big problem was a visa for Brandy. After considerable governmental correspondence started way back in Brisbane, we received our papers, including Brandy's, to enter the nation of 13,000 islands by competing in the Darwin to Ambon, Indonesia, Yacht Race.

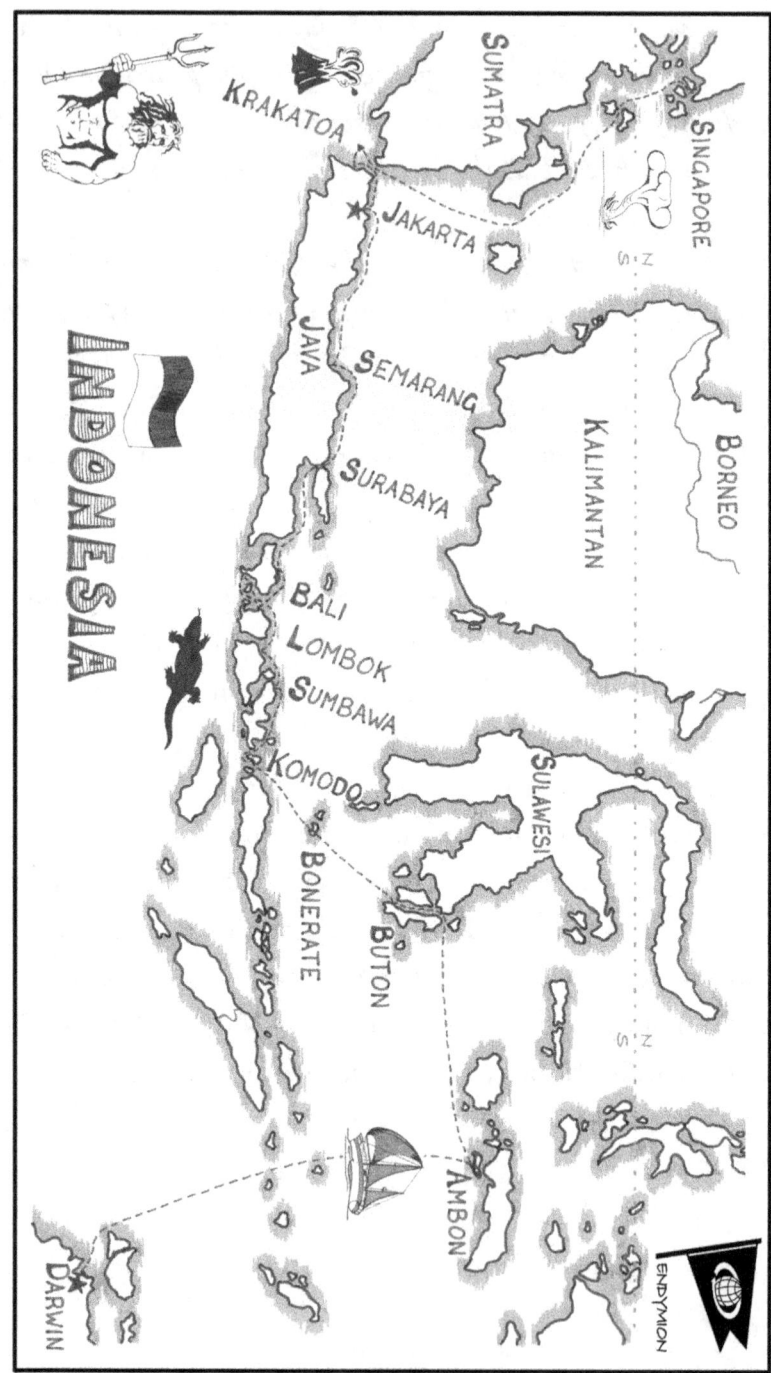

CHAPTER 36

DARWIN TO AMBON YACHT RACE

It sounded like fun. *Endymion* was fast for a cruising yacht. I looked forward to the 600 nm dash across the Timor and Banda Seas. Another competing yacht, *Bagheera*, was a sleek new 38-foot Benetau owned by our previously mentioned friends Andy and Liza Copeland from Vancouver, Canada.

We had shared several anchorages since tall ships. Now we would compete with *Bagheera*. Andy, a big but gentle soul, was highly competitive. I believed he would bet with me on raindrops running down the window. For this race *Bagheera*, rated as faster than *Endymion*, had to give us an hour on corrected time. Andy and I bet a Darwin Stubbie beer on elapsed time, the first of us to cross the finish line. (Darwin's Territorial government ruled pubs must close between 0400 and 0600. Boozers were permitted to drink a beer served before 0400. Thus was born the Darwin Stubbie, a 72-ounce can of your favorite suds.)

The 600 nm race was exhilarating, with the wind the entire distance perfect for our best sailing conditions. Shortly after the start gun, freshening winds had all yachts flying spinnakers. Through the second day and night we were literally sailing side by side with *Bagheera,* almost close enough to reach out and share Liza's breakfast scones. If they got a puff or slight wind shift they might move a few hundred yards ahead. Ditto for us when we were favored.

Tracking Bagheera in the Banda Sea.

We could see every move they made adjusting sail, as they could see us. It was competitive fun sailing at its best, made better because we really liked these Canadians.

On the morning of day three the wind had risen. We were on the edge of safety flying spinnakers. Mike turned to me, "I wish that damn spinnaker on *Bagheera* would blow out."

"Yeah, me too."

"Be careful about wishing," cautioned Denise.

Not more than a minute later *Bagheera's* custom spinnaker burst to shreds and she fell out of sight behind us.

"It wasn't a prophecy," claimed Mike.

"Yeah, maybe it's a lesson. We should douse our spinnaker." I said, noting the power of increasing wind.

Barely had the words left my mouth when "BLAM' like a cannon shot our spinnaker was in shreds. In the following confusion I hadn't looked for *Bagheera* but wondered if they had seen the retribution. Apparently they had gone off on an altered course.

The following evening, with twenty-three miles to go to the finish line we were charging on a close reach at nearly ten knots—streaking through a pitch dark night toward a strange harbor. Looking ahead through a myriad of flickering shore lights we strained to pick out the lights of the finishing line committee boat. The only prominent steady light was the portside running light of a yacht slightly to windward and exactly even with us. It was going to be close. We couldn't make out what competitor it was so Mike played with the radio, attempting to tease the mysterious yacht into disclosing its name. No dice. We jockeyed with each other in williwaw wind shifts barreling down from the surrounding hills, concentrating on every puff.

With less than an hour to the finish the wind piped up to thirty knots. At five nautical miles to go we thought we saw the finish line lights. Our adversary held position just to windward. He would have us if he had to bear off a few degrees, increasing speed. It would be close. It was exciting. In the final minute before crossing the finish line we recognized the challenger. *Bagheera*. This was our Churchill Downs, the 12th round, the Super Bowl last second point after. Both yachts, now coming together, were being sailed to the max. We would cross the line in a dead heat—bow to bow.

BOOMBOOM—the gun fired twice nearly simultaneously as we crossed the line astonishingly close together. In the end *Bagheera,* our friend and rival, finished 1.56 seconds ahead of us in the 85 hour 6 minute dash. We beat them on corrected time. Who says yacht racing isn't close?

CHAPTER 37

HEADS ON STICKS— I WANT HEADS ON STICKS!

The citizens of Ambon threw one hell of a party for competitors. Volley-ball, tug-o-wars, football and outrigger races kept us enthused and bruised. Food was delicious and speeches too long and boring, causing Denise to write home:

Yesterday the committee and the Indonesian Government gave us prizes and a wonderful lunch, but SO MANY speeches in a stifling hot giant hall. I had to hit Skip twice. He was snoring. Guess what though—we finished fourth out of forty two boats. Skip says I did great at the wheel and standing my watches but I told him that doesn't mean I want to do more races.

At the festivities we met Dop Barr, an Indonesian Race Committee member with a keen interest in someday cruising. He was serious about it so I gave Dop several of my books about navigation and living aboard. Denise and I were invited to his beautiful home for dinner. There I learned Dop was the Electrolux franchise holder for much of Indonesia. Aside from equipment, his company sold janitorial products.

"Dop," I asked, "are you familiar with Simple Green?"

"No, never heard of it."

"Simple Green is currently the hottest cleaning product in America. My former partner Chip and I helped the company, early in its development, to get on the shelves in what we call 'big box stores.'"

"H'm, interesting. We have stores like that, but not as big. We don't have what'd you call it, simple what? Should we be stocking it?"

"Simple Green, and yes, and here's why—it's biodegradable. It cuts through grease and slime but it's safe enough to swallow."

"What?"

"You heard right. Safe enough to swallow. Tell you what Dop. I've got plenty of it aboard *Endymion*. Before we leave I'll bring some to your office and give you a demo. And if you like it, I'll put you in touch with Simple Green's president."

At a lunch meeting with Dop and his sales reps I polished off two shot glasses brimming with Simple Green. Electrolux in Ambon added it to their product offerings. Dop Barr was grateful and though we didn't know it at the time he would soon repay the favor by playing an important role in our near future.

Getting out of Ambon wasn't as easy as anticipated. Local authorities, confused by numerous governmental snafus were only granting continuing sailing permits for yachts participating in the upcoming Sulawasi race to Bitung, north of the equator.

"No way!" exclaimed Denise. "It's time to drift and blend again. No more racing for me—not now. Not ever—at least for a while."

I sympathized however we were in the midst of clearing when the race edict was announced. For two days we scrambled among authorities seeking "chops" on our papers and answering multiple invasive questions as to where we wanted to go, and why.

"Bali. It's simple, Sir," I said to paunchy man with the most sour expression this side of Olongapo, "we want to go to Bali."

"Why?"

"We hear it's beautiful for one thing, and it's on the route to Singapore, our next destination."

"And why else?"

"Officer, we have heard so much about your beautiful Bali. I once sailed on *Baruna,* a beautiful yacht named for one of your beaches. I have always wanted to go there."

The Immigration Officer was unimpressed.

"Sorry, if you are not in the Bitung race you must wait one week and clear from downtown."

"OK, OK," rankled with frustration I agreed, "We will go in the Bitung race. Sign me up."

Endymion was cleared to sail to Sulawesi. However I had no intention of crossing the starting line, and no uneasiness that they might give a damn.

On August 2nd, 1989 we sailed north with the race fleet, shadowing them for a few miles. Then we split tacks and sailed instead to Buntung Island some 294 nm distant, heading directly for Bali. I had no idea what would happen when we show papers in the wrong port, but I gambled. Indonesia comprised 13,000 islands. I hoped it wouldn't be a big deal.

Two possible stopovers lay before us. The large island of Buru was off limits according to Admiralty Sailing Directions. It had been a prison for political dissidents during former president Suharto's ruthless "New Order" administration a decade past. We chose instead to sail to Ambelau, only 55 nm from Ambon and notorious for nothing other than having been a Dutch colonized island.

What a mistake.

The island was beautiful. I'll give it that much. Two small villages existed, one on the eastern side exposed to southeast trades and annoying swell. We gave it a miss, choosing instead a village on the island's northern side. Approaching from the sea and within only a quarter mile, the bottom rose suddenly from 1,000 ft. depth to less than 50 feet. Tall stately palms lined the beach off which we anchored, with rugged mountain terrain as a backdrop, shrouded by the same rainforest clouds hanging over the verdant hills that we had so loved in the Society Islands.

We arrived slightly before sunset and were surprised to see *Kinta III* from Australia, already at anchor—another deserter from the Bitung race. Before our anchor even hit bottom the air filled with Adhan, the not so melodic sound of Muslims called to prayer. It would be repeated many times every day—loudly.

"I'm not liking this," said Mike, looking toward the mosque while cracking a beer.

"Not *my* tune," added Roo.

I went below to make a log entry. I could hear Denise on deck; "Look at all these kids, will ya! This is great!"

Outrigger canoes surrounded us. Some, relics of an ancient past, needed constant bailing. Others carried up to six youngsters, mostly teens, waving and shouting, welcoming us to their island. Or so we thought.

Soon enough, waving hands became open hands. None spoke English but they could surely gesture "cigarette, smokum or drink." Attempting to be polite, Mike offered two packs of 'smokum' to a couple of paddlers. Chaos ensued. A stampede of outriggers crowded and shoved closer to *Endymion* and the handouts. The children's cheerful greetings became screaming demands: "Hey meester, cigarette! Hey meester, me —you," pointing to the boat, wanting to come aboard. Nearly twenty paddlers crowded along our port side, yelling, demanding, smiling, and whooping. A few over-turned their outriggers in glee, attempting to win our attention. Kids wanted the small trinkets Denise happily showered upon them. Some were no more than five years old, paddling like they'd done it since birth.

At the same time the Mosque's loudspeakers bellowed again. Not what we expected in an idyllic setting. Yet who could resist these adorable Muslim children? I wondered, *how strict is their religion? Was what I had heard about treatment of women under Sharia law true? And that thievery is against the rule of order? Were these small boys in outriggers being unnecessarily cruel to the small girls, some in burkas?*

We went to bed exhausted from fending off cute little beggars.

Before breakfast dishes were returned to galley cupboards the kids again descended like locusts on a savory crop, hovering around *Endymion* in their semi-submerged dugouts. The braver boys would thump our hull, then babble to us in rapid fire Bahasa Indonesian. So intense was their assault we forgot it was Mike's birthday. For a few moments even I got into the spirit of doing nice things for strangers by handing out Clairol samples to the girls and Billabong stickers to the young lads. It was bedlam. Suddenly it rained, a welcomed forceful fall. I mean it poured. Grabbing soap and shampoo we turned our faces skyward.

Mike, all lathered up on the foredeck first noticed something amiss.

"Hey—where's my damn fishing pole. OK, c'mon Skip, no joke, which of you dummies has my telescoping fishing pole?"

Blank expressions. Then it struck Mike.

"Screw this. The little bastards stole my pole, my prized pole I carried all the way from San Francisco."

Mike was furious, shaking his fist toward shore. "I want *heads on sticks*!"

"Calm down big fella, you probably stowed it below."

"No fuckin way. Hey Skip, better check this out." Mike pointed to the starboard boarding gate in our lifelines. "The pelican hook was missing."

"What the hell—no way." I said, irritated and scrambling forward. But it was gone, along with the stainless wire connecting the gate on the upper ends.

"Little bastards!"

The cheerful smiling little prick faces had robbed us. While I was Santa on the port side they robbed us to starboard. The children of Islam had cleared our decks of fittings, thongs, lures, Mike's prized fishing pole and anything that wasn't securely tied down.

Poor Mike. What a crappy birthday.

We radioed *Kinta III*. Peter spoke Bahasa. They were waiting for authorities to paddle out to clear them, and volunteered to swing by *Endymion* with the officers to help us with the language and customs. We sat in the cockpit, pissed off, awaiting justice.

We had obviously been robbed. I was concerned about the section of lifelines. We didn't carry spares so something would have to be jury-rigged. Mike was pacing and cussing about his telescoping pole. The man took his fishing seriously.

An official and *Kinta III*'s crewman Peter approached in *Kinta's* inflatable. Mike couldn't resist gesturing toward them; "I'm tellin ya, damn it. Heads—on—sticks. I want heads on sticks."

"This *is not* going well," offered Roo.

"I'm going below," said Denise. "Mike's outta control. Poor guy. Poor birthday boy."

Looking aft, two officials, one an Indonesian Army Sergeant brandishing a Sten gun, similar to an AK-47, were climbing our swim ladder. He did not look happy. Roo put both hands firmly on Mike's shoulders forcing him to sit, but Mike was fired up and carried on blaming the thieving children, one of whose fathers was possibly about to take a seat in our cockpit. It was tense.

"Sticks I'm tellin ya. I want heads on sticks!"

Kinta III's Peter spoke in Bahasa to the officer, who certainly didn't speak or understand English or we'd probably all be dead or in the local slammer. Peter turned to me;

"I told them Mike said what a lovely Island it is."

"Yeah, good. What'd he say?"

"He said they would like a beer."

"I'll get it." Said Denise, smiling at the Sergeant while Mike continued to call him an ass-hole in English.

"And some smokes if you have them. He wants some smokes." Peter hollered to Denise.

"Mike," Denise spoke gravely, "Get four packs of your cigarettes. Do it now and be polite."

"I thought Muslims didn't drink?" Roo commented to no one in particular.

"Times they are a-changing," I said as I presented our papers for approval. Our government visitors didn't read English either, so they approved, not realizing we were supposed to be headed to Bitung, Sulawasi. Same for *Kinta III*.

The beers went down quickly during an awkward silence. The cigarettes were indiscreetly pocketed before our "guests" departed.

Roo took Mike ashore to look for the crooks. All the faces looked the same. The only policeman they could locate pointed to a beat up diploma from a school in Germany. May have been his—or maybe not.

Back aboard, Mike was still brooding when he recalled leaving his new deck shoes on the aft deck where the officials had boarded. He went to retrieve them. No shoes. Mike again faced shore lamenting, "Some guy came aboard today thinking, 'I wish I were in that guy's shoes,' and now the bastard is."

That night we posted a deck watch. Mike drew the 0200 to 0400 watch. Poor Mike. Or as Roo put it; "The hell with him. It's not his birthday anymore."

Denise later said in a letter home:

We left the next morning thinking, Oh no—Indonesia's full of thieving poverty stricken children. We were on guard, but our next anchorage at Sumbawa was just great!

CHAPTER 38

THE KID WHO WILL SOMEDAY BE KING

At Paleau, Sumbawa, we anchored close to shore, this time befriending an industrious, charming lad of about fourteen years. Clean and polite, our new friend Aladan was a child entrepreneur. He took us to a fresh water spring outside of his small village. Denise and ladies from other yachts decided to do laundry. Afterwards Denise excitedly told me; "It was a riot, Skip. The whole village was hiding in the bushes gawking at we white ladies with fair skin doing bags of laundry. When we caught them looking, they came out laughing. We hired two villagers to do the rest of the laundry and we ladies went upstream to a shower behind a rock to wash our hair. It was great."

How'd you get them to do your laundry?" I asked.

"Easy. We used our dictionaries and phrase books to communicate, quite successfully I might add."

Aladan paddled out to introduce village elders who introduced their sons. The sons arranged to fill our water tanks by taking jugs ashore, filling them with spring water and returning them for 100 rupiah a jug. From their standpoint they were extorting us and from our side it was a hell of a deal with the exchange rate hovering at 1750 rupiah to one US dollar. As organizer, Aladan got a cut, same as he did for fresh fruit delivered in bundles. If the island someday builds roads he will surely have the first Mercedes.

That leads me to another Mike slice-of-life incident. Somewhat plastered from too much grog on a sunny windless hot afternoon, Mike knocked his prescription glasses overboard. He either jumped or fell (I'm not sure which) over the side to find them. He couldn't locate the glasses but in his thrashing about, the rupiah that had filled his pockets came loose and floated over the reef, delighting locals casting their nets nearby. While Mike was thrashing about, Aladan arrived with his canoe full of fruit. Mike hauled himself onto the canoe, turning it over, launching the fruit and Aladan into the water. Recovering and realizing his faux pas, Mike, a generous man, rewarded Aladan with the future down stroke on the aforementioned Mercedes.

Joined by Steve and Joansey from *Vintage Port* and John and Ines Bentley from *Quahlee of Sydney*, both Australian yachts, we gunkholed the shoreline finding secluded anchorages for perfect beach BBQ and bonfires. No locals. Long into the night we sang songs off-key or recited poetry for which we'd long forgotten the major lines. What we all shared was living the drifting and blending lifestyle.

Crew of Vintage Port *aboard.*

CHAPTER 39

KOMODO DRAGONS

We'd been advised to give a wide berth to Komodo Island, home of the legendary dragons. That advice was an invitation to me. We made Komodo our next anchorage, dropping our hook in 15 feet close to a sandy beach fringing heavily wooded jungle. Crossing the beach, we spotted a sign: *BEWARE KOMODO DRAGONS!* It went on to warn we should proceed with caution, listen carefully and if chased '*move in a zig-zag fashion as the dragon has short legs, a long body and cannot turn quickly.*' It also advised us that the dragons, largest lizards on earth can be 10 feet long and weigh 300 pounds.

Reading further Denise said, "Hey, no need to worry. It says they have poor eyesight."

"Yeah, but they compensate by having a keen smeller and lots of serrated teeth. We can use Mike for bait. He stinks."

"Screw you, Roo. Let's go." Mike was ready.

"This way—follow me." Roo turned into the forest. Pretending to throw caution to the wind we stayed a good 10 feet behind him.

We followed a reasonably definable trail that led us to a strange scientific station. A tired looking bearded man of maybe 60 years greeted us. He wore a badge announcing he was Alfred. Below his name was printed 'Reptile Scientist.' He invited us to sit in a small area with bars, much akin to being inside a slammer cell. He spoke with authority telling us to look through the bars to a wide pit 30 to 35 feet deep. It was hot and sultry. The hushed air had a deathly scent I couldn't identify. The scientist-cum-zookeeper said our timing for coming to this remote place was exceptional.

"What you will see you probably won't like," he said with a heavy German accent, "but it is how we study habits of these large lizards."

Roo took this shot of substantial Komodo Dragon from inside the protection of our cage—too close!

We watched his associates, with armed guards for protection; string a goat, most likely drugged, to a tree. It wasn't fighting, but it let fly a terrifying scream when a guard slit its stomach. The knife wielder and guards retreated rapidly to the small, protected cell where we were and took up camera positions. Three Komodo dragons approached the helpless crying goat, one from low in the pit, sauntering directly up toward the goat, and the other two from the goat's right flank. Thankfully the poor creature never saw them coming. The dragons' attack was savage, ripping the goat apart directly before us. Blood was thrown everywhere. It was over in seconds—suddenly deathly silent. We were all shaken. Denise wept openly.

"Why do you do this?" Roo inquired.

Met with mostly silence, one attendant told us in broken English; "It keep native people safe to understand lizard movement."

"Makes no sense. It's stupid, really stupid." Denise sobbed, "You should be ashamed."

I was stunned by the cruelty. Even Mike felt sad. None of us saw even scant scientific value. This wasn't the world we came from. I wondered, as we slowly left that dismal place, *was this a legitimate scientific study? Had we been duped? If so, why? Or, maybe we just came across some truly sick people.*

Roo led us back to the beach. Still tied in emotional knots and sick to our stomachs, caution was our middle name on the ten-minute walk. We had newfound respect for Komodo dragons, knew they really existed and legitimately feared for our safety. At one point Roo thrust his hands up, signaling us to stop. We did—dead in our tracks. "Hush, shhh. I hear something." Not true. Not funny.

Back at the beach with a wide stretch of sand between the jungle and us we pondered our food supply and shortage of meat. A goat nearby appeared to be pigging out on a coconut. Despite what we had seen, Mike, Roo and I hatched a plan to capture it for dinner, and not as a guest. The goat was wise to our amateur stalking talents and ran off easily as we dashed after it, with Denise shouting, "You bring that damn goat on the boat, you'll have to name it."

We ate more fish.

CHAPTER 40

LOMBOK ISLAND IMPRESSIONS

Lombok Island, east of Bali and west of Sumbawa, was in sharp contrast to the primitive, pristine jungle environment of Komodo. Lombok's population was dense, yet primarily poor. Bicycles with seats ahead of the handlebars were basic transportation. The wealthier had a motorbike with passenger seating, or one of the few automobiles we observed. It was a dramatic display of "haves" and "have-nots" coexisting—*but what if food became scarce?* I knew who would benefit.

Much of the population here didn't bother to work at all. Those that did averaged about $30.00 US per month as a laborer, or potentially $60.00 a month for skilled office workers. Granted, food was cheap and a house may cost $1,000 US, but none of us would live in it. What about those who don't work? They steal, beg and live a marginal existence.

We saw children who will do in a second what we would not consider in a lifetime. For the equivalent of an American quarter a young man will dive into the disease and pollution ridden harbor to free a snagged line or fix a broken prop. Old men push carts heavily laden with teak through smog-saturated air to the center of town. Most were barefooted, working in blistering sunlight, for fifty cents a trip. Human labor, so readily available, was cheap. It was also sad.

Yet, somehow there was dignity in poverty. Being Hindu and Muslim, those folks didn't drink alcohol. Thank God for that as an adult population of alcoholics would certainly have created starvation for ignored children. There were a lot of observable traffic accidents as well, though not from alcohol—just because the roads were a virtual free-for-all.

Indonesians' strong adherence to faith, especially Buddhism, placed high value on family relationships. Purity was essential. Throughout the islands we never saw signs of prostitution or teen pregnancy, even in areas of dense population. Bodies seemed to be travelling in every direction, getting little done—but smiling, always smiling.

Scarcity of food was frequent. Many areas with abundant children have no stores at all, so it's a given there are no frozen foods. Somehow they make it work. The farmer feeds the fisherman, the fisherman feeds the farmer and they all feed the builder or educator. Barter. Not money.

So everything is fresh. Great!

Well, not really. It's hot. Miserably hot. Fresh foods don't last long. A lot has to be tossed and there are no supplier markdowns in price. How would one mark down something that is nearly zero to start with? We have purchased limp lettuce with weevils, cabbage with brown bugs, fruit with worm species not yet cataloged, and eggs so rotten they were stinky when cracked. But hey, we didn't pay much.

Poultry was plentiful however scrawny and certainly best purchased while still alive. Denise didn't take to beheading chickens. She became downright hostile to one native vendor who paddled up to the stern of *Endymion* proudly offering a small monkey—not as a pet. One of few times I heard Denise curse as she shooed the sales rep away.

Meat. At smaller islands it was often scarce. At bigger places like Lombok, knowing its source and what it had been fed were just as critical as knowing how long it had been dead.

Fish, a dietary mainstay on all islands since humans first carved wood or cast a net, was in jeopardy of disappearing. Looking seaward at night, a line of dugout canoes was visible as far as could be seen. Working only twenty feet apart, fishermen with bright lanterns to attract fish slapped the water to bring prey to the surface. The fisherman took them all, some we saw were five or six inches. This went on every night, mile after mile, regardless of weather. There are no holidays from the need to eat—until, guess what—there are no fish, and that time may be close.

CHAPTER 41

THE BALI COCK BROKER

We chose, for no special reason other than to avoid Bali's Kuta Beach, to sail around the northern side of the Island to Singaraja. We found it a dirty and unpleasant anchorage. *Quahlee of Sydney's* John Watson radioed, inviting us to sail twenty miles further to Lovina Beach where he and wife Ines were entertaining Balinese friends aboard their yacht. Once anchored, we flopped our leaking tinny over the side and motored over for a chat.

Our Balinese hosts were talking about "must see" places.

"Ubud, up the hills from Denpasar is an artist colony you should not miss," we were told. We also heard about a secluded 115 foot vertical waterfall a half hour inland of our location, and of a Lake Batur, formed from an ancient volcanic eruption located at the foot of Mount Abang, elevation 7,000 feet, the highest point in the Batur volcano caldera.

Over breakfast the next morning John and Ines shared that they had once been to the lake, staying in the tiny village of Trunyan. Roo asked for a further description.

"Here's what I recall," offered John, "The village follows ancient traditions including 'burying' their dead in cages above ground. It relates to having once survived a massive volcanic eruption where thousands perished."

"How long ago? I inquired.

"Don't know for sure, at least several centuries I think. One local had told us it's been erupting since the last time the earth shifted on its axis."

"Sounds like you Skip, talking about the poles shifting." added Denise, referring to my interest in variation versus deviation and how I believe ever so slowly declination from the North Pole will in some distant day cause the earth to shift on its axis. Water melting from polar ice caps must relocate somewhere, and evaporation over landmasses is creating imbalance.

"Screw the poles," Mike said, "I'm going to Kuta Beach. No way I'm gonna spend a day with the dead. You with me Roo?"

"Don't think so mate." Roo replied and turned to John, "Did you visit the burial ground?"

"We didn't. It was a graveyard of great suspicion. Locals don't go there unless they have to, like a funeral. I'm not suggesting it's haunted but I can tell you it's across the lake. You'll have a hell of a long hike on a very narrow trail to go around, and the water transport Ines and I saw looked unreliable. We decided to pass."

Denise, Roo and I unanimously agreed. Let's go. Gruesome as it sounded, curiosity got the best of us. We wanted to see what others wanted to miss.

"Behold my friends. You guys are flat out nuts!" Mike scowled, showing his distaste.

Would John & Ines join us? No. Were they apprehensive? Yes.

"First for me is the waterfall, then if Captain Skippy here and Denise are keen to visit the dead, I'm booking into that one too. OK?"

"Good on ya Roo," Denise said with a smile, "I agree, waterfall before graveyard."

I agreed, "Yup, I'm for the falls. I foresee a power scrub for our aching bodies."

John introduced Wayan, a local lad of about twenty and his younger brother, also Wayan who would guide us to the Gitgit waterfall.

'Whoa here!" Denise was curious "Wayan and Wayan, two guys with same name from same family taking us to the Gitgit. Sounds bizarre."

"No." said John as the brothers looked on flashing broad smiles. "In Bali there are systematic names for the first four male children and the same for girls. When a fifth child of the same sex is born the Balinese revert to the first name. Thus Wayan, age twenty and his brother Wayan, age nine."

"Be a bit dicey in a courtroom." I softly uttered.

"How many kids in your family?" asked Roo.

"Eleven." Wayan proudly said in reasonable English. "In our country it is a caste system. From our name we know the order of birth. We are free to take a popular name as well, like someone from history or a nickname as you would say. After death we assume yet another name. In our family three of seven brothers are same name."

"Crapola." Denise was pondering the situation. "Too confusing. Supposing every man friend I have was called, Pete. I say 'Pete, I love you' and a dozen men all want to et laid. No thanks!"

"It can be worse," said Wayan, "girls have the same names as boys but with a Ni in front. So I have a brother Wayan and a sister NiWayan."

"Enough. Tell us about Gitgit waterfall."

Gitgit, we learned, was actually three falls with the first being the tallest falls in Bali and to this point undiscovered by world tourism. Cool pleasing water cascaded with a roar heard a half mile away into a refreshing, surprisingly large pool allowing us to bathe or stand under the falls soaking in beauty and feeling blessed. We spent hours at the falls, and never saw another person. *How long will this last?* I wondered. *It won't be Niagara but it will be popular.*

Skip lathers up.

We next met up with Mike and Dan in Ubud where we rented two bungalows close to the monkey forest. I was blown away by phallic symbols everywhere—as doorknobs to the bungalow, a key ring or carved wooden souvenirs. One was a handle on a water faucet. Most Balinese were Hindu and the penis, we learned, represented the supreme God, Shina Linga. Wayan and his brothers wore penis charms around their necks to fend off bad spirits.

Mike bought numerous such charms for his friends in California. I wondered what Customs in San Francisco will think.

We sat on our bungalow deck looking out over rich green rice paddies. Lovely Balinese girls were serving a beautiful fruit and nut assortment when Mike asked, "Skip, you and Denise are going into that monkey forest. Do you have a guide, a Wayan or a Komang (third in line)?

"Hadn't planned on a guide Mike. The place is supposed to be well marked."

"I've a suggestion then," Mike offered "You should take some of this fruit to feed the monkeys. Not the fresh stuff that's cut up already. Jam a few bananas under your shirt, Skip. Whadda ya think?"

"Sounds OK."

"Sounds stupid to me, more like a trap," offered Denise.

Stupid it was. Denise had never seen me scramble so fast. The monkeys damn near tore me apart. They knew where the bananas were. My shirt wasn't a challenge. They came from all directions, jumping on my head, tearing my shirt to shreds, clawing and crying for fruit I couldn't dump fast enough. Though not wounded I departed the forest shaken and plastered with mud.

"Check that out, you dope," said Denise pointing to a sign reading, "Rules—DO NOT feed the monkeys."

Watching a cockfight was a cultural must do at Ubud. Mike drew me aside to convince me that we should buy a cock.

"Are you crazy?"

"Naw, course not. It'll be fun. Listen, you saw how these guys bet. The way to win is not to bet on someone else's cock—it's to own one. Let's get one. We can make a fistful of rupiah from these locals."

"I don't know, Mike."

"Come on. Look at that swarthy guy—over there. He's a cock broker. Wanna bet."

"That guy?" Now I was pointing. "He the most sinister looking person I've seen since Capone. Awww, what the hell Mike, I'm in."

Unsavory guy to right was our cock broker.

We bought a cock. I named it *Predator*. The little killer with a blade taped to its claw looked evil enough to Mike and me. Alas—we paid too much. *Predator* went to battle in his first match—and was dead a minute later.

"This sucks. Let's get a beer," mused Mike, looking toward a vendor with beer bottles floating in lukewarm water with sparse pieces of rapidly disappearing ice.

"Gimme two," Mike signaled the bar keep, holding out two fingers and a wad of rupiah.

"Damn," I exclaimed, "will ya look at that!" Our vendor was opening our bottles with a penis shaped opener.

"That's gotta hurt."

CHAPTER 42

'BURIED' ABOVE GROUND

Denise and I returned to *Endymion*. Mike and Danny left for their chosen environs, the *Hard Rock Cafe* in Kuta Beach. Roo found a guide to take us to lake Batur—reluctantly.

"Lake OK. Volcano OK. Graveyard bad bad place. No go there." he explained through an interpreter. Now we wanted more than ever to go. I negotiated a fee. The driver would take us to the edge of the lake, but no further. He would wait for us to return. We piled into his small bus type vehicle and headed for Trunyan Village on the shores of Lake Batur.

Climbing into the mountains was akin to driving into any mountain range with two exceptions. Never had I seen so many flowers growing in wild profusion. Poinsettias, daisies, orchids and frangipani—a kaleidoscope of beauty waving in cooling breezes as we neared the mysterious lake. And there were the bathers, men and women. Normally in Hindu fashion they would be heavily dressed but here were stripping to the birthday experience to bathe in mountain streams that flowed along the road. Nude, smiling and waving as we passed they were a sharp contrast to what we would soon see.

For a bone jarring hour we lurched and swayed through hairpins and switchbacks as the terrain became more forbidding. All of a sudden we burst into a vast open space. Thirty miles away we could see the distinct rim of an ancient volcano. It was hard to believe we were on the opposite rim, looking across thirty miles of world that had been blown apart creating vast openness. Now thousands of years later there was a lake, vegetation, commerce—all where glowing liquefied lava once flowed. Some areas perhaps from more recent eruptions still had no growth, appearing as bleak black areas.

Lake Batur was a breath-taking part of the Pacific Rim of Fire. Our driver took us to the small lakeside village of Trunyan. Locals wanting to be friendly asked the same questions we heard throughout Indonesia; "Where you go Mister? Where you from Mister?" They vanished when we said "to the graveyard."

While eating lunch at a shore side restaurant, more a bamboo shack, local hawkers found us and swarmed. They didn't care at all where we intended to go.

"This is cultural," said Denise.

"Not to me. I feel I'm back in the monkey forest. These kids are worse than monkeys."

The persuasive but charming little brats hocked anything that wasn't anchored to the ground, but wanted no part of crossing the lake to the cemetery. We didn't get the impression it was because the cemetery was sacred ground, more that it was a remote place where people who had not been good in real life were exiled to spend eternity with others who had been dishonorable. We eventually located Nyoman, the third, or seventh, or eleventh son of a Bali merchant. Nyoman spoke some English. He was a keen negotiator. For an enormous fee (about $20.00 USD) would take us across the lake and wait one hour—no longer. We asked if it was true only bad people not worthy of cremation were buried in the cemetery.

"Yes yes, true true," whispered Nyoman as if sharing a state secret. "And no children. Only bad people. Many times bad things happen. If woman go to take body away we have earthquake. I take you now." Pointing to Denise he added, "She can go now too. Not go to carry dead, only go to look."

Scrambling into his slow moving jakung, an outrigger with canopy and motor, we crossed the lake in twenty minutes. Afternoon winds caused a short chop. Roo, sitting forward, was spray soaked, something he found cool and refreshing in the blistering heat.

Approaching shore our guide explained. "Only the bad rest here. Full up, only ten persons. When more die, bones of oldest get kicked down the hill, make room for next bad one."

With the jakung bow on the smooth black pebble shore, the cemetery gate was immediately in front of us with stone walls to either side, adorned by human skulls.

"Damn, this *is* eerie," said Roo.

I questioned our judgment— perhaps we should not be there. Then Denise piped up, "Pay attention Skip, you won't see anything like this ever again,"

I sensed a strange reverence in her voice as she gently patted a skull.

The cemetery was on a steep hillside. We paused under a giant Banyan tree rumored to be over 1,000 years old and able to absorb odors of death. The tree was the gravesite guardian. Perhaps it worked. There was no foul smell.

On a reasonably steep rise, close to the mysterious tree and with an exceptional view over the lake, we found ten above ground gravesites in a small area, thirty to forty feet wide, about the size of an ordinary tract home. Each deceased was partially protected from the elements by a loosely arranged bamboo tent-shaped shelter inside of which the former citizen rested eternally—or until kicked down the hill.

"Are we ready," I asked, "to have a face to face confrontation with death? Do we really want to see what a human corpse looks like only weeks after death—several months or a year? What if it makes us sick, or we have nightmares?'

I didn't scare anyone. We each knelt to look inside.

"This one is just old bones," remarked Roo, sounding disappointed.

"Don't see much in this one either," said I.

"I'm looking at one here," said Denise "that looks pretty new. Maybe dead a couple of months—my guess."

Leaning closer Denise held an arm behind her like a relay runner awaiting the baton. "Hand me the camera, I'm going to ... Oh crapola! This stinks! Oh my God!" Denise jumped backwards nearly tumbling down the hillside. Roo and I cautiously came for a closer look and quickly backed away.

"What gets me," Roo said, "is the litter. Like our boatman said, someone must kick the remains of the longest dead one down the hill to make room for a new body."

I hovered over another site. I saw no bones inside the bamboo, only personal or household items. Then I noticed bones on the ground all around me, so many I had to be careful where I stepped.

Bending to inspect a skull half covered in leaves and debris I said to Roo, "Looks like some of their worldly possessions are sent to the spirit in the sky with the dead. See the plate, and the basket with the spoon in it."

"Wow! Look at this skull," said Denise, "that's a coin wedged in its teeth, isn't it?"

Notice the coin in this skulls teeth.

We looked and agreed, wondering why and what that soul may have done. Was the coin an accident, honor or the sign of a thief?

From death only a few weeks ago to several years ago we witnessed unsettling decay. It wasn't shocking or scary or spooky. In a way it was peaceful. In a stranger way this place made me more comfortable with death. I know, as I always have known, that our spirit will survive, though as we have now witnessed the body will not.

Whatever our initial skepticism, this strange place was peaceful and the occupants had a marvelous view.

"When tourism discovers this site people will pay good money to see what we just saw."

"Maybe if that happens, they can clean it up a bit. Show some respect," added Denise.

Back aboard *Endymion* Denise included the following in a letter home:

"Skip called it the Valley of The Dead, but it was a hill instead of valley. Honestly Mom, how many people can you think of who have had such an experience? Or who would want to? I guess we want to see it all. That's what we are here for. Next stop is Jakarta, the largest city in Indonesia.

CHAPTER 43

JAKARTA

We sponsored a rousing farewell dinner for Mike and Danny in Denpasar, the Capital of Bali and a city about the size of San Francisco. Crossing streets with a plethora of motor bikes, carts, taxis and trucks all vying for the same chunk of pavement was daunting for our laid back status.

"If this is city life," I confided to Denise amidst honking horns, "please stamp 'out of order' across my forehead and I'll call it a day."

"Relax Skip, it's party time. These are good friends."

"How can I relax in this mob?" was my question.

But relax we did to the point where son Danny had to help pour Mike into the taxi to the airport for their morning departure to California.

Before we set sail a senior friend from Seattle came to cruise with us as far as Malaysia. Denise grew fond of Don McMillan. Don's wife had passed from cancer seven years ago. At age sixty-nine this "real nice fellow" as Denise referred to him, hooked up with us for one last shot at adventure before marrying his forty eight year old Spanish teacher in January.

"My hero," I confided to Denise.

On Thursday, September 28th, Don took the helm, we upped anchor and departed beautiful Bali headed for Jakarta, a distance of 600 nm for the course we had projected.

Rounding the southern tip of Bali, Don set our course at 345º magnetic, delivering us comfortably into the Java Sea after negotiating the narrow gap between Bali and Java.

Roo took the helm for the 2000 to midnight watch. Assisted by our Perkins and sailing only a few miles offshore in calm conditions he began to notice strange flickering lights ahead of us—not steady bright navigation lights, but more like flashlights from a gaggle of people walking across the ocean.

"Hey Skip," Roo called to me at the chart table, "either I'm going daffy or hallucinating. Can you check the radar? We have weird lights ahead."

"Roger, Roo. I'm on it. How far?" I asked wiping sweat from my brow.

"Can't tell fer sure Captain. Come have a look while the radar fires up."

"Radar's already warming. I'll take a peek and then come up."

A few minutes later I traded the stifling navigation station below decks for the stifling muggy evening heat of the Java coastline.

"Roo, you're spot on. I get several returns just inside the five-mile ring and a whole bunch further out. They're faint. I can't tell what they are. Best to exercise caution though nothing shows on the chart."

"Bloody dark one, she is tonight," said Roo. We're making six knots. Probably won't be running anything down. Whadda you say, skipper. Should I cut our speed?"

"Naw, not yet. I'll monitor the radar."

Denise and Don had come topsides, wanting to be part of whatever was breaking monotony. They passed our binoculars back and forth, thinking they saw something as well. Our running lights were on, as they *always* were after dark. I went below for another look. Definitely there was something ahead. Something small and stationary, perhaps an anchored fish boat. I picked up the VHF radio; "All ships, all ships, please respond with lat-long if you are able to see a strobe light flashing at 7.32.5 South Longitude- 115.9.2 East Latitude." I switched on the masthead strobe.

Silence.

Back at the radar the return was still faint but steady at 1.6 nm ahead. I called topsides with distance and bearing. "One of you guys up there should see something. It's close. 1.6 miles dead ahead."

"I do!" called out Don. He stood, grabbed the binoculars and headed to the bow pulpit for a better view.

"What the hell! Looks like a giant wicker basket. I see lights. Hold your course. Damn, this is crazy ... looks like a small fire burning inside a basket."

At our speed we were approximately fifteen minutes away. "Hold course for now Roo."

"Roger skipper. Holding course." Roo repeated the command.

Not once did we get a radio response. A few minutes later a platform structure ten to twelve feet above the sea surface loomed clearly into sight. Passing within a quarter mile we saw it was a fisherman's lodging, perhaps his family's home. A bamboo platform about forty feet square sat atop stilts buried into the mud below. And yes, there was a cooking fire in use. In what could only be a life of poverty we concluded, and later verified, the inhabitants eked out a meager existence harvesting the small pelagic fish found abundantly in these shallow waters.

Bamboo fisherman's home in Indonesia.

"Jeeze, I feel sorry for them." Denise said as we passed the second platform. "Look at all we have, how bountiful our lives are. What's a future is there for these people and their children?"

"What about storms?" I asked.

"Strikes me," answered Roo as he gave Denise the watch, "from weather we've seen it's hot, muggy, and windless. Probably more chance of being flipped over in a Rim of Fire shaker than in a storm."

"And what's a 'shaker'?" asked Don.

"Earthquake, dummy."

"Get a heart!" Denise said before repeating course and sightings back to Roo, and assuming the wheel for two hours of dodging dozens of platforms, all occupied by locals seeking small shallow water fish.

Our only stop en route to Jakarta was Semarang. We tied to the city's municipal dock the following afternoon. What a place—what a toilet! We fashioned rat guards for our docking lines. The water was foul, horribly polluted and emitted an oily stench. Buildings near us were deserted. High water marks on sides of structures indicated levels that had driven people away, but there was no river. An official checking our papers told us global warming had raised the sea level. Buildings around the harbor had been abandoned. There was no fresh water at the pier, nor was electricity available. The place was a mess. Denise felt sick to her stomach just breathing the air and wrote home about it:

The four of us were in the cockpit when evening prayers bellowed from a nearby Mosque. This guy couldn't sing. I can't describe it except to say it's worse at 4:00 am. I screamed at Skip, "That's it!"

I already had Bali Belly and a temp of 100 and wasn't feeling well when I lifted my head from the cockpit cushion trying to catch a breath of air. Sixty feet across the channel two disgusting men had their butts hanging over the seawall and were pooping into the harbor. I said to Skip, let's go NOW!

We stayed the night, casting off at 0500, headed for Jakarta, an easy 200 nm sail. Wind was slack but we were in no hurry so we sailed slowly and uneventfully. Nearing Jakarta late the following afternoon, the raw water pump cooling the engine seized. I radioed for repair advice. A man named Paul with a strong Chinese accent told us; "There is a small docking site in a nice park. It's not far from city center and a mechanic lives close by. I am moored here," he said. "It is peaceful."

"Sounds like my kind of place!" Denise was happy.

"Peaceful, huh? Wonder what the hell that means?" Nobody answered me.

We headed for the peaceful place.

Planks were missing from the rickety dock we tied to. The park was a five-minute walk through dense brush on a dirt trail and the city wasn't even in sight until you crossed railroad tracks. There was one rickety boat tied to the rickety dock, a Chinese junk with guess what—a guy named Paul, who told us about Ivan, also Chinese, who had opened a small mechanical repair shop.

"Probably his brother," lamented Roo. He and I removed the pump in stifling below deck heat. Ivan, actually from Singapore, picked it up. He also lingered to tell us about his friends on Singapore Island. He thought we should visit. I promised we would.

We spent the next morning locating the Jakarta Post Office. Allegedly they held mail for us, but there was none. That troubled me. We had resolved a business dispute with the IRS. Important papers and payments had been forwarded to Jakarta. We taxied to the US Consulate for advice and help. The OIC (Officer in Charge) and his government associates there to help, had taken an extremely l-o-n-g lunch break. We eventually left without seeing anyone. It was a hot, humid day. City people had not been friendly or helpful. We were disappointed.

Ivan came by *Endymion* the next day to install the repaired pump. He noticed our rat guards affixed to our dock lines. Apologizing profusely, as if chairman of Jakarta's rat control authority, he also captured a rat right in front of us, and sent the poor critter off to sea on a scrap piece of wood. Denise found Ivan's wife and children charming. She invited them aboard. Before leaving hours later we discovered they still maintained an apartment in Singapore that we were invited to use while there. Ivan's wife Theresa gave us a phone number for her Singaporean brother John, insisting we call when we arrive. John, she promised, would pick us up and deliver us to her apartment, a gracious offer.

Ivan volunteered to "swing by the post office to forward our mail." Much as we liked him my caution flags flew. We declined with a lame excuse he politely accepted.

Before heading to Singapore I wanted a one-day detour. Since writing a junior high school paper about volcanoes I had been captivated by the history of Krakatoa. We were close. I was keen to go there; however British Admiralty sailing directions strongly cautioned mariners to "avoid the area of Krakatoa in the Sunda Straits between Java and Sumatra." The ocean floor was considered unreliable, meaning volcanic disturbances could occur at any moment.

I read the caution aloud, following it with a question; "Roo, Denise, Don—what say you guys. Are you up for treading where we should not tread—going where we should not go?"

Agreement was unanimous. We sailed for Merak at the northern tip of Java, my one stop for a last mail check before heading to Krakatoa.

CHAPTER 44

MYSTERIOUS KRAKATOA AFTER A BUS RIDE FROM HELL

Hold the presses. Stop everything! Forget about the dead buried in baskets above ground, pass on the hurricane at Hamilton Island and scrub the frightening overfalls. We have a new winner for terror: an Indonesian public transportation bus ride.

Anchoring by a small island just off shore of Merak on Java's northern tip, Roo and Don stayed with *Endymion* to do clean up chores while Denise and I found the bus station and transport back to Jakarta for one last Post Office visit.

Climbing aboard the bus we were lucky enough, after moving two small crates with live animals, to find seats together halfway back on the right side of the bus. I wish I had taken pills—been stoned or drunk. What followed were two insane hours of nerve tingling, stomach churning, and occasionally breathtaking excitement being catapulted across the Java countryside to Jakarta. There were no rules for that frenzy.

We were jammed aboard a ten ton smoke-belching diesel-eating bus, along with forty-some odd babbling Indonesians, their luggage, chickens, dogs, a small pig and one very freightened goat. Other than we two Puritan Yanks returning to Jakarta for missing mail, nearly every other traveller puffed away on something foul.

Our driver defined the missing link between Neanderthal stupidity and modern space cadet. He put Richard Petty back in a go-cart, blew his horn more than Gabriel and passed more traffic than an airliner. The two hour ride was a game of inches played out at 70 to 100 km/h: an inch behind the vehicle ahead, an inch to spare pulling out to pass or an inch apart passing head on.

"Don't wave," I said, holding Denise close, "Your hand will belong to someone else. James Dean couldn't play chicken like this."

"I'm in the crash position already," muttered Denise.

"I suppose travelers' insurance is out of the question."

Locals took it in stride. Luggage, crates, boxes and duffels banged from side to side as we careened down the "almost" highway.

The pig barfed.

In a flash of bravery I peeked though the cloud of cigarette smoke attempting to see what the driver saw. Hurtling towards us on the two-lane road, closing at close to 180km/h was a giant fuel truck. We missed in an ear-shattering triumph of horn blowing. Near-miss wind parted my hair. I looked at the pig and checked my shorts.

And this entertainment bonanza had a stewardess. Pardon me—steward.

"Must be a prison trusty."

"Yeah, can you imagine anyone *wanting* that job, or *applying* for it?"

Like on airlines the steward passed out free drinks and little cakes as he picked and weaved his way aft. Unlike airlines, the bus offered no cups or glasses. Passengers were expected to drink from the bottle while the bus jolted, praying not to acquire an instant hair-lip. I envisioned a week at the dentist.

When a passenger wanted off, the driver would almost stop. It's different than boarding with your luggage. De-boarding belongings, hopefully yours, are tossed to you after you jump. The most outrageous sight was watching the bus driver roll a smoke while passing a funeral procession on a curve. The horn was his wrong way beacon, probably floor operated because he had a soft drink in the other hand. I hoped he was praying for his passengers. I was.

What did two hours of terror cost? 1,700 rupiah per person or 93 cents each, including a transfer token.

I lost mine.

Finding the post office, we also located the pile of mail awaiting us. We were settled with "Uncle Sam" and had a nice check to boot. We cashed it at the American Express office and treated ourselves to a taxi ride returning to Merak. We found Endymion looking sharp thanks to Roo and Don. They reported Brandy had stood a proper deck watch and had a scoop of ice cream..

Brandy standing deck watch.

Our moods were good casting off for Krakatoa, 40 nm across the Sunda Strait. Nature had other plans, throwing high winds, pesky seas and strong currents at us for the first four hours. With the remains of mighty Krakatoa looming before us the wind died. We motored on at a comfortable five knots, Roo at the helm, Don reclining on a beanbag and Denise deep into her latest Stephen King novel. I was anxious to share my enthusiasm.

"OK you guys, here's a couple of facts I researched. Pre-eruption, Krakatoa was a 2,600 ft mountain island spread over 5.5 by 3.2 miles. Only a third of it remains and we are about to see it."

"And didn't that same research say not to go here," said Denise, lowering Mr. King momentarily to favor my words of wisdom.

"Indeed," said Roo, "the exact Admiralty quote says; Owing to volcanic eruption, the area between Palau (island) Rakata and Palau Sabesi, 10 miles north, must be considered as unsafe and routes outside these islands should be taken."

"So, there ya go. And we're where... right in the middle?" Dense questioned.

'Yup, pretty close, but remember we agreed. I don't believe one of us has ever *known, heard about or read about anyone* who has sailed here.

We motored along the edges into the shadows of Krakatoa. The day became sunny, peaceful and mysteriously quiet. 103 years ago, almost to the day, 36,000 people were blown from the earth during modern history's most powerful volcanic eruption. It created a wave 100 feet high. Smoke and ash rocketed at 80 miles per hour, seven miles into the sky circled the globe for months. Ashes rained on Paris, 7000 miles away. The explosion, it was said, was felt in Australia. A ship off the coast of Java, with 128 aboard was driven a mile inland. All perished.

Roo, at the helm, added, "I read the dust cloud was so big the sun over South America was blue."

"Bull shit," said Don.

They could joke. That was fine. I was humbled. I believe Roo was as well. Soon we were there, right in the center, where loved ones holding hands, children playing ball and pets enjoying a Sunday afternoon died an unimaginably agonizing, hopefully sudden death. Entire small communities vanished in seconds. I felt reverence and profound sadness moving slowly alongside jagged rocky hillsides and sheer cliffs jutting hundreds of feet straight up from the sea. Vines, and flowers grown in the last century clung to the rugged terrain. Our depth indicator could not sound the bottom, indicating it was more than 500 feet deep, yet we were only 100 feet from the silent remains.

Before us Anak (The Son of) Krakatoa was rising. There was no foliage on this barren, bleak, yet intriguing lava island.

'ENDYMION' sailing under the smouldering menace of Anak ('son of') Krakatoa with Pulau Rakata (background) as an awesome reminder of its violent past.

Courtesy of Roo Biram

Anak Krakatoa

Don suggested we anchor, and climb it. Roo agreed. Me too.

Denise said "You *are* nuts." She didn't look up or miss a sentence in her novel.

We managed to sail within a few hundred yards of Anak Krakatoa but the bottom was poor holding. We couldn't anchor but clearly saw lava creeping down the side and steam venting from a fissure—heady stuff it was for me, to be alone, absolutely alone at the very location of the explosion heard around the world. No other people, no boats, only a deep haunting feeling of being in a time warp. Much as we wanted to explore further I couldn't risk climbing partway up the smoldering new volcano to look out and see *Endymion* dragging anchor, drifting away. I had no desire to be Anak Krakatoa's first permanent inhabitant. We sailed on, headed next for the Equator, roughly 400 nm north.

CHAPTER 45

FRIDAY THE 13TH — EQUATOR CROSSING

The sun had yet to punch the clock Friday morning. While others slept serenely I sat alone with my thoughts, behind the wheel, a cuppa Joe in my hand. I enjoyed peaceful crack-of-dawn hours immensely. This was my domain, my castle. Behind the wheel was my favorite position—I loved it. An important day lay ahead.

We would cross the Equator that morning, into the northern hemisphere after eighteen months in southern latitudes. I had mixed emotions. It would be nice to be back in the hemisphere from which we came—but what difference did it really make to sail over a line we couldn't see anyway? Wherever we were, north, south, east or west, cruising life had been remarkable. I made a mental note to write a book about it someday.

Daybreak was still a half-hour distant. I looked toward the nearby unnamed, uninhabited island we were anchored close to. Yesterday we'd been "Robinson Crusoe" exploring for treasure, curious about a hundred-yard section of topless coconut palms, apparent victims of a vicious wind event. We discovered sun-bleached remains of a large dugout canoe and discussed our theories; what had become of the paddlers? Roo, like natives we observed throughout the Pacific, had scampered up fruit-bearing trees to toss coconuts to Brandy, running in endless circles below him, tail constantly wagging. This was "drifting and blending" at its best. No pressure. Sure, we've had stress—in storms, during the Fiji Coup (*Leg One- Chapter 40*) or after losing our non-sacrificial inflatable to thieves. But problems had been short lived compared to the continued stress of business while living in congested, smog-laden cities.

Sipping my Joe I had a talk with God, Who mostly listened while I gave thanks. Then I read some poetry in the light of a lantern, one of my favorites: *"The Man From Snowy River."* I reflected on another time at another island with crews from *Vintage Port* and *Quahlee of Sydney* when one cool evening we sat before a roaring fire taking turns reciting favorite passages. I had chosen two; Canadian Robert Service's *The Cremation of Sam McGee* as my first choice. *Vagabond House* by American Don Blanding as my second. A poet and military man, Blanding served in both US and Canadian military. Following the fall of Bataan in 1942 he reenlisted in the US Army as a private, at age forty-seven. I believe Don Blanding's writing capable of inspiring any person with a twinge of wanderlust.

I snapped back to reality when Denise appeared in the companionway, looking radiant with the first rays of sun highlighting her long blonde-streaked hair.

"Good morning, Beautiful."

"Thanks, my captain. I had a great sleep. Hey, today's the day isn't it," said as a statement. " I become a shellback for crossing the big E."

"That you do, and Roo as well."

I turned off the lantern and joined Denise at the head of the companionway. We hugged and looked toward the sun rising over the deserted island.

"Kinda red," said Denise "means bad luck, doesn't it?"

"It does, though many believe it's only mariners folk lore. Red sky at night, sailors' delight. Red sky in morning, sailors take warning. Actually dear lady, it goes back to biblical times. Jesus said 'When in evening ye say, it will be fair weather for the sky is red. And in morning it will be foul weather today; for the sky is red and lowering.' That's the derivation of the common quotation."

"Ha, good one! Trying to trick me again, Skip?"

"Nope, look it up. Book of Matthew. Actually Jesus was right. Fact is moisture in the atmosphere and impurities raised by wind contribute to the brilliant red hues of sunset. Impurities usually settle by morning. Red sky in morning signifies impurities in the air caused by wind, potentially heavy wind creating lumpy seas, thus the expression "sailors take warning."

"Humph, looks calm to me. Want some breakfast. I'm doing something original, à la Denise—flapjacks with coconut."

"Count me in."

"Me too. And by the way, Captain's right. We could be in for some breeze." Don, climbing through the forward hatch, had entered the conversation.

Roo, Don and Denise had breakfast at the salon table. I ate at the nav station to study our route north to Singapore. There were many islands and areas of shallow water I feared might not be well marked. Coconut flapjacks proved too sweet for me but I held my tongue. After another cuppa we stowed loose items, gave Brandy an "evacuation run" ashore and prepared to get underway. The sky was reddish brown.

"Don't like this much." I said to Roo as he set the jib.

"Wanna turn back and re-anchor?"

"Sturdy vessel, Roo. We'll be OK." I said, convincing myself.

"Too damn hot for me!" Declared Denise, a trickle of sweat running down her tanned forehead. "Let's go north. I like it where Christmas is in the winter."

"And I," said Roo, "am pleased to step into the Northern Hemisphere—where my friends at home have not been."

Don had crossed three times and was nonchalant. He and I planned to welcome King Neptune and his able assistant Davy Jones aboard for a crossing ceremony. King Neptune will confirm Denise, Roo and Brandy have shed their lowly pollywog status to become shellbacks, the definition for centuries of elite seafarers who have crossed the Equator.

At 0800, after a short first watch, Roo went below to log our position, weather info and comments.

"Hey guys," he shouted from below. "Do you know what day this is?"

"Friday!"

"Yeah! October 13th. Friday the 13th."

"Red sky, sailors take warning, Friday the 13th. I can dig it." I said with authority. "Sail her over or sail her under. That's another weather expression. No worries mates!"

We were in the South China Sea hugging jungle along the east coast of Sumatra. I wasn't worried. Winds were light. There wasn't much fetch between charted islands and visibility was good, plus we had our trusty Furuno radar.

Next at the helm, Don called below to Roo, "Got a position fix? What's the ETA to Equator?"

Roo responded, "Eighteen nautical. Allowing for current we should cross, in my opinion, at 1146."

This was good. Assuming Roo's time, speed, current and distance calculations were correct Don would be off watch to take part in the crossing celebration. On we went under power, though our fuel was nearly spent. I figured the nearest refueling opportunity was 60 nm distant. It would be close. Clouds began filling the horizon that only an hour ago was so red. Wind had taken a holiday. There wasn't any, not even a whisper.

Having risen before dawn I ducked below for a catnap, dozing off straight away.

Commotion awoke me. I bounded topsides. Threatening black clouds hung ominously all around us. A mean monster cloud at 10 degrees starboard was birthing a waterspout. We watched it thread its way to the sea. It looked to be ten miles or more away.

"Whatcha thinkin Captain?" Roo asked.

"I'm thinking I know bloody little about sea twisters Roo, except they are dangerous, don't last long and we should stay the hell away."

I went below again. Shortly there was more commotion. I returned topsides. Directly in our path was a dangerous fully formed waterspout. Radar had it 3.2 nm distant.

In the moment I stood watching, lightning and thunder, blazing and intense, closed in from two opposing storm cells, one to either side of us. Using compass, I determined the spout close to connecting with the ocean was moving toward us, while the storm cells appeared stationary.

Endymion and I had confronted odd situations before. The sea alongside was spooky calm, yet we were surrounded by immediate threats.

I eased into my two foot zone, where confidence reigns and decisions are effortless. All I had to do was pick our way through a couple of storm cells and avoid the twister. Piece of cake. A minute later the spout connected to the ocean creating a giant ring of surface spray. Giving the Perkins full power I altered course to avoid it. Confidence—no problem. Then it dissipated, right in front of me, leaving a thousand foot tower of water to cascade back into the sea. The spout, an incredible display of nature to witness, had lasted nearly fifteen minutes.

I heaved a sigh of relief and thanked our creator for another save. Denise took the helm. As she told us how uncomfortable she was with the situation, the same cloud produced another spout charging toward the ocean surface. Its disjointed partner reached up from the ocean to join it, creating a spellbinding black curtain of swirling water.

Normally reserved Don: "This is freaking unreal!"

Though we were only two nm from the Equator Denise had to divert course, taking us away from the spout and "the big E," at the same time dodging thunderheads and frequent lightning. Denise, resolutely calm asked only one favor. "Fetch my rain hat, will ya?"

Good on ya, Honey, I thought to myself, *you didn't ask to be relieved.* In the South China Sea this young nurse from Pasadena was half a world from home, in freaky weather at the helm of a yacht about to cross the Equator.

But not yet.

We were aware weather was changing rapidly. Roo was below counting down distance to the Equator. Denise had been with me in electrical storms. She knew the dangers but I reminded her, "keep your hands off the wheel when you can. Only nudge it or tap it to stay on course." Then all hell broke loose.

A huge black cloud above us split in half, belching lightning, heaving thunder in ear piercing volume and dousing us with sheets of stinging rain—conditions sailors seriously want to avoid.

I looked to Denise, asking if she wanted to be spelled. No way. The moment was hers to conquer.

From below Roo shouted out distance. "Point oh three miles to crossing."

More rain. Huge pelting drops—gallons and gallons. We could not see beyond the bow, except in unnerving lightning flashes every few seconds. Scary conditions; a lightning strike at sea could be catastrophic. *Endymion* had exceptional grounding but could possibly lose everything electrical, all of it from our primitive sat nav to compass light.

In the storm's darkness Roo read latitude: "000.000.04 south. 000.00.02 south … point 01 south—we're *OVER!* Mates, we're in the northern hemisphere!"

A pleasing smile crossed Denise's face as she looked from below her yellow rain hat. "Here, take the wheel! We're over and I'm finished!" She looked directly at me.

I took the wheel thinking what a crappy crossing we had. "We will have our celebration, but after the storm."

Simultaneous with my declaration Roo, still at the nav station shouted out, "here we go again, we're going over the damned Equator again."

For a second I was puzzled. Then it dawned on me: lightning had caused enough static electricity to confuse the sat nav to give us false position readings. The storm was subsiding. The sat nav wanted us to know we hadn't crossed. We had another quarter mile to go.

We put Denise back on the helm. Unanimous decision. At 000.00.00 we let out a contagious *whoop,* said congratulations all around, broke open a bottle of champagne, shut down the Perkins and drifted. We had our ceremony, presenting Denise and Roo the following certificate:

On_*13 October 1988* (date), at *1906* hours Zulu time, *Denise Marie Rowland* US Passport # xxx-xx-xxxx did cross the earth's Equator aboard the Documented US Flag sailing vessel *ENDYMION*.

By accomplishing this in desolate waters, and having been duly introduced to the Northern Hemisphere by King Neptune himself, *Denise M. Rowland* is now elevated to the lofty position of "Shellback" and is joined through eternity to the fraternity of Mariners who have challenged God's restless, peaceful sea.

Sworn by my hand *Captain Skip Rowland* (signed) *13 October 1989* (dated)

Captain, US Yacht *Endymion* USCG License # *248631*.

Roo received the same honors.

CHAPTER 46

NOT SO SECRET NAVY BASE

Skies softened and a light breeze favored us in the lower northern latitudes. Timing couldn't have been better. Our fuel gauge registered empty though the Perkins hadn't coughed or sputtered—yet. My concern, looking at charts, was our approach to Singapore. While sail trumps power in the rulebook we have seen ample "don't give a shit" potentially causing trouble. Singapore was one of the world's busiest crossroads for maritime traffic. "Not to worry" Roo cheered us, "we'll stay alert."

Close to mid-day our wind died. *Endymion's* jib hung limp in scorching afternoon heat. The main flapped in windless air causing deck block and lines to pop and snap as they jerked up and down, pounding the deck. Comfort played hooky. Only current kept us from doing doughnuts. If we got sideways we went backwards faster. I ordered the main lowered and sun awning raised to protect us from the blistering sun.

Now we either motored or found a spot to anchor until we had wind, possibly days later. We fired up the Perkins keeping rpms at 1000—just above idle speed. It gave us steerage in a desolate area with reefs, wrecks, sunken rocks and floating hazards we wanted to avoid.

Don had chef duty. He produced a meatloaf with mystery ingredients poking though the burned ketchup topping. Serving it to a tired crew on deck he said only, "Pay no attention, it won't kill ya." It didn't. He never said what was in it.

During mealtime Roo and I worked charts and depth sounder. We were in the midst of small islands, some uncharted. Our depth indicator was set to sound an alarm at ten fathoms (sixty feet). So far, no problems.

With binoculars I scoured the horizon, slowly moving the glasses across each island. Whoa big fella! What's *that?*

I focused on a tiny lagoon tucked so tightly into a miniscule island that it would be easy to miss completely. I judged the distance at five miles and as something Gilligan would be proud of. First I thought I saw, and soon was certain I saw a tiny compound on stilts with a couple of buildings atop—and a large boat, looking to be swift, tied alongside. Patrol boat?

"I don't believe this! Look there," I pointed. "Come hard-a-port Roo. Let's see if these guys have any fuel."

Approaching, I saw people through the glasses. They weren't very animated, just seemed to be sitting or standing around, paying no attention to us. Then I noticed red flags in the water on either side of the compound. Were they a warning? Coming closer I put the glasses aside. Clearly the boat I had seen was now two boats, one behind the other. The closer boat had dive tanks and gear on deck. The second larger vessel was an Indonesian Navy patrol speedster. Why, I asked myself, was an island with a naval presence not charted? *Oh shit*—had it been intentional?

"Here we go again," said Denise, recalling the military boarding incident in Fiji (*Leg One- Chapter 40*). "We don't need more trouble. Skip, this means you."

At this point there was no turning back. A skiff with armed men aboard signaled me to pull alongside the dive boat. Even before our lines were secure, a navy officer jumped aboard *Endymion* demanding I produce our papers. He was unfriendly. So was Denise. She scolded the massive armed man, "Take your boots off on our boat, and be respectful—please."

I gathered our papers before a scene erupted between normally sensible Denise and the navy gorilla, the length of whose fuse we didn't know. He wanted papers *now* and Denise wanted him off *Endymion*—*now*!

Short of losing my spirited wife, we managed a tense peace. I explained our fuel shortage and urgent need for diesel.

"Surely you have some. We have rupiah."

"Tidok solar. Tidok solar." (no fuel.)

By this time other military had jumped aboard with weapons and boots. Roo held Denise in check.

I offered our papers.

"No camera," one of them ordered in good English, followed by, "you," pointing at me, " you come with me."

At least he wasn't yelling. Our world was calmer. I didn't know where we were going but thought fuel might be possible—a hope quickly dashed when two soldiers fell in close behind me, rifles pointed at my back. Strange how things get in your mind at times like this.

I dropped into my two-foot zone, taking in surroundings I might need, recalling my USMC training to escape early if a prisoner. But I wasn't one—or was I?

Being escorted toward the more prominent building I worried about Denise, Roo and Don. Would they be safe? Would anyone hurt or take advantage of Denise? I stayed in my zone, remaining calm. Shortly I stood at attention before the Commanding Officer while he examined our papers. Eventually, slowly lifting his head the CO looked across his orderly desk and addressed me in fluent English.

"Relax, Mr. Rowland. Stand down if you please. Your papers are in order. May I ask, sir, why an experienced captain is without sufficient fuel?"

"A judgment error on my part, sir, I'm reluctant to admit." I said figuring humility the best course. "We fueled in Ambon but required our engine more than expected en route. I took on fuel in Lombok. It wasn't quality diesel. We use what's called a "Baja filter" (homemade filter) when fuel is suspect. Even that filter clogged so we took on only a small amount. Now we are nearly dry."

"You are in good fortune Captain Rowland. I will gift you a fifty gallon drum, courtesy of the Government of Indonesia."

"Thank you sir, thank you kindly and very much."

"Now, one other thing. No, two additional subjects. I must have your word there will be no photographs. I'll repeat. It is not advisable for you or your crew to use cameras while guests at my base."

"Agreed, sir. You have my word."

(Author's note to readers: remember the Ambon race chapter and a man who would play an important part in our futures? Here it comes.)

"To my second point. I see on your cruising permit the name Dop Barr. Are you acquainted with this man?"

"Yes sir. I am. Dop was a race official representing Indonesia in the Darwin to Ambon race—a real gentleman. My wife and I came to know him well, even having dinner at his home and speaking to his Electrolux sales team."

"Your unusual luck continues. Captain, may I call you Skip?"

"Of course."

"There are over 175 million people in Indonesia. We are spread among many cities and remote islands, as you know. To meet two who know each other is rare. Dop Barr was my university roommate. Now, meeting you completes a circle. May I invite you and your crew to tea?"

I was blown away. The red sky morning had become a four-leaf clover.

Returning to the wharf unguarded I was surprised to see *Endymion* casting off and the dive boat moving from its position between *Endymion* and the wharf. Denise was handling lines, Don was on the bow and Roo at the wheel. Before I could yell out, a soldier explained they needed to get the dive boat free. He spoke politely. Apparently the word that we were "friendlies" had reached the pier. Neither Denise nor Roo had experience docking in shallow water. But dock it they did without incident.

We enjoyed our evening with the Commander. He gave us T-shirts from the Indonesian Dive Service, a cover we suspected for an underwater demolition service—otherwise why all the secrecy about the base? We also suspected, because the Commander with a nip under his belt, let it slip he would be attending a US Navy UDT (Underwater Demolition Team) school in San Diego.

He ordered fuel delivered to *Endymion* and was comforting: "Unsettled weather. Stay as long as you wish."

So we spent the night and half the next day at Indonesia's "secret" navy base. Want a picture? Sorry, none available.

CHAPTER 47

SINGAPORE: CITY OF CONTRAST

They must have been frogmen who cast off our lines after breakfast. They were dressed as such and never said a word—nor had anyone else from Base Commander to the teen-aged guard with a rifle and spit-shine polished boots. Nor did we ever learn a name for the base that hosted us. With just a day's sail to Singapore, we left with fifty gallons of clean diesel fuel.

"Hey Skip, problem here." Roo warned, "the freezer is pulling the batteries down again, faster than we can keep up with them."

"Aww double crapola!" Denise contributed, "that means no ice and or cold drinks until Singapore, whenever that may be."

She knew it was only a day ahead but the heat, the constant sweltering equatorial temps with humidity close to 100% was getting to all of us.

"Tell ya what honey, if it comes to choosing between no roaches or no ice, I will opt every time for adios to bugs over having cold beverages."

"Dope."

We argued the point heading north in heavy rain between Pulau (island) Batam and Pulau Bintan, in plenty of deep water and steadily increasing traffic.

"Where all these boats are going?" Don asked anyone who might be listening.

"Somewhere, can't remember exactly, I read that a huge new vacation city for Singaporeans is somewhere around here." said Roo.

If there was, it was closeted by jungle but seemed possible as much of the traffic was high speed people carriers. Nearing the northern point of Pulau Batam rain became so astonishingly dense we slowed to three knots, depending heavily on the radar.

"Seven nautical to Singapore Island," Roo called out.

"Seems like eternity!" Denise wanted a bath in a real tub.

Moments later, like a theatre screen rising to reveal a scene, the clouds lifted, sun came out and we burst into a near forgotten world. Before us lay a massive city with skyscrapers filling the horizon—Singapore! Container cargo ships, more than we could count, lay at anchor. Tugs with tows plied the waters and above, just a mile ahead, right in our path, a jumbo JAL 747 was descending for landing at Singapore's nearby Changi International Airport.

The old is forever new. In moments we had left the uncomplicated, primitive jungle environs with bubbly happy native people to arrive in the hectic pace of teeming masses in Singapore, known as "the crossroads of the world." Four souls aboard *Endymion* were awed and excited for arrival. Welcome culture shock—and another milestone.

Changi Sailing Club's launch guided us to a mooring skillfully picked up by Roo while Denise hoisted the Singapore guest flag, and the required "Q" flag until cleared by authorities. Afternoon showers rolled in. We sat beneath the rain canopy, more soaked by perspiration than God's free wash, taking stock of our surroundings.

To one side we had a beach littered with bleached white driftwood, testimony to the harshness of the sun. In the sky above towering cumulonimbus thunderheads provided telltale evidence of suffocating tropical humidity we will share when they burst.

Toward the other shore and closer to us were three buildings, two with sparkling white walls. One was the Changi Sailing Club (our hosts) and the other a sports complex. Just visible on a rise beyond them we could see through thick jungle the forbidding guard tower of the Changi Prison. Many of World War Two's most barbaric atrocities against Yanks and Aussies occurred in that heartless place. We would later visit the prison museum and memorial where five minutes inside did more to make us appreciate our freedom than two decades of Memorial Day political promises.

Separated from Malaysia in that anchorage by only a thin ribbon of a channel, we were at the northwest corner of Singapore Island, a scant 72 nm above the Equator. Things were different than when the Japanese were here. The prison still housed social offenders but Singapore emerged from its vague and shady past into a bustling trade center. The city-state housed 2.7 million mixed-culture souls sharing a cramped 277 square miles of land, much of it reclaimed from the sea.

All of that said, we still could not reach the clubhouse, with showers, a bar and restaurant until we cleared with officials. Many were at the airport, really close by, yet for us it would take another day as those who clear vessels were across the island in a snafu of officialdom geared to clear a variety of sea traffic from around the world. Denise and I would handle that mission while Don and Roo cleaned up *Endymion*.

For the afternoon and evening we languished in the aforementioned heat, pelted by occasional showers. Thunder made Brandy scramble for her storm quarters, a hiding spot behind the forward toilet. We took turns stroking and comforting our shaking puppy.

"I feel *sooo* bad for Brandy." Don said while giving her a taste of her favorite, the last of or vanilla ice cream.

"I feel so bad for *me*," Denise shot back, "that's gotta be a pig farm across the channel in Malaysia. Between that stink and the heat I'm gonna puke."

"We've got electrical clips in the toolbox. How 'bout I put one on your nose." My joke. Only I laughed.

Early the next morning the club's "bum boat" (launch) took us ashore. Recalling promises from Ivan, the mechanic from Jakarta, Denise phoned his brother and sister-in-law in the Bidok area of Singapore. We had no idea where it was. John and Iris expected our call. They took us to clear Customs, inviting us to their apartment afterwards.

"We'd be delighted," said Denise.

The couple, to our surprise, had only been married a week, yet insisted we stay at their tiny flat overnight.

"John will drive you tomorrow to get engine parts," Iris said as we pulled into their parking spot. They genuinely wanted to help us. I guessed we were an oddity, the only non-Singaporeans in their lives.

Walking to their building, one of many surrounding a confined central park, we learned there were nine districts in Singapore, divided into sub electoral areas, each with its own council. There are numerous cultural differences making up the city.

"The government controls everything, including where a citizen may purchase an apartment," John told me.

"You're kidding!"

"No. The reason is to keep a balance. Not to have friction. If all Hindus lived in one section and all Muslims in another we would collide. It wouldn't work. I'll make it simple for you. In our building an apartment goes up for sale. Our governor tells us there is a place for a Christian or a Buddhist family but not Hindu because there are many Hindus here already."

"Doesn't sound so simple to me, but what the heck if it works. What about price?"

"You can get what you can—and the government will finance it!"

We found John was right. Harmony, with little crime, existed in Singapore among many cultures. Hat I couldn't understand was why the seventh floor fire alarm was a large old fashioned Chinese gong. And apartment toilets were "squatters" with no seats. Ancient cultures die hard, as Denise explained in a letter home.

Apartments here are pretty basic, all high-rises. The city is immaculate and organized. The government controls everything! Littering will cost you $200, parking tickets run $50-$200 and it's a $150.00 fine not to flush a public toilet. Imagine that in LA? Is Big Brother watching? And, the toilets—you squat over them. Unlike Indonesia at least we don't have to lug toilet paper around with us.

We found the parts for our refrigeration and people to install them. Roo and Don supervised and cared for Brandy while John, Iris, Denise and I attended dinner and an amazing auction at their Buddhist temple. Over 150 people gathered at tables in the street in front of the temple for a seven-course dinner, tasty and expertly served. An auction of donated items fired up after dinner.

"You'll like this," Iris explained, "As Buddhists we believe the high bidders for items will have good luck, and be blessed with prosperity in their business."

"Meaning bids are tax deductible?" Denise asked, receiving a chuckle. I suggested it meant over bidding.

A bowl of fruit, the first item up, went for $1500.00 ($1,215 US) Two hours later the last item, a grotesque Buddha statue, was offered as the grand finale. Bidding started at $5,000.

"Watch this," Iris said. "It's auctioned every three years. Last time it went for $20,000. And," Iris continued, "The winner will have good luck for three years plus a highly successful business with huge profits."

It went for $10,000 ($8,100 US) prompting my business mind to suggest, "Must be changing market conditions, or the poor soul who paid $20,000 had no luck, or profits. By the way Iris, does the former bidder recover any of his expense?"

"Temple gets all. Good for Buddha."

Quahlee of Sydney sailed in a few days later. Also moored near us were Liza and Andy Copeland and their sons, aboard *Bagheera*. Soon enough *Kinta III* and *Vintage Port* arrived. Club management loved it. Visitors kept the bar in business and provided good entertainment for the locals.

Returning to *Endymion,* Denise summed up the sultry oppressive midnight heat, observing, "It's a riot—trying to sleep together, unsticking each other all night. Damn, it's hot Skip. The air doesn't move."

"Agreed, but for my money foreplay and love are worth the effort. Let's stay in the cockpit. It's late. No one will see us."

We slept soundly in the afterglow.

One muggy afternoon we sat with cruising folks at the club bar, reading British Admiralty Sailing Directions, drinking beer and noshing pretzels with peanut butter centers while planning our future routes. I caught a glimpse of a man in a dark suit and thought *that's unusual*—surely not routine attire for the heat and humidity.

"Hey guys, check out the suit." Everyone turned, but instead of one suit there were now five.

"Looks like trouble."

"They look like bodyguards."

Our position on the second level lounge deck looked over the anchorage and lawn below where a ruggedly handsome American and his all-female crew were washing and bagging a pair of spinnakers. We met them briefly at Hamilton Island Race Week in Australia. Howie Jackson owned an alluring 45 footer made of kauri wood, said to be the world's oldest workable wood, found exclusively in New Zealand. For a decade, because of its enormous value, this 50,000 year old knot-free wood had been a clandestine mechanism to get money out of New Zealand—build a yacht of kauri wood for example, sail it to Europe or America, sell it and eureka—tax free profit.

Howie Jackson boasted he had done that, but one part of his story had me scratching my head. He claimed to be from a prominent Newport Beach, CA, family and named several yachts the family had owned. Southern California had been my playground for years. I had never heard the family name, of their association with boating or *any* of the yachts he'd referenced. During Hamilton Island Race week Howie had been reclusive, seldom seen at social events though he sailed with an all-female crew, every one of them stunning and active socially.

The suits were walking straight toward him.

"Watch out, Howie." *Qhahlee of Sydney's* John Bentley warned in a tone heard only by us.

"Oh - my - God!"

The suits circled Howie. They were closing in. Obviously the prey, Howie hadn't yet realized it. I took a sip from my beer. When I looked up, the suits had Howie on the ground. Three remaining suits were backsides to Howie, looking outward for trouble. His lovelies screamed, acting frantic. The outward guard turned inward. Words we couldn't hear were spoken. The group, with the alleged former Newport Beach society guy in the center moved slowly under our patio position and past us. Howie was cuffed. The lovelies had reason to sulk. Their ride was over.

Roo popped from his seat like a jack-in-the-box to follow, returning to tell us, "They drove away in two black Fords with small antennas on the trunk. Gotta be the fuzz. Wonder what he did? Jerk."

"And where will his girls go now?" inquired Paul from *Kinta III*.

"No you don't Skip. They are *not* coming with us," Denise declared.

The Singapore Straits Times provided a partial answer, reporting the next day that an American, Howard Jackson from Chicago, was being held for drug smuggling.

"What the hell!" I said to all listening. "Never woulda guessed it."

"I wouldn't want to be in jail in this town."

"Or anyplace." added Denise, saying "Skip has us insured against that."

"Yeah, what's up with that captain? Me included?" asked Roo.

"None of you. It's not people insurance. It's poor man's insurance for the vessel—a bank loan against the boat, offset by funds in the bank. If we get in trouble and a foreign government seizes the boat, Wells Fargo will come after the boat and I will likely be released as part of the deal because they want the loan repaid. It's flimsy but my banker in California said it worked for one her clients held in a South American slammer."

"And you leave us stranded?" Roo was half serious, as I was with my answer. "Call your parents!"

Word eventually leaked. US DEA agents had chased Howie several years for trafficking drugs into the states by boat—large shipments originating in Thailand, to fund his lavish lifestyle. Howie was going for a double score this time—Kauri wood and drugs. In Singapore certain types of eavesdropping are legal. Agents aboard a boat halfway across the mooring area listened with devices tuned to Howie's yacht. They heard every word of conversations related to an upcoming shipment, then they nailed him.

Aside from that excitement, life in Singapore was fun. We window shopped for Rolex watches and high end clothing on Orchard Street, purchased counterfeit music for our sound system and ate copious amounts of creamy rich ice cream.

We took a cable car to Fort Siloso on Sentosa Island and sat beneath the only remaining gun battery from World War Two. With eyes closed I tried to feel the lives of men who once sat exactly where I was—likely scared to death. *What was it like to have been a worker carving the fort from solid rock in the 1870s, or to have been British Army watching the Japanese invade from the west when the fort's guns were turned East—the cutlass empire invaders coming at you with overwhelming force. Did they know death was imminent?* I could not get there in my mind so I took personal time to pray in the chapel amidst the remains of the Changi prison where so many Australians, Brits and a few Yanks had suffered and perished. I've always considered it shameful how few care about the sacrifices so many gave to make us free.

At an outside cafe on Orchard Street Denise, Brandy and I, with ice cream, discussed the country.

"Singaporeans have their priorities right."

Denise nodded and added, "They will be leaders the next century."

"Watch out America!"

"Meaning what?"

"Meaning there is a huge difference between western hemisphere kids and the ones we see here. The car they drive or what country club parents belong to judges American kids. Kids here are judged by their drive, education and ambition. America will lose jobs and leadership positions to Asians. It'll happen in the next twenty years. Wanna bet?"

"No. Probably right."

On the lighter side, we threw a Halloween party aboard *Endymion*. Denise dressed Brandy as a pumpkin. We hung ghosts made of sheets in the rigging. *Bagheera's* crew came by inflatable and Roo faked a climb from the swim ladder dressed as a pirate, scaring Brandy to shivers.

The time came to part ways. *Endymion* would sail north through the Malacca Strait to the edge of a small fresh water lake near Langkawi, Malaysia. *Quahlee of Sydney* following a day later would hook up with us for Thanksgiving dinner. The others were splitting tacks, going elsewhere.

"Here's an idea!" Roo suggested, "How about a BBQ breakfast in a park before departure? I'm cooking a corker, Aussie style."

Roo promised eggs on the barbie and lived up to his word. Over a piece of thick homemade bread Roo laid ham topped with an egg poached over a charcoal fire. Roo claimed it a "Ham-burger"— emphasis on ham. Brandy, by then nicknamed "Hoover" for her ability to suck up scraps, had a taste of ice cream and her last run ashore chasing ducks and birds in early morning heat.

I settled our bill at the Changi Sailing Club, we all lingered taking a long shower and boarded *Endymion*—It was good to be at sea again.

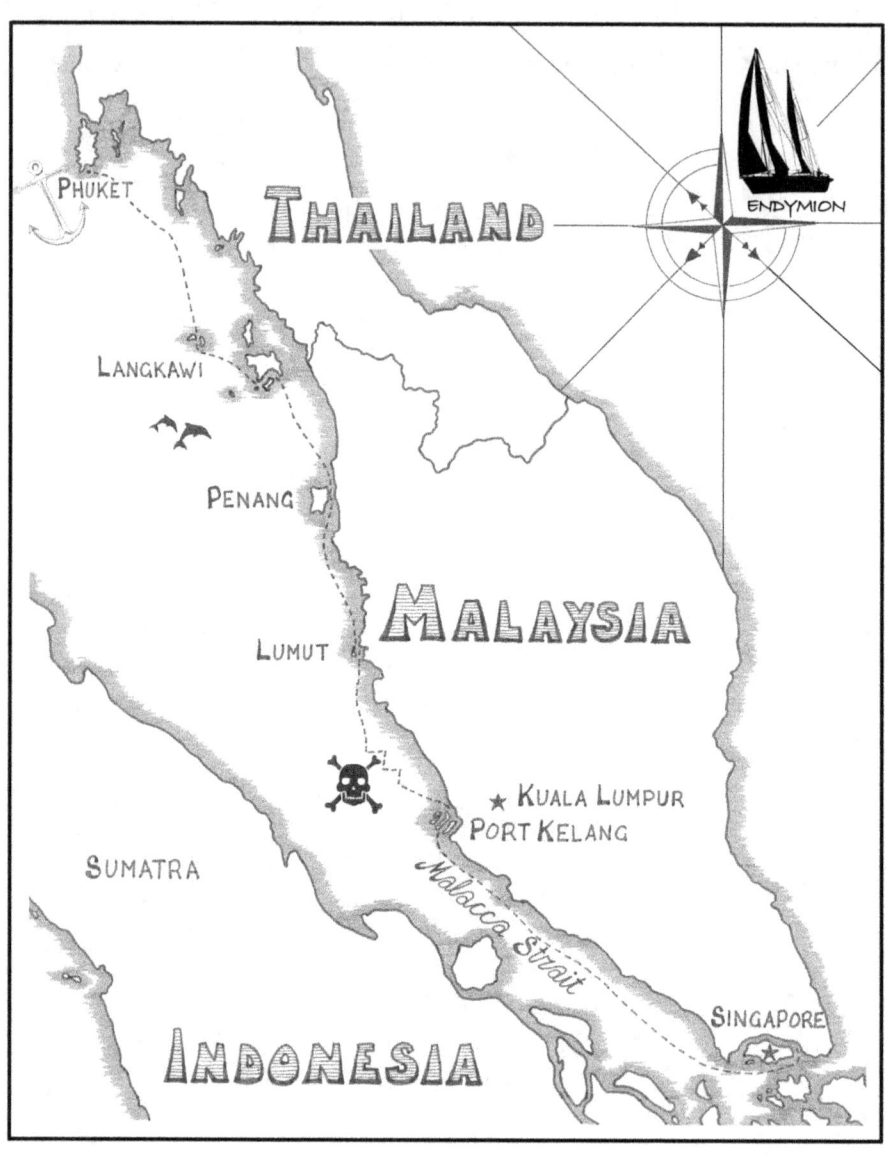

CHAPTER 48

NORTHBOUND IN THE MALACCA STRAIT

The Malacca Strait is a long ribbon of water separating the southern end of Thailand in the Andaman Sea to the north, from the island of Sumatra to the south. Before entering the Strait we had to transit around Singapore Island. We took the narrow waterway route between downtown Singapore and Sentosa Island motoring close to massive freighters in shipyard dry docks. There must have been twenty rust-buckets awaiting the mulch machine's hungry jaws. So much commerce every way we turned. Big, small, old, new, rusted or shining, we saw vessels from every corner of the world. I was surprised how many were from the USSR.

After rounding Kukup Point and firmly into the 580-mile-long Malacca Strait, I handed the helm to Don.

"Here ya go big fella. This is the last leg of your strung out bachelor party. Enjoy it. Any man of seventy who has sailed all of his life, is as young at heart as you are, and is going home to marry his Spanish teacher deserves a heap of helm time."

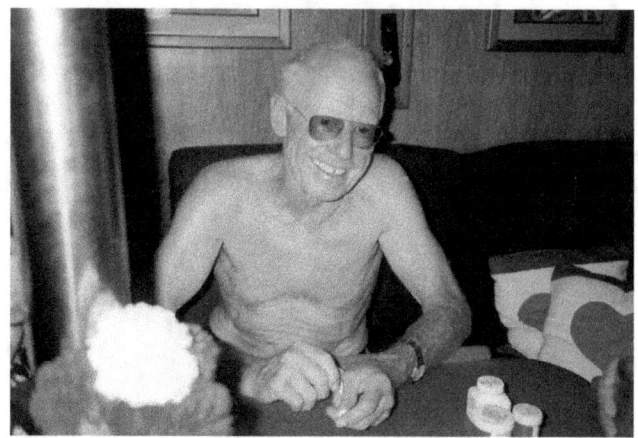

Don McMillian thinking about his Spanish teacher.

"Hope she's pretty. Otherwise you're a dummy." Roo was teasing.

Don moved to his place behind the wheel. For small sailing yachts the Strait is a challenge. Leaving Singapore it was narrow enough for us to see the forbidding jungles of Sumatra's Karimun Besar Island to the west and towering high rises of Singapore eastward.

"Check it out guys. We'll never see a sight like this again."

"You mean the view, or Don at the wheel?"

They were kidding, but for me it was another high point. I had a great crew. Don was experienced and easy going. I've touched before on Denise's beauty; now my wife and the only female aboard, I was immensely proud of her. Not only like a son to Denise and me, Roo had become a treasured friend and our resident strong man. I as skipper, was fifty-one with thousands of blue water miles under my keel. Rounding out our motley association was a real slacker—Brandy, our year old puppy, simply along for the ride.

I had personal concerns though, as Don swung *Endymion* to a heading of due north. From the days of spice trader's centuries ago to modern oil transports, the strait has been a waterway rife with piracy.

Where swords and daggers were once the weapons of choice, modern thieves use powerful speedboats loaded with high-tech electronics, or inconspicuous fishing boats with swarthy, armed, often desperate crew to do their dirty work. We know them as modern pirates.

Being the shortest sea route between three of the world's most populous countries (India, China and Indonesia), the Malacca Strait is a choke point of opportunity. Filled with reefs, tiny islands and jammed by nine hundred commercial vessels a day, for decades it has been a perfect hunting ground for imperfect people.

Smaller, slower sailing yachts are vulnerable. That was us.

Back at the Changi Sailing Club, studying the British Admiralty sailing directions we learned more about piracy in the strait. While downing world-class Bloody Marys had been fun, we talked about strategy, more in jest than seriously—but now the prospect was clearly real. I looked again at Denise and thought, *You are so loved. There is no way you will ever be a pirate's prize.*

I knew the dangers and that we must all be alert, especially on watch. Sailing into unknowns sharpens our senses. Speaking casually, we verbally rehearsed what we would do and shaped a loose plan. If attacked, first order was to get Denise below deck, out of sight. I would handle the radio. Don would take the helm, and Roo would wave fish bats from as many hatches as possible making it appear there were more of us than four. Our lighthearted moods contributed to our false confidence.

"What about that flare gun, Skip. Doesn't sound like much help," Roo inquired.

"Well, first off it's our only weapon other than your fish bats, a boat hook and maybe winch handles. The purpose ... "

"Now there's a confidence builder," interrupted Don, reaching for a sandwich Denise had set on the cockpit table, "first we read there really *are* pirates, then we make a plan while getting bombed on Bloody Marys and *now* you tell us we can't defend ourselves."

"What's with that?" asked Denise, taking a seat beside Roo.

"What's with that," I said, getting a little agitated, "is a decision I made long ago *not* to carry weapons. First—we would probably be out gunned anyway—second our weapons could be turned against us and third it's illegal. If we, meaning I, get caught the guns would be confiscated and I'd be tossed into some third world prison."

"Like Changi?"

"Funny, Denise. At least we can fire one 12 gauge shot. At close range it's powerfully destructive."

"If it works," added Roo.

"Yeah, that's always a question. Maybe it'll blow up or burn off your fingers. Least we have it. I keep the insert hidden in a toolbox. I'll go fetch it."

I dug out the pieces and gave a non-firing demo. We all agreed our one flare gun would be no match for aggressors. Were anything to happen we needed to be smart, confuse the enemy, use the radio, stay calm—using the flare gun only as last resort.

Traversing the straits we made port for the night wherever reasonable and safe. *Endymion* was capable of ten knots in the best of conditions. Malacca Strait's current could run four knots. Easy math.

We didn't berth our first two nights but they went well. Weather was pleasant, temperatures either down a welcome few degrees, or sea breezes made us falsely believe we were comfortable. There was massive ship traffic both day and night. It helped to sharpen our navigating skills. We made it a point, especially after dark, to stay clear of the primary shipping lanes. With rising confidence we put into Port Kelang, the harbor for Kuala Lumpur, tying fast at the Royal Selangor Yacht Club. We found Malaysian people we thought to be shy and elusive, were gregarious and among the friendliest we had met anywhere.

We raced in the Malaysian Offshore Series, a good party but not serious racing. We came in First Overall ... if you count backwards. Truth is, *Kinta III* waxed us.

As tourists we took a train to Kuala Lumpur for a city tour by bus, feasted on spicy dishes in an astonishingly clean open market and visited an earth tiger tarantula farm.

"Come on Skip. *Please.* I really want to see 'em, they're so fuzzy."

These ghastly, creepy looking critters, close to the size of a hand are considered a prize by serious collectors, and there apparently are some though Denise did not become one.

Heading north again in the Straits we were inexcusably too relaxed. Our worries about pirates were at low ebb, so to speak. Our tummies were full, food lockers jammed and our tanks brimming with sweet delicious fresh water. My concern was our fluxgate compass and binnacle compass were fifteen degrees apart, one pointing north and the other north-northeast. They self adjusted—luck of the coin under the mast, the kitten in the park or tiger tarantula's charm—who knows? It all helped us slip out of worry mode and enjoy comfortable sailing.

CHAPTER 49

PIRATES

By dusk the wind freshened. We clipped along at seven knots in moderately choppy seas, the confused kind that prevails where traffic is heavy and water is shallow.

At 1930 Roo, on the wheel, sniffed the first of Denise's perfume drifting into the cockpit, signaling her watch and a rest period for mighty man. Preparing to take the helm an exceptionally cheerful Denise brought a lengthy music play list. She tuned in Alabama and James Taylor to while away her shortened one hour watch, thinking, *I'll just pass my time and go back to bed.*

"Wow Denise, you're a cutie this noight" Roo said with authentic Australian twang. "She be a bit pitchy roight now and the winds hankerin to puff up. Best get your harness on there missy, before litin up the tunes."

"Thanks Roo, help me with this stupid "D" ring. The captain always complains it's important but my fingers aren't strong enough to open and close the clip—but we gotta please the captain, right?"

"Roight ee oh," Roo said. "I'll clamp it fer you Missy, roight to the survival raft. You won't be takin any trips in choppy seas that a-way, and I'll jabber with the skipper about shortenin sail. Won't be so hard for you then, drivin in this slop."

Roo found me at the chart table. We called to Denise for instrument readings and checked repeater instruments below deck before agreeing to take a reef in the main.

"Could lose up to a knot, I suspect. Hey, who cares if we can make it comfortable. Denise will be pissed if a wave slurps over the side and she gets drenched."

Roo took a small reef in *Endymion's* roller furling. An advantage of slow sailing at night was not hitting floating obstacles or sailing into shallow spots where depth was a scant ten feet—not a safe margin for our six-foot keel.

Roo took his normal dozen humongous bites of whatever tucker (food) was available before announcing he was 'a piker' (quitter) and turning in until his next watch.

Don slept soundly in the salon leeward berth. I noticed he'd snapped in the canvas to prevent being tossed from his bunk should a freighter's big wake roll us.

The ship's clock struck one bell (2030 or 8:30). Denise said, "Ohhh—only a half hour left on my watch. Bless me."

At the nav station I worked a position fix. I heard Denise again from above in a sing-song tone, "Halfway through my watch, who's up next better get tuned up." She enjoyed being on the helm—but not as much as being off the helm.

"Hey Denise, not time yet for beddy bye, so how about you calm your personal wind and shout me down your weather conditions." I was teasing.

"Wind steady at 10 knots from nor 'east. Stars went to bed like I will very soon." She was playful. "It's solid clouds. Skip, seriously pitch black like Halloween night, Captain, sir." —Added for effect.

Fifteen minutes later all was quiet. Denise reported, "I hear something—something strange, I think with our engine."

She glanced the controls. The engine wasn't running.

"What the heck?"

There was that moment we all fear.

Bathed suddenly in light from the aft port quarter Denise turned, squinting into the brilliance of a large commercial fishing boat rapidly bearing down on us.

Her blood ran cold.

Two fierce looking men stood beside the cabin, pistols in hand. A third, brandishing a grappling hook was in the bow. The light was blinding. There was no mistake. It was coming for us.

"Skip, *Come quick*! Skip! Skip! A big boat—he's going to hit us! *HURRY! GET UP HERE! OOOH SHIT!*"

She screamed in terror.

I was in the cockpit instantly, Don and Roo close behind.

A sixty-foot Malaysian squid fishing boat, seventy-five yards away, was heading directly for us. Men held on with one hand, brandishing pistols in the other. The menacing figure on the bow wildly waved a grappling hook, motioning us to come alongside.

Adrenalin fired. My heart pumped, veins bulged.

"*Fuck you!*" I yelled across the water, sliding into my two foot zone.

"Don, get Denise below *NOW!* Quickly! *MOVE* it Don!"

"Wait up" cried Denise. "Gotta get the engine fired."

"Forget it Denise. Get your ass below. *MOVE! NOW!*"

"Damn it. NO. We need power. I'm getting it, so shut up!"

I did not want Denise on deck, but the engine was important. Don was struggling to open Denise's harness as she stretched for the engine controls.

The squid boat kept closing, grappling hook swinging.

Denise fired the Perkins. "Which way skipper?"

"Hard starboard. Just get the fuck away from them. Roo, help Denise! Back the main. Spin the wheel—get us the hell away from them!"

I felt remarkably calm.

Unhooked from her D ring, Denise refused to go below. The intruder was a boat length away. The attackers were scrawny, shouting in a foreign tongue. They meant us harm but I felt *sooo* calm.

Denise had the wheel hard over, all hundred pounds of her leaning into it. Endymion responded like a horse avoiding a rope.

"Don, grab the boat hook—right behind you Don. *Look BEHIND you—damn it!*" Don was confused, stammering; "But, Denise? Gotta get her below, out of sight."

"I'm good." Denise shouted.

Don picked up the boat hook, a 'what now' expression on his face. Roo was waving fish bats.

Things moved at lightning speed.

"Roo, take the fucking hook from Don—swing it Roo! Fend us off."

Going hard to starboard helped for the moment. We turned better but the invader was faster. Now two boat lengths from our port stern quarter he had momentum and was gaining on us.

Diving for the radios I spoke calmly; "Pan Pan Pan—Pan Pan Pan—Pan Pan Pan (now faster, gulping for air)—all vessels, this is the US sailing yacht *Endymion*, (slower again; I had to be understood)

Position 02 degrees 25 minutes north, repeat 02 degrees 25 minutes north and 101 degrees, 35 minutes east, repeat 101 degrees 35 minutes east. Four persons onboard. Suspect pirates attempting to board. Repeating position 02 degree, 25 minutes north and 101 degrees, 35 minutes east. Pan Pan Pan—*Endymion* clear."

I heard pandemonium on deck as I jammed the adapter down the barrel, converting our flare gun into a single shot 12-gauge shotgun—at the same time monitoring radios. *Shit Skip, you should have had the stupid pistol ready long ago. Damn thing better work!*

Still at the wheel Denise, taking advantage of our maneuverability, plunged *Endymion* to port, causing the invader's bow to barely miss our stern. This was no drill. Gripping the mainsheet, Don worked the big sail to help us turn.

Chatter burst from the radio. "*Endymion Endymion Endymion*, this is the *Berna Marie*. We are twenty north of you, and standing by."

We knew them. Nice New Zealanders, with children aboard.

Christ, they can't help, I thought. *Can't sail backwards.*

I needed to stay in my zone.

Topsides, Roo had two fish bats and a kitchen knife. He looked BIG! It appeared, for the moment, we were holding our own. The pirate boat had one engine. So did we, but our sails, engine and the underwater configuration of *Endymion* gave us advantage in tight quarters.

Denise swung us to starboard, being evasive.

It wasn't over.

"*Endymion, Endymion, Endymion,*" a radio voice booming authority; "This is the southbound Shell tanker *Sam Houston*, passing One Mile Bank. *Endymion*, we have you on radar. ETA your position 17 minutes. *Sam Houston* standing by."

Thank God—but no cheers. The pirates had come as close as twenty feet. The foredeck barbarian had narrowly missed snagging our lifelines with his hook. He would try again. Seventeen minutes was too long.

They struck again. I saw the bastard, grappling hook in hand, a scrawny little cretin, face overrun with hair and a feral look. He swung viciously and let the hook go. It flew toward our bow but its chain tangled. The hook jerked back against the wooden fish boat, tearing away a hunk of rail.

"Damn! Ya see that Roo?" I shouted.

"Hope the bastard sinks. That was way too damn close. Looks like we're further apart. Take a breather, Captain."

I almost laughed.

The fishing boat bore off after the grappling hook snafu, and shut off its lights. We vaguely tracked its silhouette still visible against a murky sky. We also had radar.

"Go 90 degrees port," I directed Denise.

Our adversary anticipated the move.

"Fuck 'em. We should ram 'em."

"Yeah, but we gotta hit 'em broadside or it won't work, Roo. He's too fast."

"But he's no match for our fiber hull!"

Roo was right. *Endymion* packed two inches of extra fiberglass in the knuckle, reinforcing the bow at waterline. For strength we owned the upper hand. We could probably sink them, but it would be difficult to get broadside.

Chaotic as it was I would never have pictured Denise at the wheel when she ought to be hidden below. She wasn't much bigger than the wheel she was turning. If boarded they would find her anyway.

Topsides she knew her stuff and worked well with me. She was fearless, and freed another man to fight, if it came to that.

The *Sam Houston* broadcast, "*Endymion, Endymion, Endymion,* we're full power. ETA now twelve minutes."

"Listen up friends. Whadda we have?" I answered myself, "Fish bats, one 12 gauge shot, a boat hook and a filleting knife—anything else—anybody?"

"I can half fill coffee tins with diesel. Might help blind them," offered Don.

"Get to it then Don."

"Allow me Captain." Roo reached and took the flare gun from me. "I'm half yer age."

The fishing boat was a quarter mile astern. Moving slowly, then increasing speed the squid boat came again, straight for our stern, lights out, trying to catch us unprepared.

Squid lights bathed the spectacle again. He was close.

Our aluminum tender hung over the stern, swinging wildly. Boarding from behind would be tough.

But the fish boat was closing. This would be a collision or very near miss. Denise worked the wheel. No dice—not fast enough. The invader's bow careened into our aluminum tender. The wicked sound of ripping metal filled the air. Our tinny crumpled like a candy wrapper, leaving sharp ragged pieces. The grappling hook cretin swung again. He missed. The starboard side gunman started firing—*Pow. Pow. Pow.*

"Down! *Get down!*" I shouted, bullets whizzing past, but nobody took cover. Brandy barked non-stop.

Roo squeezed the flare pistol trigger. Nothing. It didn't fire. He tried again. It didn't fire.

"Throw it to me," I yelled to Roo while watching the bow of the fishing boat tear further into our tender, locking our vessels in combat.

This was it, happening fast, all at once.

Climbing over the clutter, the gunman with knife in hand, struggled to board us. Profanity and screams rang everywhere. It was a fight to the end. I fired the flare gun. Piece of shit! I threw the pistol at the intruder.

"Damn! I missed. Gimme *that*." I reached into the cockpit. Denise, now showing fear, handed me a fish bat.

"Get the fuckers!"

"Roo, *portside*—take the bastard with the hook!"

"Got 'em Captain."

Drawing compliments of Roo Biram.

Sure-footed on an unsteady vessel, Roo bolted past me to the aft deck, snatched the boat hook Don had dropped and *shoved it,* with all his might, into the knife-wielding pirate's gut.

The pirate cried out. Wrenched in pain he doubled over breathlessly trying to grasp the boat hook. Roo showed *no* mercy.

Shots rang out, one different. A pirate dropped a gun. It had misfired, wounding him.

With a cut inside my left leg I wrestled with the grappling hook fool. Hearing his buddy scream he turned to look. Wrong move. My fish bat smashed his left knee.

He went down.

Roo pulled the boat hook from his pirate's blood soaked gut, savagely swinging again at the staggering pirate's head, and missed.

Determined, my adversary was slowly regaining wobbly sea legs. I decked him.

"Look *RIGHT* Roo."

Roo swung again, this time the business end of the boat hook found the pirate's back just below the neck, knocking him squarely into the opening for our swim ladder. Bewilderment crossed his face. He lost balance, stumbled and cried out, falling into the churning sea, possibly to be run over by his own vessel.

"One down!" yelled Roo. We became attackers. I chased the limping dirt-bag I had fish-batted, now scrambling through the jagged remains of our tinny, trying to get aboard the squid boat.

"Roo, gimmie a hand. Don, watch for anyone coming. Denise, full power to starboard on my command!"

Roo and I straddled the ripped up tinny, pushing hard to separate us from the hull of the intruder.

"*NOW* Denise!"

Denise leaned into the throttle, bringing the Perkins to full power and turned the helm to starboard. In moments we were free. The squid boat dropped off astern, making no apparent effort to re-engage.

"Holy crapola that was scary!" declared Denise breathing sigh of relief.

"Friggin tinny's a loss."

"May be, but that piece a shit probably saved us."

"Should we cut 'er free? She'll no doubt sink." Said Don.

"Naw, let's stand down, rest easy. Anybody seriously hurt? How about you Don? You're leg is bleeding pretty good."

"It's OK. Doesn't hurt. Geeze, I have no idea how it happened."

"Here skipper, take the helm," Denise said, "I need a break anyway and I'll tend to Don. Anyone else?"

She noticed my leg. "Damn it Skip. Lemme see, is it bad?"

"No problem a few kisses can't cure."

Denise tended immediately to Don who needed painful sutures. I later required a few. For the present she steri-stripped my leg.

I went aft to assess damage. The tinny was a goner. My prized teak rail was broken in several places, the swim ladder twisted, and two stainless stanchions that previously held the teak rail in place, were seriously bent. I figured that caused the two hulls to lock together.

Don appear in the companionway holding Brandy, her little tail wagging. He handed her to Denise. At that moment, when our guard was down, Roo shouted; "Shit, here he comes again!

"What the fuck!"

The pirates were coming at us from the starboard stern quarter one hundred yards from us. No lights.

"Get the fuck away!" cried out normally polite Denise, grabbing the wheel after suturing Don, who was groggy from sedative.

"Hang on." Denise pushed the throttle forward.

"No Denise, *NO!* Slow down. Throw it in *REVERSE* when I say so," I called.

"Are you nuts?" asked Denise, " This isn't tea and biscuits time!"

Shots came from the fishing boat, now sixty feet away and determined to get us. Nobody hit, but two bullets ripped our mainsail and they were still coming.

"Jesus. These fuckers are serious!"

" NOW Denise" I shouted, "Hard starboard. Full reverse throttle!"

The Perkins screamed displeasure at grinding gears. *Endymion* spun, turning 120 degrees in her own length. We were headed away, opposite from the intruder who could only turn slowly.

"I don't believe it!" Roo said breaking into a smile and happy dance.

"Me either." I said. "Everybody OK?"

We all were.

"Roo, go below. Check the radar. Denise, nice job!"

"On my way." Roo slid down the companionway just as the radio burst to life half scaring us all over again; "Seven minutes to you," came from the *Sam Houston*.

"See anything Roo?" I called after him, "Wooden vessels are hard to see unless they are close."

"Gimme a sec Captain, I think, yeah, gotta be them. Our enemy is almost a mile away, running dark and—away from us."

"Not sure I could take another round," Denise confessed.

"Probably won't have to." Roo appeared on deck. "I checked again; no traffic within the two mile ring."

I went to the radio. "All ships, all ships, all ships. This is *Endymion, Endymion, Endymion*. Stand down Pan-Pan-Pan call. Situation clear.

Repeat, stand down, Pan-Pan-Pan call. Thank you *Sam Houston*. Thank you all ships. *Endymion* clear."

"God speed to *Endymion* and her crew. *Sam Houston* out."

Breaking one of my rules, I passed the bottle of "Johnny" around, only once because you never know, and Roo relieved an exhausted Denise from the wheel.

Don was hurting. Denise put eight stitches in Don's leg with only a 'local' for pain relief. I excused him from further duty. His leg looked nasty. This guy in his sixties, sitting here sipping whiskey with his mates, would have made his Spanish teacher mighty proud tonight. I announced, "Don, from this day forward you will be known as The Ancient Warrior."

"Hear, hear! For Don." We all cheered and motor sailed on, each of us retreating to our private worlds and thoughts as a somber quiet fell over the yacht. There would be time for Monday morning quarterbacking—but no rush.

CHAPTER 50

HAD WE KILLED A MAN?

We sailed on, keeping a wary eye. We were thankful to be alive, but felt troubled by a weighty question for which we had no answer. Did a man die? Was it accidental or had we killed a person? Most pirate attacks in this area, to our collective understanding, didn't result in loss of life, but these guys had been stirred up. What ended badly for our adversaries could well have ended tragically for us. It happened hours ago but scarcely a word had been spoken.

Roo was first to address our moods speaking quietly, "I have said a prayer for the pirate who went overboard. I hope you all will say one too."

We did, in the cockpit holding hands, and we prayed for Roo as well. He seemed so low.

"Roo," I spoke up, "It was a chaotic, confusing time. You didn't hesitate. You acted with valor. You may well have saved *all* of our lives, but the one thing you *did not do* was kill that man. He was very much alive when he went overboard. Excuse me, please, but I suspect, Roo, that you are feeling some guilt."

"Aye, I am." replied Roo.

Denise captured the moment.

"Mighty Man," she said, "I was gripping the wheel and turning to you, trying to see what you would do when we were stuck to them because of the smashed dingy. I was scared, and I mean really, really scared—but it's like I saw the whole thing like in slow motion. Pardon me Roo, the man had a gun! He raised the gun—at you! He was going to *shoot* you, Roo. He could hardly have missed, crapola—you were nearly holding hands. When you swung the hook he had to duck, and I can't remember exactly if the gun went off then or not, but I think it exploded, probably toward his feet. I did notice he was barefooted because I remember thinking how strange that seemed for a pirate. I always thought they had big black boots. I *saw* him stumble and lose balance, like one leg gave way and went from under him and he hit the rail right by the gate. Then he tumbled sideways over the stern. You did not kill him. Hope that makes you feel better!" She leaned over, hugged Roo, gave him a kiss on the cheek saying, "My hero."

"Echoes my sentiments," said Don, "but no kisses from me."

"How many shots were fired? Anyone count?" I asked. No one had.

"Roo suggested it didn't seem like many, maybe because they had older weapons or weren't familiar enough with them. We found two holes in the mainsail, one in and out of the dodger and a slug embedded in the soft flotation of a 'man overboard pole.'

"We were lucky," said Don. He then added the dumbest questions heard anywhere in the Pacific since clocks began recording time, "Do you suppose they were trying to sell us fish?"

"Do you suppose you're an idiot?" Denise shot back.

And on we sailed through the night, working together as crew—each again closeted in our private emotional worlds.

I know where my mind took me. I had gained enormous respect for Roo. His action was almost sacrificial, yet there had been no hesitancy. I knew he was paying a heavy price in his mind after the fact.

Denise had also climbed a handful of notches on my opinion ladder. She had shown her mettle. I often complained when she talked too much or packaged half a dozen subjects into one sentence. Tonight she showed her mettle with the rest of us and handled the boat like a solid professional. She did what was needed in the moment. No way would she would hide below deck, though I'm certain she knew full well she'd have been a major prize if captured and kidnapped. And that begs the question: were they after electronics and ship's fittings, or were they after people?

We never learned the fate of the man who went overboard. Did shipmates pick him up? Was he struck by their hull, or ours? Or did he swim the mile or so to shore?

I believed I was justified calling it an attack. I felt it was correct to have made a Pan-Pan call instead of Mayday. Mayday indicates loss of life is imminent. Pan-Pan means loss of life is possible. I felt we held our own, kept our composure—and we were damn lucky.

It was my job to report this. Not an easy assignment. I feared how it might be received by authorities, most likely also Malaysian, and wondered whether my story would be believed at all. Would there be consequences for us, and for me particularly?

Don looked at me as if reading my mind and suggested; "Maybe, Skip, this is one of those times you'll be happy some distant bank has an interest in your boat."

We would know in the morning when we put into Lumut and checked in at the Navy Base.

The ship's bell broke another prolonged silence, announcing my 0400 watch. I gave Roo another "atta boy" for his bravery, trying also to implant confidence that there was nothing for which he should feel at fault. He did though. I just felt it. He'd need to be cared for and nurtured. He had been courageous but it wasn't what he would have chosen. It wasn't what Roo had been raised to do. We had met his dad. We knew his lineage and the caliber of person Roo was.

I coached Denise in making a proper log entry before she turned in for well-deserved sleep. Having as detailed a written record of how the night developed may someday be crucial. Roo volunteered to put more thoughts on paper following Denise's effort, but I told him I would do it. I didn't want that 'too many cooks for the broth' thing.

The whole event, from Denise's first scream to Johnny Walker, couldn't have taken more than fifteen minutes. We were drained—totally exhausted, yet on we ploughed through the night as sailors have done no matter what takes place, for as many years as the romance of the seas has fascinated humans.

CHAPTER 51

REPORTING TO AUTHORITIES

With the sun high the next day we were a sliver south of the narrow channel between Pangkor Island and the town of Lumut at the mouth of the Dinding River, when there occurred a surprising reversal of roles. A fishing boat hailed us for help. From hand gestures we concluded they were trying to tell us they had wrapped something, probably netting, around their prop and couldn't get it off. Did we suspect trickery? Absolutely. Closer inspection with binoculars indicated they spoke not with forked tongue, as we could see netting running from the stern deck to the aft waterline. It looked taut.

We didn't want to get too close and had only remains of our tin dinghy, so Roo, an excellent swimmer, volunteered to swim over. He was shown the problem and for the next half hour dove on their bottom with a long knife, eventually freeing the culprit netting and enabling the fishermen to resume their trade. Swimming back to *Endymion* Roo was dragging a Styrofoam container packed with fish so fresh their eyes hadn't hazed.

It was a boost for all of us. Really good! I don't mean just eating gifted fish. It was substance for the soul, nourishment for our spirits to know there were other good people out there, and that we were for-real good people too.

And Don didn't ask if they were selling the fish.

We docked at the Malaysian navy base about 1500. I asked Roo, Denise and Don to stay aboard while I cleared us and made my report. I didn't want to be in a position where Malaysian military people speaking broken English (if any at all) asked multiple questions of us, resulting in confusion, mistaken answers or worse yet, wrong answers. Also because they may know English and feign otherwise, catching us speaking amongst ourselves.

Armed with our log, official papers, passports, proof of ownership, and US Government documentation, I reported to the commanding officer. He was casual, offered me coffee, and listened politely while I told of last night's events. I could not read his face. A tombstone could have told me more. He looked at the papers I handed him, though not carefully, and looked across at me only a couple of times.

I completed my story with something inanely limp, "and that is my report, sir." The ranking naval officer leaned back in his chair, clasped both hands behind his head, and there followed, a long awkward silence. I said nothing, thinking, *first one who speaks loses.*

Finally he spoke. "I am not surprised, Captain. It is a problem in my country and in these waters. Do not worry. We will investigate. We bring many bandits our form of justice. You are free to go."

That was it. He had no comment about the man overboard and asked nothing about the guns they used. (I left our flare pistol out of my report.) I was confused. In Malaysia the use of a gun can be punishable by death, same as drug use. It's a powerful punishment, an effective deterrent to gun crimes and drug abuse. Why had he not said anything? I didn't have good vibes—but hey, not my problem any longer.

"Do you suppose the Navy is in on it, that they're in cahoots for dirty profit?" I asked my crew when I returned aboard.

Denise lightened the moment, saying, "I'm surprised the moron didn't say, 'Got any cigarettes or whisky for me?'" We had seen this behavior previously.

It was dark when we passed through the channel to the Royal Perak Yacht Club. Nearly all of the river's navigational aids, from day markers to lights, were missing or not working. The night was clear, so with radar help, we found find our anchorage opposite the yacht club. It was close to 2200 when we dropped our hook in fifteen feet and shut down the Perkins.

CHAPTER 52

BOTULISM—
THE ERIE AFTERMATH

Anchoring in front of the Perak yacht club after dark, we felt the place resembled a Stephen King novel. Eerie silence. We were not prepared for what morning light disclosed. The "Clubhouse" was more suitable as a lean-too. Spanish moss hung in abundance from trees and a truly spooky 30-foot sloop with no mast lay at anchor close by. Correct that; it had the stub of a broken mast. The hull was covered almost to deck level with remnants of seaweed, indicating a troubled past.

We sat at the cockpit table with toast and morning cuppa Joe.

"This place looks haunted."

"You gotta stop reading those King books. Feelin uncomfortable there Denise? Think it's possessed?" asked Roo.

"Well, I don't see how they can call that dump on shore a *Royal* yacht club." Shot back Denise.

"I'll answer that. Because these Provinces were once ruled by Sultans and if one of them came here the ground then became *Royal*," I explained.

"No foolin?"

"Yup, simple as that. I read it in Singapore."

"Still, it's a spooky place. Whatta ya suppose was the situation that created that derelict boat? Denise motioned toward the nearby moss covered hull.

"I figure she musta had a female skipper who couldn't handle the weather." Don jabbed at Denise.

"You sure are prejudiced, Don. Sexist too?"

"I bet it was a well handled boat that got caught in a bad storm. All persons were saved and they drifted until picked up by a passing Australian frigate." Roo at least was civil.

We will never know for certain but were told the boat hailed from the UK. A man and women aboard were on a two-year voyage and were in the Indian Ocean. One balmy evening they sat across from one another. The man opened a can of outdated mushrooms. The can was defective.

Botulism.

The man perished. His mate continued sailing through foul and fair weather, we assumed with the corpse still aboard. A pocket size freighter eventually spotted the floating tomb and towed it to where it sat in front of us, at the Perak Yacht Club on the Sungai River close to Lumut. I don't know if those were true facts, but for certain, none of us were inclined to board the boat. We did however question what would become of the boat, and the surviving lady.

Life at sea, so wonderful, can also be brutal. God bless their souls.

We rowed ashore for a look around this quiet, mysterious place. A logbook for visiting yachts invited us to enter details, and we did. We found cooking utensils begging use but passed on the opportunity. The fragrance from an outside dunny suggested a wide berth. Brandy enjoyed her romp on solid ground, fetching sticks and rolling in Spanish moss. Never once did we see another person at or around the most informal "yacht club" since Dick's Place at Malolo Island in Fiji. We left the following morning, our destination Dayang Bunting Lake on Langkawi Island, Malaysia.

CHAPTER 53

DEALING WITH SUBMERGED DEBRIS

Nearing the northern end of Sumatra to our port side, the Strait became the Andaman Sea, no longer narrow and with plenty of deep water. We kept the coast of Malaysia close to starboard.

"Damn, it's hot! Never ends, does it?" complained Don, shedding his T-shirt at a moment perfectly timed to catch a brief heavy rainfall, cleansing and cooling our over-heated, over-ripe bodies.

"It's monsoons, Don. We're in them—northeast winds and heavy rain until May. Get used to it."

"You mean *you* get used to it." Don corrected me. "I'm getting married, may I remind you, in Seattle, a long way from this sweat belt."

"But with plenty of rain, right? So there ya go Don."

The weather fined up, as Australians say, and we held Penang Island in sight the next morning—back again into a bustling world of commerce.

Motoring north between Penang to Port and mainland to starboard we were awed by a bridge we hadn't seen on our chart. Spanning

8.5 km of water, and towering to allow taller vessels to pass beneath it, the bridge connecting the mainland and Penang Island was stunning and architecturally superb. An hour after passing below it, we anchored at the edge of the commercial district on the northeast corner of the island. The water around us was disgustingly polluted, surprising because it moved with tide and current. People versus nature we figured, and too many people.

We needed to provision, to sightsee, have a good meal ashore and play ball with Brandy. With our tinny tender destroyed we relied on "bum boats" (water taxis) and there were plenty. Our first stop was a local watering hole, said to be a favorite of westerners. Plopping onto a barstool I was thumped heavily on the shoulder by more than an accidental passing patron. Turning to engage, I saw the entire crew of *Kinta III*. How they arrived in Penang ahead of us I'll never know. How heavily we partied that evening I'll never remember.

We toured the island on rented motorbikes, Brandy hitching a ride in the basket of mine.

We provisioned, including exotic spices that Denise promised to sprinkle on our Thanksgiving turkey dinner with *Quahlee of Sydney*. At a local chandlery I stocked up on belts and parts for our engine.

"Hey guys, do one with me." Don implored.

"One what?"

"One visit to the rubber tree plantation!"

"Are you fucking nuts?"

But we did, *only* to satisfy Don. It was without question the dullest afternoon of my life. Watching rubber slow drip from trees into little buckets wasn't a priority for me. Roo and Denise agreed. We didn't speak with the 'ancient warrior' for hours.

Penang would have been more enjoyable if the water was not so polluted. We were happy to hear the anchor rising and get underway.

"Go ahead forward." Roo shouted to me from the foredeck.

I put the Perkins in gear and headed *Endymion* slightly to port to clear the island's tip. Nothing happened. Heads turned toward me. Roo came aft.

"Problem, Captain?"

"No forward speed. She's in gear."

Roo looked at the speed gauge and then over the side. "Try puttin er in neutral, then in gear again."

"You've got rpm's" Denise was looking at engine gauges.

"Crap, we're drifting down on that old shit boat!" I said, motioning toward an anchored fishing boat of dubious quality. "Anchor! Free the anchor, Roo."

Roo sprung forward to release the big CQR anchor from its chock while Denise grabbed the remote control letting the anchor plunge to the murky bottom.

We took stock of our predicament. There was no apparent engine problem, no smoke, overheating or other warnings, but we had no forward motion.

"Problem's got to be the prop." I declared.

"Could we have lost it?" Denise inquired.

"Doubt it. We replaced the feathering prop after the Tall Ships race. Roo replaced zincs in Darwin. Crap—you did didn't you, Roo?"

"Yeah, they weren't bad then either."

"Plus the raw water's been OK except maybe Singapore."

"Tell ya what skipper, I'll take a sticky beak, said Roo, opening a cockpit locker for his swim goggles.

"*No way!*" Denise was loud, jumping up from her seat to caution Roo.

"That water's hepatitis city. You can't go in it. Not today. Not ever. Not you, Roo. Let's find local divers used to this water. You could get seriously sick from polluted water like that."

Nurse Sluggo had made her point. This is what she said in a letter home:

Neither Roo or Skip wanted to get into that water nor did I relish treating one or both of them for hepatitis, a real possibility.

She was right. I took to the radio. In short order we had a swarm of native teens in outboard skiffs wanting to dive below *Endymion*. The sound of jingling ringgit coins was loud and clear. We chose three brothers who went to work.

Our prop was not missing or damaged. The culprit was a huge tarpaulin, maybe twenty feet square that had come free from a coal barge, either blown away in the monsoons or perhaps lost from carelessness. It had lain just below the murky surface and somehow wrapped around our propeller, tie lines and all. The boys had it free in short order and we were on our way. It was Wednesday, November 23rd.

CHAPTER 54

A CRUISING FRIEND JOURNEYS TO HEAVEN

Our meeting place with *Quahlee of Sydney* was a scant 75 nm sail. We were to rendezvous the next day, Thanksgiving Day. Soon after sunrise we anchored beside Dayang Bunting Lake, a small body of fresh water separated from the Andaman Sea by a quarter-mile-wide stretch of hillside—a picturesque place.

We were the only yacht there, no *Quahlee of Sydney*. We figured we would be surprised as happened so often, like with the sudden appearance of *Kinta III*. Denise dove into holiday meal prep. Don and Roo pumped up a swim raft and took the tom-turkey we had overpaid for ashore for plucking in fresh water. I called *Quahlee* by radio—without success.

By 1100 the bird was in the oven and table set but still no word from, or sighting of Ines and John Watson's *Quahlee*.

"Why not give the ham a yak?" Roo questioned, almost choking on a warm diet Pepsi.

"Yeah. Can do but I don't recall they have ham, at least not that I remember."

Microphone in hand I started, "Yankee Poppa Tango.... this is *Endymion*." I repeated, then asked if anyone out there had QSO (contact) with *Quahlee of Sydney* or could give me a last known QTH (location). I wasn't an accomplished ham operator so I didn't stick with it. I shut the radio down, not wanting to embarrass myself.

Ines prepares to bake bread. John sips a brew.

"What now?" asked Denise.

"We wait I guess."

"With champagne! After all, it's Thanksgiving." I pulled one of two celebratory bottles from our fridge.

The metal wire wasn't twisted free of the cork when our high seas radio went live.

"Endymion, Endymion, (pause) Endymion?"

"This is *Endymion* back. Skip speaking."

"Skip, my name is Rusty Parsons. I have a Peterson 44 *Serendipity*, in Singapore. You are looking for John Watson and his wife Ines?"

"Yes."

"For what purpose may I ask?"

That's a strange question I thought to myself. "We have been buddy boating since Tahiti and are meeting today for Thanksgiving dinner. You're free to pull up a settee?" I gave Rusty our location.

"Hmm. Actually, we met once in the bum boat at Changi. You would remember me as *Dr.* Rusty Parsons, also American."

"Of course, you're the solo sailing doctor."

Denise remembered Rusty and whispered out of radio hearing range, "He's 80. Sailing by *himself*. Crazy huh?"

Dr. Rusty; "Skip, John had an accident. Ines has gone back to Australia."

"Good God. What happened?" I asked. All aboard *Endymion* were silent.

"John had a heart attack. He's dead."

"*WHAT?*" We all said it. Disbelief. "Oh my God! What happened."

"Leaving the sailing club, heading for Thailand," there was a pause, "John had an engine problem. Andy Copeland went aboard to help out. John was going down his companionway. He never made it—had a massive coronary on the companionway stairs. Andy made a "Mayday" call. Two trained nurses were there in minutes as was an ambulance. But John was dead before he hit the salon floor."

We all gasped. Denise broke into sobs and tears.

I could only mutter "I can't believe it."

"I was the attending. He didn't have a chance, Skip. Sorry."

"No, you shouldn't be. I'm in ... *we're* in shock. They were coming to meet *us*. *Today.* Then we were going on to Phuket together. When did this happen?"

"Been about ten days now. Ines flew home with John's body on Monday, just a few days ago. They—excuse me, *she* put *Quahlee* on the hard here. I guess she'll return sometime."

We talked a few minutes, bits and pieces, agreeing to meet up in Phuket if we are not yet headed for Europe when Rusty arrives in Thailand. After the call we sat—still stunned.

I led a prayer asking God's blessings on John, Ines, the unknowns who suffered botulism, and even the pirate we feared had drowned. It saddened us to think that on Thanksgiving Day we would hear of the death of a friend we all admired. Our mood was subdued. Denise particularly, was grieving.

"What *bothers* me is how John died. Maybe, just maybe, it wasn't necessary."

"Meaning what?"

"Remember the night Ines made beer bread, and John was suffering from allergies?"

"Vaguely."

"He was having a hard time breathing. Wheezing a lot. I asked if he'd seen a doctor and he hadn't, but showed me some antihistamine he was taking. I forget where it came from, Australia or somewhere in Indonesia. I didn't recognize it."

"So?"

"So," said Denise in a cheerless voice, "I'm not a doc but I'm a damn good nurse and know antihistamine would be contra-indicated for *any* person with a heart condition or John's breathing difficulty."

"Sorry Honey. You didn't know. You're feeling partly responsible, I can tell—but you shouldn't."

Denise agreed. We had our turkey dinner on a lackluster holiday.

We turned in early. Denise and I in our aft-cabin with a wind scoop deployed through a large hatch hoping to divert any breeze to our berth. I couldn't sleep and went topsides.

The night was whisper still. Not a human voice, a breaking wave, call of a bird or even the buzz of a mosquito. Our friends, the stars who guide us (I think they have personalities), were out in force. Lying in the cockpit, looking at the heavens I thought again how astonishing and improbable all of this is: what I am looking at, and what I am seeing. *Sure,* I thought, *if light from our sun rips along at 186,000 miles a second and it takes eight minutes to reach us, how distant in human terms, are these star friends winking to me now? Our fastest space vehicles would take 40,000 YEARS to travel as far as light in one year—and so many stars are hundreds of light years away from me tonight on this boat, at this island. Their light shines not only on me, but on every person in the world—and the star could have been dead for centuries. No wonder the glory of it all is overwhelming. What is out there that we don't understand?*

As a speck in the sand in this big picture, how do I put it all in order? I lay in this moment captured by the wonders of life and my little place in it?

It was time to contact God. I did, asking that he take John Watson into his kingdom for life everlasting, and seeking guidance to keep my friends and I safe on our journeys. Then, as a tribute to John I turned to the music of Wolfgang Mozart, and let Roger William's piano piece *To Amadeus With Love* drift over the anchorage as I fell asleep and first light of a new day blossomed.

CHAPTER 55

IN THE ANDAMAN SEA

We hadn't cleared customs in Langkawi as required. It was my plan to slip quietly and illegally into Bass Harbor before leaving, do a little duty free shopping, top off our fuel and slip quietly out. I carefully planned our approach to be after 1800 when officials would have left for the day but facilities would still be open. We flew our Malaysian flag—a textbook version of fraud since we flew no Q flag, having not cleared.

We tied to the seaplane dock and hadn't gone but a few feet toward the village when two uniformed officials approached.

"Oh shit, we've been had." Roo quietly said.

"Be calm," I said and turned to the uniforms, "Good evening Gentlemen. Selemat Selam." (Good evening in their lingo)

"Same to you, Captain. You'll have to move your vessel." He spoke perfect English.

"Can do. Why?"

"Our new hovercraft is due momentarily. There will be a celebration tomorrow. You are in the way."

Just when I thought we were home free he asked, "Did you just arrive?"

I lied. "Yes."

"I am the Port Captain. You are not allowed ashore until cleared. I will see you in my office first thing tomorrow, 0800 sharp!" He looked past me at *Endymion*. I hoped he hadn't noticed we were missing the required Q flag.

I felt a sense of doom seeping into every pore. The penalty for entering illegally by boat can be severe. I tried to sound casual. "Yes, sir."

The Port Captain walked away. Relieved, we did our duty free but the fuel guy couldn't fill us until 0600; his system was locked. He expected to be busy in the morning, celebration and all. The government intended to make this a tourist destination. Apparently that plan was in motion.

I didn't sleep well.

We fueled by 0620 and slowly proceeded east, headed for Thai waters as inconspicuously as possible. After a mile I gradually increased speed, constantly looking aft for signs of a patrol boat—none in sight.

A few minutes later Roo said "Look again. What do you think, Skip—looks like patrol! Whatever, he's coming fast!"

I snatched the binoculars. "No doubt Roo. It's blue, throwing a wake and headed straight for us."

My mind went to overdrive. *I don't want to go to the slammer. Better to tell the truth. CRAP! Why did I get us in this jam? He's getting closer, can't outrun him. Be calm Skip. You dope—the same day as the hovercraft, reporters—Christ, that'll be humiliating. Can't be the hovercraft, too big a wake. Who will bail me out? Probably get buggered by some Malay mob guys. You idiot, Skip!*

"Looks like it's turning!" Roo said "Unless he's playing a game with us."

"No, he's veering off." I sighed with relief. Looking again I could see it was a large blue high powered speedster with no interest in us.

But we were not out of it yet. God was about to show us instant karma. Clear of Bass Harbor and headed north toward the alleged Thai drug haven Buntang Island, we were hit by a murderous storm. We expected squalls in monsoon season but this developed into hours of 30-knot winds battering us right on the old nose. To make headway we resorted to a reefed main as close hauled as we could make it, an engine and no other sails. Occasionally the squall would clear for a few minutes before battering us again. At least the rain was warm.

Near dusk in a dying wind we dropped our hook in a rolly anchorage at Buntang Island. With a depth of seventy feet I felt it insecure, but we were on the lee side, so no direct wind waves to deal with. Roo and Don dove over to take a look around on shore. Denise went below to curl up with a book and let the wind scoop blow her to pieces. I stayed on deck but kept nodding off.

A powerful gust awoke me. On shore sand was being wildly whipped by another squall. This one was fierce. I raced to secure hatches. Too late—it hit, ripping away the sun awning that I grasped while hanging to the mizzenmast with the other hand. Denise came to assist me, barely containing the fabric and stays before losing the whole thing. I stole a glance at our instruments—wind was peaking at 48 knots, steady at 40. The depth indicator read 78 feet-82-90 feet. We were dragging. Denise and I'd been through this drill before. She took the wheel and started the engine. I went forward to the anchor winch and motioned Denise to bring *Endymion* slowly ahead to reduce strain on anchor chain while it's rising. She motioned by hand for me to look ashore. Roo, looking frustrated, was ready to swim out to us. I motioned him to stay put.

Denise had us headed away from shore when I realized that while I was napping some twenty trawlers had also sought refuge in the shelter of the island. We stood off a quarter mile waiting for better conditions. A skiff from a trawler delivered Roo and Don back to mother ship. We took them aboard over the port rail because our swim ladder remained non-functional after the pirate experience.

Rain and wind squalls continued well after dark. I didn't want to anchor again. The trawler guys know when to seek refuge but I didn't feel right, so we turned tail, close reefed the main and sailed for Phuket during the night, hugging the Thailand coast.

CHAPTER 56

HEADED TO PHUKET

All night we worked our way slowly and painfully against short nasty seas. At some instants I couldn't believe the monsoon energy whistling past us—white squalls where we couldn't see through seething wind spray, rendering it difficult to determine what was water and what was sky. Nonetheless we were safe, on a fine yacht, and eventually skies cleared.

"Damn glad not to keep staring into the radar!" Roo exclaimed climbing topside to greet the day. Sunrise gave a crystal-like appearance to mist still clinging to dying wind waves, giving the Andaman Sea an ethereal beauty.

There was something about entering the Andaman Sea from the Strait of Malacca that was comforting. Nothing really changed. It just felt right after a stormy twenty-four hours to be someplace I considered less threatening. Fact or fantasy, we had heard a lot about Thailand, its beauty, friendly handsome people, food and traditions. We would get our first taste earlier than expected.

Before us lay one of many tiny islands dotting our route to Phuket. This one was Koh Bulon Leh. (Koh or Ko means island. The formal name follows Koh.) The island looked interesting. Don had landed a 10-pound mahi mahi we wanted to cook, so we stopped. Dropping a day pick in fifteen feet with good holding had us 100 yards off a serene sandy beach protected by a thin spit of a reef to the north and barely visible. Not much protection should it blow.

Preparing our raft to float us to shore we looked up to see a Thai "longtail" approaching. We'd never seen one before, a long narrow dugout shaped boat with a man standing aft holding a steering rod connected to a noisy motor connected to a drive shaft nearly twelve feet long, allowing the prop to be close to the surface. Two young men aboard waved and smiled as they approached.

The youngsters wanted to take our trash ashore, offered to fish for us and told us a new resort had just opened beyond the sand spit. By gestures we learned there was only one guest, however the restaurant was "peid." (Open)

"Sounds cultural," said Roo, digging for his Thai dictionary.

"Ask if they have showers?" Denise was anxious.

" It's what drifting and blending is all about. Let's blend." I added. "Let's climb aboard this contraption."

After being welcomed like royalty we tasted our first fresh pineapple on a stick, and Denise got her fresh water shower. A large audience of Thai ladies fussed over the texture of her skin and shade of lipstick.

Brandy, however, was the hit of the day. Most Thais are Buddhist and love dogs. A dozen at least sniffed greetings with Brandy, a petite creature compared to the less kempt island dogs. Brandy created a lasting impression at a new construction site by leading a parade of admirers through fresh cement. Thai people laughed, repeatedly telling us "mai pen rai" (it doesn't matter).

Don's mahi mahi was prepared Thai style for us, topped with fresh fruit including a mango sauce to die for. Brandy had her little stomach stuffed with a special chicken dinner cooked doggie bland style by the same Chinese chef who treated us. I was told he did not feel it honorable to cook for a dog. Brandy was an exception, and had ice cream.

During our visit ashore a trim 36 foot wooden ketch went by, all sails flying, then tacked sharply to set anchor too close to the barely visible reef, a good maneuver but not smart seamanship. I yelled out to make them aware of the reef and got in return a gesture indicating 'we know.' We later met the Scot who owned *Ganesh* and his two female back-packer crew. He had purchased the lovely vessel in Singapore. His first boat and first voyage.

Though invited, even encouraged, to stay the night thus increasing the guest count, we stayed only through the first evening thunderstorm, returning to *Endymion* to find she had dragged precariously close to shore. My fault for setting a light weigh day anchor instead of our standard 90 pound CQR.

We opted to sail through the night, anticipating arrival in Phuket the next morning. It would be a wild ride. Don was at the wheel when wind shifted to west-northwest piping up to thirty knots. We reefed both main and jib, and doused the mizzen totally.

Then an unexplainable event took place. I was trying to find a rock on the radar called Koh Rok Nok reported to be fourteen miles west of a large mountain on Koh Lanta. We were about midway between the rock and the shore heading in a direction that would take us close to the rocks. Though actually three rocks jutting from the sea they were only seven feet high and returned an excellent radar image. But the mountain on Ko Lanta was radar invisible. "What the hell?" Nothing I could do produced a return from the mountain. An hour later we passed close to the nasty looking rocks but they appeared to the east on our radar instead of west. Something had infected our Furuno radar. It showed images in reverse. Roo, up most of the night with me, was also amazed so I knew it wasn't my mind going crackers.

Anyway, we sailed through the night in lousy conditions. Poor Brandy was frightened when *Endymion* pounded in harsh seas . She took turns curled up in someone's arms, not wanting to let go.

We later learned the Scot and his beautiful wooden ketch set sail shortly after we had, also bound for Phuket. He didn't make it. He cut Koh Lanta too close and lost his lovely boat on a rocky outcrop. They all survived. It made me wonder if there had been a poltergeist in our radar. Had the Scot had one as well?

We arrived safely at Patong Beach on the west side of Phuket Island.

CHAPTER 57

THAILAND—
THE MAGIC KINGDOM

It's OK if I never get a second chance for a first impression about Thailand. I didn't need one. We anchored midmorning, close to shore in the center of half-mile-long, crescent shaped Patong Beach. Hundreds of beach umbrellas already shaded thousands of sun lovers. Speed boats zipped about towing people in parachutes. Music with a hint of delicate bells drifted from shore on a light morning breeze—a whisper of wind that also carried scents of intriguing food. We took in the magic of Thailand.

Denise first heard light tapping on our hull. She peered over the side. Standing in a beat-up dingy was a shirtless tanned man with beard and Hollywood smile. As he extended a hand to Denise, his beltless trousers fell to his ankles exposing his 'Johnson rod' and support equipment. Not missing a beat Denise said, "Welcome aboard, whoever you are—just zip it up before climbing up."

"Hi. I'm Rowdy Taliaferro. Welcome to Thailand."

"May I pour you a cold one?" I asked.

It was midmorning. Our guest said "yes." We semi knew Rowdy from listening to his ham radio net from as far off as Singapore. With a beer in hand and pants pulled to his waist he gave us the skinny about Phuket Island. For a population eighty five percent Buddhist and twelve percent Muslim, Christmas, only a few weeks away, was a non-event.

"That's my trimaran *Allegra* anchored in front of us, near the beach."

I looked but couldn't believe it. I didn't say anything but thought, *what a mess! Allegra would have to be painted before it could be condemned.*

Alas, *Allegra* was Rowdy's home. His castle. From it he conducted his ham radio net that had surely saved lives and avoided groundings. However, his castle was crumbling. While *Allegra* may have been held together by seaweed and scotch tape I'll say this for Rowdy; the man was a gentleman. It was rumored he came from wealth but wanted no part of it. Our first impression of Rowdy Taliaferro was of a happy high-value soul—truly a fellow drifter and blender.

"Looking ashore," Denise commented, "I'd say they're celebrating something."

"Thais are happy, always celebrating something," said Rowdy. "You'll love it here but I don't recommend extended anchoring at Patong Beach. It can be rough and noisy. I'm here only today and go to Ao Chalong for permanent anchorage. A place there called Pan's Lighthouse is where yachties gather."

I explained to Rowdy that we had mail forwarded to us care of Pan's Lighthouse, thanks mostly to his ham radio advice.

Denise explains it best in this slice from a letter home:

Pan's Lighthouse was a 38 km taxi ride from Patong Beach. Well worth it! With the exchange rate it was $4.00 US—round trip!

We asked if there was mail for Endymion. The man said 'Hi Skip, we have heaps of mail for you plus a Christmas box.' That's how we met the proprietor Pan and his wife Julie from Canada. Great people and Phuket is lovely. It costs less to eat out than it does to feed us on board. Beware of Thai whisky called Mekong—Holy shit (excuse me Mom) but that's the only way to put it. Add lime or sip it if you want to see morning. Never again!

We later anchored close to Pan's Lighthouse in Ao Chalong, but that arrangement didn't last. The harbor was too commercial. We moved to the southern tip of Phuket Island and fell in love with Nai Harn Bay, a beautiful quiet anchorage with a sandy beach, small restaurant and motorcycles to rent. Brandy became her usual hit, paddling ashore from *Endymion*, chasing crabs, playing ball (fetching one) with anyone willing. She would patiently sit, still as a statue, waiting for a vendor to drop a niblet of fresh pineapple or chicken roasted over wood fires. We blended easily into island life—no agenda and no pressure.

With two weeks to Christmas, yachts gathered at Kata Noi, a quiet cove on the island's western side. We were there for a Christmas party and a roasted pig BBQ on the beach. I sat in the aft cabin writing home while Denise baked cookies in the galley. Our anti roll devices were deployed to keep her cookies from spilling. (Take that any way you wish.) Our wind scoop delivered gentle breezes to help fend off tropical heat.

Endymion was more than 14,000 miles from home. It would be hard to be further without leaving the planet. All around us were anchored yachts with hailing ports such as Sydney, Glasgow, Stockholm. Miami, London, Breckenridge, London, Vancouver, Grimeaux, Perth, Newport Beach and even Halifax. A few were multi million dollar yachts with nannies and paid crew. Some were like us and many were smaller.

For some the long journey here had been hard, sometimes dangerous. Our ship's clock struck 4 bells (2:00 pm). The smell of fresh cookies brought Christmas to life.

Last night Santa visited the anchorage—by radio. Youngsters were surprised Santa knew them by name. A kid from one vessel was shocked to learn Santa knew about his Dad's involvement in a brush fire back on Lizard Island in Australia. Another lad had been spreading a rumor that Santa was a fake. His astonishing recognition by Saint Nick reversed his position.

Bagheera was stage center yacht for children cruising with their parents. As their laughter rang across the water I was intrigued by the diversity of accents and the harmony in their voices. There was no racial tension, no political friction. No sign even of cliques or favoritism. Cruising children were vastly beyond their years in wisdom and compassion, products of solid families that define typical cruising parents. I counted fifteen shouting, laughing kids on *Bagheera's* deck waiting their turn to grab the spinnaker line and hurl themselves with abandon into the sea. In their glee I doubt those young friends realized how fortunate they were. But I'll bet you this ... they will someday... when they look back at how they spent Christmas, 1989. Powerful stuff. That multinational collection of youth has seen more of the world and life in the last year than most kids will glean from the sum total of a book education. Should these youngsters be the leaders of tomorrow we will all be better for it.

I went to join them.

Eventually the festivities moved shore side for the roasted pig BBQ arranged by Bob Gay from the American yacht *Shenghei*. Bob

Skip swinging from Bagheera's *rigging.*

put days of effort into the event but Santa stole the show. Apparently the old gentleman had 'wet his whistle' with Mekong. Coming ashore plastered, he fell from the dingy transporting him.

Denise and I returned to *Endymion* to share a quiet evening with a bottle of wine and carols from the folks at the Mormon Tabernacle.

Roo helped me string holiday lights throughout *Endymion's* rigging. We filled the air with Christmas carols and invited every yacht in Nai Harn Bay to join us on Christmas Eve.

Denise & I went to Phuket town to shop for the party. Toting party foods we opted for a Thai tuk-tuk instead of motorbikes. We had lunch in town, shopping went well and our backpacks were overloaded. The reader probably doesn't need to hear this but I swear what's next is true. Returning to Nai Harn the tuk-tuk stopped frequently to pick up or discard passengers. It was a s-l-o-w annoying

Denise lends Santa a sympathetic ear.

trip. Somewhere midway through a patch of jungle something from lunch punched me in the gut. We've all been there. Lunch was seeking a way out of me. I desperately needed a sit down toilet. Crapping in the tuk-tuk would be embarrassing.

"Denise, I'm in trouble—can't make it back."

"Sure you can. No choice, no worries."

"I don't think so."

"Ute nee, Ute nee," (stop NOW) I boisterously shouted in Thai.

Thinking someone was dying, the driver ground to a stop. He wasn't far from wrong. I jumped from the rig, backpack with groceries over my shoulders and pushed into the jungle. Snakes or poisonous brush be dammed. This was an emergency. I squatted just out of sight. I took my sweet time. Passengers gave me every scornful dirty look they could muster when I stepped aboard again.

Back aboard *Endymion*, sorting groceries, Denise innocently asked, "Where's the pumpernickel?"

Getting no answer she turned to me and asked again, "OK Skip, where's the pumpernickel?"

"I used it."

CHAPTER 58

AN AWESOME SEA NOMAD

An immediate chore after arriving in Thailand was finding an inflatable to use as our shore boat. Rowdy showed me a marvelous Thai-made Sea Nomad model. New methods of separating air chambers were involved. The boats were made of Hypalon, the best and most expensive material for extended exposure in the tropics and withstanding general mistreatment. Sea Nomad had also developed an elaborate system to glue Hypalon, using additional bonding agents to give the inflatables outstanding rigidity and stability. More impressive was a design feature I had never seen on any inflatable. Rather than the standard conical shaped stern end to the two principal tubes, the inventors had cut out the major portion of the conical end and replaced it with a solid fiberglass step-like fitting. It served two worthy purposes. First it allowed the boat to accelerate more rapidly. Most important it provided an easy way for anyone swimming to board the craft. Accidental inflatable deaths were most often caused because the swimmer was too tired or too drunk to pull their bodies over the large rubber tubes. We bought a Sea Nomad inflatable. The company, for a slight fee, glued the name *Endymion* to port and starboard tubes in contrasting color fabric. We loved this new dinghy. I wished we had had it when Denise fell out of the Avon during the overfalls adventure back at Hook Island. (*Chapter 32*)

Roo was pleased to hang around. Phuket was a young man's paradise. Roo was not one to take advantage of anyone. He was respectful of everyone. He simply enjoyed island living.

Toward June, with monsoons due, we took one last fair weather sail to Koh Ngai, a deserted island 30 nm southeast of Phuket. Harry, Pauline and Caroline, ski crazy friends from Aspen, were with us. Roo called depth and Denise handled the anchor, dropping it in fifteen feet with a sandy bottom. We were on a lee shore at an island south of Koh Lanta, not our normal territory. I generally avoid lee shores but in this changing season any shore might become a lee shore. Harry and the bikini-clad girls lowered the Sea Nomad and sped to the beach. Roo rigged his new windsurfer, shouting up to me that he wished for more wind to challenge his muscular frame.

"Roo, you'll be twenty-two in five days. How about wind for your birthday?"

"Works for me," he replied, casting his wind machine free of *Endymion*.

I sat under the sun awning, reveling in solitude and watching Harry and Denise with a Frisbee playing 'keep away' from Brandy. Caroline and Pauline were walking aimlessly, toes in the water, along the beach.

The sky to our north turned dark. It happened fast. I watched with seasoned eye, thinking *no worries. It will play billy hell with someone somewhere, but should pass well clear of us.* A Thai cruise ship, *Seatram*

Princess, set anchor a mile south of us elevating my lee shore comfort level. Overhead, small puffy clouds with heavy bottoms scudded across the sky. *Coming our way?*

I saw lightning. Intense lightning. I watched it increase. I saw Roo's scarlet sail in contrast with the darkening sky. I still had sunshine where I was, and little breeze. Something wasn't right. Upper clouds were moving away. Lower clouds, dark and unfriendly were sweeping toward me. *Crap. I don't like this.*

Harry returned to leave Brandy with me and for his camera, wanting to get a shot of *Endymion* against the storm sky.

"Be careful Harry, conditions may get nasty!"

Harry sped off in the Sea Nomad. *BOOM-CRACK-BOOM!* From almost directly overhead my little world was shattered. Brandy dove for the hatch and her toilet hiding place. *We're in for it now.*

I looked seaward. I couldn't find Roo. On shore everyone was looking toward me. I signaled all is OK. Looking more intently I saw that Roo was down, a half mile from me with white water, rain or maybe sea, closing over him. I took a bearing. 040 degrees.

I was battening hatches when *Endymion* heeled forcibly to port. The storm front hit at 35 knots. I could barely make out Roo trying to get his sail up. He wasn't managing it. A puff hit 43 knots. Seas building rapidly behind the initial surge were too much for Roo's small board and big sail. *Endymion* pitched in the growing swell. Now I *was* concerned. *Concentrate Skip—get into your zone.*

I radioed *Seatram Princess.* Yes, they could see Roo, took a bearing of due north and offered to send their longtail to assist Roo. The longtail radioed me. "Roo turned down our offer to help."

It wasn't the time to be macho and I needed his help. *Endymion* was jerking, pulling hard on the anchor chain. A small reef was 100 yards astern. No rain yet for me but with rising sharp seas I had to get my home ready. I worked my way forward on a deck strewn with clutter from our guests, making a mental note to have a fireside chat about this. As I freed the safety wrap of chain from the capstan *Endymion* pulled hard, causing her bow to be buried in a wave and nearly knocking me overboard. Without a harness I clutched rigging, moving aft to start the Perkins. A quick glance to shore showed Harry pulling the inflatable further up the beach. *Good, no heroics.*

I had to decide—leave or stay put. I was alone. Can't make a mistake. Seas were up, anchor strained and reef too close to let out more scope. On the other hand, no rain and wind had dropped to the high twenties. I kept the engine running in neutral. Up the beach the girls were walking toward a beached longtail, pointing seaward. I followed. I saw Roo. He would be OK. I sensed the critical moment had passed. The wind gauge hovered around twenty knots. I could handle that. Soon I saw the longtail headed toward me carrying a sailboard and one exhausted strong Australian. Roo was all smiles.

Those ashore made no move to return to *Endymion*. Roo swam ashore to learn why. They had sheared a pin on the outboard and could not have come out anyway. When seas calmed the longtail towed them out.

Total elapsed time, first concern to finish—no more than twenty minutes.

Miller time.

CHAPTER 59

REACHING OUT WITH LOVE —14000 MILES OUT

Not all of our time in Thailand was stormy. There were endless days of pleasure sailing amidst the cliff-faced islands of the Andaman Sea, nestling into snug anchorages where privacy was the rule rather than exception. One night we lay on our backs in the cockpit, listening to our favorite music and watching an awesome lightning display. A jagged, fierce bolt from nature's arsenal ripped earthward striking the boat next to us. We were momentarily enveloped in an umbrella of static electricity. Thunder shook the boat. It frightened us at the moment. In the afterglow we appreciated the experience.

In midsummer we received word that cancer of the jaw invading Denise's dad was advancing. It was expected in a way. Her dad had hinted about cancer when he visited in Australia. The letter from her brother hit Denise hard. She wanted to be with me yet wanted in the strongest way possible to care for her dad. She made the 14,000 mile journey home, as she should have.

During her long absence Roo and I worked day and night preparing *Endymion* for December's King's Cup races. For years Bhumibol Adulyadej, Thailand's King and the world's longest reigning monarch, had been an enthusiastic small boat sailor. The country revered their King. The cup races in his honor attracted talented competitors worldwide. There was a division applicable to *Endymion's* specifications and we were keen to compete.

I wrote daily to Denise, mostly words of love and encouragement for her dad. After that I told her about our daily life. Here's a portion of one letter:

Things have gone to the shits. Yesterday I had an offer to charter Endymion for $500 a day for several days. I turned it down because I had a commitment to the boatyard. Three hours later a fax from the yard was delivered telling me not to come. They are closing for four months for, get this, modernization. I faxed back that I had a reservation. They faxed back 'so sollie." Assholes.

Last night me and Roo went to a Thai kick-boxing match. Before each fight contestants pray in the ring and do an entertaining sort of spirit dance. Then they beat the crap out of each other. Get this ... They dress in the men's toilet room where girlfriends help to prepare them. I won't say more other than I couldn't tell working girls from lovers.

Roo and I go to tomorrow Phang Nga for a few days to investigate the jungle shrouded mountain cliffs etched by lime deposits. We'll do rigging work aloft because water is calm. Roo will dive to change the broken thru hull fitting since the boatyard screwed us by closing. I join Roo in hoping there are no jellyfish like the one that stung him in Ao Chalong.

Last night it pissed rain and thundered for hours. Brandy was shaking. Poor thing. I looked for something to read when your diary of personal poetry fell in the way of my wandering gaze. It wasn't locked. I thought you would be OK if I read it or you wouldn't have left it on open display. Denise—it's wonderful. It's lovely, just like you!

As always, I send my love.

Roo went to the masthead in calm waters and found the same jamming spinnaker halyard problem Denise went aloft to repair in the Tall Ships race. He made proper repairs.

View from masthead on calm day. Imagine Denise up here in a storm
—Chapter 9.

Denise's father's condition was serious but under best care. She returned in mid October, perfect timing for relentless monsoon rains. We decided to try our hand at living ashore for a spell and rented a cute cabin on a steep hill above Patong Beach. Thai cottages are not air conditioned unless they have closets. If one couldn't afford AC they couldn't afford anything to put in the closets anyway. Shelves are open air to avoid mildew. Usually nothing is on top shelves because Thais can't reach them. Our place had a refrigerator on blocks that came to my chin. The manufacturer had labeled it 'The Big One.' The kitchen had no sink because Thais washed everything outside in a stream or under a hose. Our only sleeping room was Lilliputian tiny with a bed I suspected was borrowed from a prison. The shining feature was a small living area with a stunning view of Patong Beach below and Indian Ocean beyond.

The place came with a dog, abandoned by a shameless former occupant. We named him "Woofie." The sorrowful gaunt creature had fleas and ticks. He loved us, he loved Brandy and we learned to love the unloved pooch. While an outside dog, Woofie possessed uncanny ability to arrive at my feet, even when doors were locked, taking an hour to rid the residence of freeloading ticks.

Denise nourished the skeletal animal, managing to put some meat on his bones. One day Woofie disappeared, never to be seen again. God rest Woofie.

We spent lazy days at the little shack on the steep hill. Brandy enjoyed shore life and shadowed us every minute. We made a deal; she doesn't pee on the floors and we won't eat her treats. We kept our word.

CHAPTER 60

FLEE IF YOU'RE THE DRIVER

The principal road between Phuket Town and Patong Beach lay 300 feet below our tiny rented cottage—a busy two-lane LeMans challenge with steep sharp curves. Thais believed anything motorized was powered by the horn. They 'toot' horns continually, filling the air with a melody (if you choose) of mechanical brass sounds. Sometimes a blaring horn signals opposing traffic to 'get out of my way' and is followed by a horrendous crash. Only days ago a tractor-trailer roared over the hill, started his perilous descent to Patong Beach and lost control. The entire rig flew over the hopeless rail, took out trees, rolled a few times and came to rest 300 feet below. Most Thais stop, not to help, but to watch. That one drew enough crowd to attract cart vendors so spectators could choose sausage rolls, pineapple on a stick, chicken legs (foot attached) or a soft drink while they watched death and carnage. Should one be unlucky enough to be a driver, passenger or first at the scene, it was best to flee quickly. One never knew who would be blamed for what.

Cops doubled as graffiti artists. Following a collision they outlined positions of the vehicle or persons flung to the roadway in white paint, fortunately water-based or some roads would be solid white.

Kids drive young. When you're old enough to walk you're old enough to barrel across the countryside on a 500 cc bike. Few Thais took driving tests or had a legitimate license. They bought them. I decided to be honest, took the high road and studied for my test. Asking the examiner where I should sit for my exam he replied, "mai pen rai cup." (Never mind) There would be no written exam. The agent motioned to a second store window.

"You get in jeep. That one yours, yes?"

He pointed to The Leopard. (Name painted on my jeep) I acknowledged ownership.

"Drive out parking lot there, and come back there," he said pointing to openings fifty yards apart. "I watch from window. Driving test."

I passed but never saw anyone in a window. I liked driving in Thailand. It was challenging. We drove on the left, but to count on that was folly. Traffic lights were few. Those working were fewer. Police at intersections directed motorist by signboards hung over their shoulders. The chest side read 'GO' and backside read 'STOP.' I saw one with 'GO' written in red and 'STOP' written in green.

One day I missed the grim reaper by milliseconds. Work crews using hand shovels were patching potholes with a stink-bomb tar substance. Portions of the road over a hill I was approaching were closed. No flagmen or warning signs. There I was burning along toward home, over the crest of the hill and *BAM!* I *slam* the brakes praying a cement truck wasn't inches behind me. The road before me, open an hour ago was now closed. Coming at me on the one open lane I was about to enter was a giant dirt truck going a good 100kph. Fast reactions make it to adulthood.

I estimated the road below our cottage as 7 or 8 out of 10 on a danger scale. One night there was a deadly head-on meeting of a jeep and a motorcycle. Denise, with me in tow, ran down to render emergency aid to victims; one Denise suspected had a broken back, the other a badly smashed jaw. When the ambulance arrived they simply heaved the wounded into the back and sped away. One died.

A small contraption called a 'sam law' (sidecar) can be attached to a motorcycle, making the impossible possible. I've seen them laden with heavy-eyed doped chickens headed to slaughter, suckling pigs, untied furniture piled high, huge sheets of glass, and one with ten people aboard.

Thai family outing

My biggest double take was a lovely Thai lady whizzing down the hill with an enormous cobra snake wrapped casually around her neck and body.

Thai motorcycles, millions of them, were very dangerous—not because manufacturers built them for power but because Thai's didn't get it that metal is stronger than flesh. As careless as they were, I never saw one angry person. Thais were high-spirited wonderful people. Their life-styles and values were different than ours. That was OK. We adapted.

CHAPTER 61

KINGS CUP REGATTA

December's King's Cup Regatta attracted fine-tuned racing yachts from afar as well as local competitors keen to take advantage of 'local knowledge.' We fit somewhere in the middle, having cruised a year in Thai waters and having a fast cruising boat. With inviting weather, incredible hospitality and fascinating islands I couldn't imagine anyone not wanting to be a part of King's Cup.

Major sponsors were two of my favorites: Mumm's Champagne and Sea Nomad. We would compete seriously and for pleasure. We practiced by pretending we were racing when sailing to islands, including those mentioned in previous chapters.

Life got in the way of practice. Sailing from Phi Phi Island I took a squirt that started in wretched pain and ended in euphoria. Somewhere midstream (not to be punny) I had ejected a small stone.

"Ahhh haa," said Denise with too much of a smile, "sounds like kidney stones. Try to catch one. We'll have it analyzed."

"With what? My hands?"

"No dummy—use a paper cup."

"Jeeze- could one get stuck?"

"Sure."

"And what happens then?"

"They go in and blow it up."

"No friggin way Denise. No testicle demolition team is going into me."

"OK, we shall see."

Two weeks later Dr. Neil Thrasher from Phuket's Adventist Hospital arranged the necessary surgery.

In the interim Roo, first mate and in charge of crew made his selection of deck apes and girl friends. The five days of racing met expectations for fun and showing our stuff. Our crew worked together under Roo's guidance, and with Denise as the sandwich machine, kept twelve souls and a dog fed. It worked.

Endymion *racing around Ko Phi Phi in King's Cup.*

We became the only cruising configuration yacht to trophy in the highly competitive series. The highlight through all of it for me was watching beautiful Mrs. Denise Rowland curtsey with style before the King's representative to accept our trophy and the Olympic style medals for each of our twelve crew, and Brandy. Super size bottles of Mumm's were a pleasure as well.

In a feature regarding the races Phuket Magazine said of us: "Skip Rowland showed uncanny sailing skills with his ability to pick wind shifts. The whole fleet saluted his choice of path for the final tack to the finish line in race three."

Enjoying the King's Cup award ceremony.

January came too fast after King's Cup. Denise and I, in our trusty Leopard jeep hauled what came ashore back to *Endymion*. We were ready to depart for Europe via the Red Sea. It would be a long haul for our out-of-tune bodies so we spent plenty of time working out in the Meridian Hotel's lavish gym.

Then one day our world came apart!

CHAPTER 62

A LIFE SO PRECIOUS

Discourteous drivers showed little regard for the life of others, aggressively fighting for road space with the ambulance clawing through Bangkok traffic. The ambulance siren drilled holes in the sky and the robust horn warning rose two decibels above the din of one of the world's busiest cities.

"*Code two, Code tw*o," the drivers urgency obvious in his tone. Serious stuff. A fragile life was teetering, balancing between today and eternity—a precious life.

Beneath her restraints Denise's arms and legs were in constant motion, out of control, her motor senses had lost communication with her brain. I searched her eyes, dull and glassy, broadcasting confusion and fear I had never seen. Denise's words were jumbled. A cherished nurse I loved with all my heart was in *serious* trouble. For a flickering moment her eyes locked on mine, dredging for signs of fear in me. Those deep beautiful eyes, once big, brown and bright were dim and sluggish —barely responsive.

I worked to hold back welling tears, fearing I might never see Denise alive again.

Her hand brushed mine. I held it.

We'd had so little time to love. We'd tested each other in our early days but following Denise's arrival in Tahiti, became as united in life as humanly possible. Together, always together, we had dined with royalty, eaten with former cannibals, been attacked by pirates and made love in the majesty of the Great Barrier Reef. Side by side we survived storms and political coups, hurtled down a flood ravaged river, made more sweet love under canopies of endless stars, competed with Tall Ships, laughed with friends new and old, and became—well, became *one*. Denise was my world. Our lives were so powerfully intertwined we *knew* we were the essence of soul mates. I prayed, *Lord, help us please.*

The ambulance barely moved. Police, wearing masks in Bangkok's noxious air directed traffic, but were ineffective. When a few feet cleared in front of us it instantly filled with motorcycles or a truck. So jammed was Bangkok traffic, some people cooked their children's breakfast over open fires on truck beds just to get to classes.

Denise's breathing became sketchy. The attendant put a mask on her face. Seeing her suffer—I lost it. Jumping from the ambulance, I ran before it like a lunatic, pushing motorbikes and drivers aside. No one mistook my wrecking-ball urgency. They moved. The ambulance driver called for additional police help. We were moving again. Ramkhamhaem Hospital was minutes away.

Denise and I had been working out, pumping iron to tune up for the next leg of our voyage, when Denise developed a massive headache. Unknown to us two cerebral aneurisms were attempting to take control—and end her life.

The left side of her face sagged when she smiled. Her sentences became confused. I took her to Adventist Hospital. Dr. Neil Thrasher startled me.

"Skip, get Denise to Bangkok *NOW!* I'll call ahead. Don't stop home or buy a ticket. Just go! She needs surgery we can't provide. *Go*—I'll have it set up for you at the airport."

The doctor suspected a stroke. A Bangkok Air flight delayed take-off waiting for Denise. An ambulance was on the tarmac at Don Mueang International Airport in Bangkok. They rushed Denise to Adventist Mission Hospital

I waited, paced and worried—and I cried.

"Kuhn (Mr.) Rowland," said the Thai doctor, "an angiogram confirms your wife has experienced multiple aneurisms. Very dangerous. One is leaking blood into her brain. The leader of our countries Neuro Surgeons, Dr. Sirah is in Bangkok. He waits for you at Ramkhamhaem Hospital. You are a fortunate man. He is on call for the royal family. Your wife is in the best hand. They put her in the ambulance now. Come, follow me."

Thai drivers are not known for patience or skill. The ambulance transporting Denise rushed leaving Mission Hospital, accidentally tapping a motorbike while backing up. It fell over. The domino effect took out another twenty similarly parked bikes. The driver did not stop.

We were blocks from the hospital when Dr. Sirah came on the radio, giving instructions to the attendant. To me he said, "Mr. Rowland, I am Doctor Sirah. I will attend to your wife. What you need to know now, Mr. Rowland, about an aneurism is that it is a weak blood vessel. Until it swells up before erupting you don't know it's there. There is *nothing* you could have done. Aneurisms are sneaky, like saboteurs doing dirty work undetected. There, I see you. Your ambulance is coming up the drive. I'm under the portico waving, do you see me?"

Standing outside with a gurney waiting for Denise was an amazing doctor. God had answered my prayers. The President of the Association of Neuro Surgeons, Thailand's finest, was attending personally to my Denise. I thought; *This is my miracle.*

"She's going straight to surgery. Aneurisms will burst." He told me in perfect English.

I was overwhelmed—as I would be for the rest of my life.

The clock on the wall struck 9:00 pm. I'd been in the operating room waiting area for seven hours. Only once had a team representative reported; all was going as expected and Dr. Sirah had help from associates. Language differences made communication difficult. Aside from cleaning staff or nurses tapping a vending machine, I had been alone for the last hour. I used the solitude to telegraph to Denise my thoughts and prayers in a comforting soft tone, letting her know I will be with her through all the days to come, sending strength I knew she needed, letting her know I will be her rock forever. I was sooo tired. It was difficult to concentrate, but I carried on, determined this would not be our last love song.

It had been a tumultuous day. Thai time seems to operate independently from the rest of the world. A Thai 'prunee' (tomorrow) can make a Mexican mañana look like a rocket shot.

At twenty-two minutes into the new day, the door to the waiting room swung open. My heart sank and legs wobbled as Dr. Sirah approached without a smile, and then he said, "Kuhn Rowland, your wife is alive. She made it through surgery, eleven hours with three Neuro surgeons. She is an exceptional lady—but very weak now."

"May I see her, please Doctor?"

"Not right now. She is in intensive care, under constant monitoring. Perhaps in the morning. We have set aside a room for you so you will be close."

"Will she be OK?"

"It's difficult to say. There were two aneurisms. We managed to clip them both. Considerable blood leaked into her brain and that created pressure. There is also bruising from the procedure. It will be some time, maybe weeks before we know the extent of the damage."

Denise remained in the ICU for twelve days, and in the hospital for more than a month.

I was startled when I first saw her. Half of Denise's head had been shaved of that thick, richly scented hair I so loved and of which she was so proud.

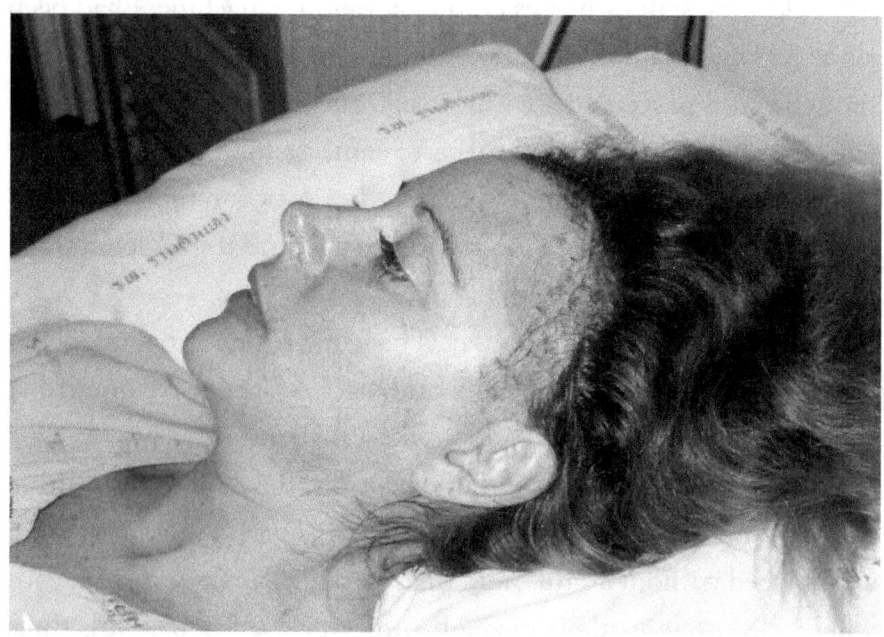

Denise following brain surgery—she always looked radiant.

There was a huge cut, with ugly black stitches, running from one ear, across the top of her skull, down to the other ear. They had opened her skull with a saw, and folded her scalp forward to get at the invasive aneurisms. She couldn't speak—only mumbled incoherently. Her arms and legs moved without command and her eyes, those lovely deep pockets of love, wandered aimlessly. I felt so hopeless. I spoke in whispers to Denise, hoping she could hear me, praying for a connection to her, any connection. It was a terrible time.

Eight days into her stay I came into ICU one morning to see her sitting up, reading the Bangkok Post newspaper. Joy flooded through me and I ran across the ICU to her bed. But the Denise I knew wasn't there. The Denise I was looking at held the newspaper upside down, uncertainly, eyes unfocused, her head swaying softly side to side.

The Doctor explained, "Her mind tells her to do things familiar to her, like reading the paper, but she doesn't have control of her motor faculties. We believe she will, but it may take a long time."

And it did. I decided we would remain in Thailand for as long as it took, certainly more, I was told, than a year.

Many people of different colors and unfamiliar languages testing their skills worked their magic enabling survival for another living soul. Myfavorite soul.

Though challenging, sad and tearful, in my heart I felt Denise, the feisty little fighter from Pasadena, would live to laugh again, that she would make one of the greatest comebacks of all time. Denise didn't have the competitive urge of the yachtsman who crosses the finish line with a broken mast, or the marathon runner who stumbles across the line nearly unconscious, but she had always been determined to do her *very* best. Winning the invasion of her brain may not yield trophies, but it sure as hell beat the odds.

Her victory may not show in the record books. Sometimes they don't; they're personal.

We would awaken one day with hope replacing fear.

God bless you, Denise.

EPILOGUE

WHERE ARE THEY NOW?

DENISE AND SKIP ROWLAND

Most important—Denise lived.

Denise and Skip remained several years in the Kingdom where Denise received excellent care. They built *Pirates Cove*, the first theme park miniature golf course in Phuket and later built a second course in Guangzhou, China. *Pirates Cove*, located directly behind the Holiday Inn on 'The 200 Year Road' in Patong Beach was destroyed the day after Christmas in the 2004 Tsunami.

Skip bought into the Sea Nomad Company, obtained US Patents and arranged for distribution in America. Unbeknownst to Skip, two of his three partners had a date with Interpol. The company folded. Oops! Sorry Skip.

The Rowland's shifted to Canada, became citizens and built *A Snug Harbor Inn,* a waterfront accommodation high on a cliff overlooking the Pacific Ocean. The Inn (www.awesomeview.com) caters

Denise with friends on Pirate Cove "ship."

to romance, has won numerous awards and was featured on TV's travel show Best Places to Kiss, as well as in USA Today.

In 2001 Denise lived through a third aneurism, thanks in part to having a helipad on *Snug Harbor's* property. The Rowland's later auctioned '*Snug*' as a trophy property.

They are currently coasting through their twilight years on the slopes of Red Mountain Ski Resort in the picturesque British Columbia community of Rossland.

BRANDY ALEXANDER ROWLAND

Brandy had the worst of moments and the best. Mostly she lived a dream dog's life and passed away peacefully in Denise's lap at age 14 — while eating ice cream.

ROO BIRAM

Roo met a tall, beautiful, educated traveller while in Phuket—and married her. Another genuine love story. Working for a small manufacturing firm in South Australia Roo was so appreciated he was invited to become a shareholder. The company thrived. Roo retired at age 45. Traveling the world in 2016 with Paula and their two remarkable daughters they honored the Rowland's' by 'hangin' with them for two weeks. Skip says of Roo to this day; "Put a visit to him on your 'bucket list.' There isn't a finer human being on the planet."

Roo, Paula Ava and Grace Biram in Canada 2016.

LARRY DENT

Larry owns and operates Crown Yacht Charters in Anacortes, WA, and is enjoying the best years of his life. That's what he says. Personally I think they were with us! (www.crownyachtcharters.com)

MIKE MULHOLLAND

Mike is a happily married man retired in Oakland, CA. I understand he is flying to Brazil this year to fish, most likely because he didn't catch anything there the last time. Some things never change. :)

KYLIE & CAETLIN JOPSON

Both sisters became what they wished for. Caetlin is a MD in Queensland AU and Kylie a Veterinary Surgeon in South Australia.

(Little) JAMIE COPELAND

Jamie still awes people, only now as an Air Canada pilot.

LIZA & ANDY COPELAND

The Copeland's sailed *Bagheera* over 123,000nm, enjoying 114 countries. Liza has written three books about their adventures and currently writes for magazines internationally. Andy co-authored a fourth 'how-to' book with Liza and now enjoys retirement from his Yacht Brokerage business. (www.aboutcruising.com)

CHARLIE CONLEN

Is semi-retired as a Manufacturers Rep living in Long Beach CA. with his charming wife Salli, and a rescue dog.

TOM & JOAN WEST

Tom passed peacefully. Joan lives in Palm Springs, CA.

❊ No Return Ticket – Leg Two ❊

Whether the weather is cold
Whether the weather is hot
Whether the weather is fine
Whether the weather is not
We'll weather the weather
Whatever the weather
Whether we like it or not

—Author unknown

GLOSSARY

Aft: Rear of vessel, as in *aft* end. Non boaters call it the 'back end.'

Avon: Brand of inflatable boat made of PVC or Hypalon.

Binnacle: Ship's compass and a useful thing to have.

Bosun's chair: a board fitted to a harness with compartments for tools. One sit's in the *bosun's chair to be* hoisted up the mast. Usually not much fun.

Bow: Front end of a vessel.

Clew: Lower aft corner of a sail, usually with metal eye where lines may be attached.

Chubasco: Violent short duration squall. Used in Spanish-speaking countries. Also known as "Willie Walls."

Eskie: same as an American cooler; an Australian term.

Gaff: An iron hook that could have several claws.

Gunkholing: Cruising along a coastline and anchoring in sand or mud anchorages.

Halyard: Line used to raise or lower a sail.

Head: Toilet, but then you knew that already—didn't you?

Heel: Indicates how far a boat is tipped, eg. on a *heel* of 20 degrees. A 90 degree *heel* would be lying sideways, which is not a good idea. (see *Knockdown*)

Jenny: Nickname for Genoa Jib, the forward sail. Reference to 150% means it covers 100% of distance from headstay to the mast and 50% additional further aft.

Ketch: Two-mast sailboat with the aft mast shorter than the forward mast and placed aft of the rudder post (if anyone cares).

Knockdown: When *w*ind or sea conditions lay a yacht on its side possibly causing severe damage or sinking.

Knot: One knot equals one nautical mile per hour, or 1.1508 statute mile per hour, or 1.852 kilometers per hour (Thus 5 knots = 5.75 mph or 9.26 km/h. Confused?

Knuckle: The area below the waterline in the bow (front) of the boat that we reinforced in case we hit something...like a rock.

Koh (or Ko): Thai word for Island

Lee: Away from the wind. The side of the boat closest to wind is *windward* side, farthest from wind is *lee(ward)* side. A *lee shore* means the wind is blowing onto it instead of away from it, and is therefore often dangerous. *In the lee of* means "sheltered from the wind by" perhaps and island. Ie: "I sat to the lee of his bad breath and was disgusted.")

Longtail: Narrow canoe-shaped Thai vessel used for passengers or light freight. The helmsman steers by holding a long rod connected through a motor to a propeller that skims the waterline keeping it from snagging coral, seaweed or mermaids.

Luff (as part of a sail): The forward edge of the sail

Luffing: Refers to a shaking or flapping of a sail, such as heading the boat closer toward the wind causing sails to shake.

Mizzen Mast: The aft (back) mast on ketch or yawl.

Mizzen Sail: Sail that goes on the mizzen mast. (see above)

nm: nautical mile; equal to 1.15 statute miles. Based on the circumference of the earth, and used in navigation.

Painter: A rope used to tie a small boat (dinghy or inflatable) to a dock or a mother ship.

Perkins: Brand of diesel engine. We had a 4/102 meaning four cylinder- 102 horsepower model.

Port (side): Left side of vessel when looking forward from aft.

Scope: Indication of the length of anchor line relative to the depth of water when anchoring. *Scope* three times would indicate 3x as much chain (or rope) as the depth in which the boat is anchored.

Shroud: Stainless steel wire rigging used to hold a mast in place. (good stuff)

Sheet: Line used to adjust the shape of a sail. Thus, *trim* the sheet to bring the sail tighter or *release* the sheet to give the sail more belly. Older schooners had a topsail. A watch commander might yell; "Hoist the top sheet and spank 'er," frightening feminine passengers.

Spinnaker: Wind gathering balloon sail seen in many pictures. Used when the wind is aft of abeam. Causes problems and occasional divorces.

Spinnaker pole: Metal pole attached to the mast at one end and spinnaker at the other end, helping to prevent the sail from oscillating.

Starboard (side): Right side of vessel when looking forward from the stern

Stern: Back end.

Tinny: Small open aluminum boat. We got a 12-foot outboard powered tinny, to replace our stolen inflatable tender.

Tuk Tuk: Thai bus carrying more people than it should, their luggage, animals, groceries and grand-parents. No express routes.

Two foot zone: An expression adapted from rock climbers, who, with vast vistas to enjoy, must concentrate on what is before them at the moment. Hence, in the *two foot zone*.

www.ingramcontent.com/pod-product-compliance
Lightning Source LLC
Chambersburg PA
CBHW071151300426
44113CB00009B/1171